Dear Reader:

The book you are abou[...]m the St. Martin's True C[...]w York Times calls "the [...]h, we offer you a fascinating account of the latest, most sensational crime that has captured the national attention. St. Martin's is the publisher of perennial bestselling true crime author Jack Olsen whose SALT OF THE EARTH is the true story of one woman's triumph over life-shattering violence; Joseph Wambaugh called it "powerful and absorbing." Fannie Weinstein and Melinda Wilson tell the story of a beautiful honors student who was lured into the dark world of sex for hire in THE COED CALL GIRL MURDER. St. Martin's is also proud to publish critically acclaimed author Carlton Stowers, whose 1999 Edgar Award-winning TO THE LAST BREATH recounts a two-year-old girl's mysterious death, and the dogged investigation that led loved ones to the most unlikely murderer: her own father. In the book you now hold, BURNED ALIVE, veteran reporter and bestselling author Kieran Crowley investigates the brutal murder of Kimberly Antonakos, a beautiful and promising young woman betrayed by her own best friend's avaricious lover.

St. Martin's True Crime Library gives you the stories *behind* the headlines. Our authors take you right to the scene of the crime and into the minds of the most notorious murderers to show you what really makes them tick. St. Martin's True Crime Library paperbacks are better than the most terrifying thriller, because it's all true! The next time you want a crackling good read, make sure it's got the St. Martin's True Crime Library logo on the spine—you'll be up all night!

Charles E. Spicer, Jr.
Senior Editor, St. Martin's True Crime Library

In the clearing air, Fred was startled to see a shocking sight for the first time, like something out of a horror movie—a charred figure slumped in a chair, burned from the waist up. It was the worst thing he had ever seen in five years on the job. It was upsetting to see a human being dead in a fire, but it was more upsetting to realize that it had been a woman. The body, whose face was unrecognizable, had been gagged. The arms were behind the back, as if they had been tied. The fire had apparently burned away some of the restraints. As the air in the basement cleared, Fred removed his mask. He smelled gasoline. It was obviously some kind of foul play . . .

—from BURNED ALIVE

CRITICAL ACCLAIM FOR KIERAN CROWLEY'S *SLEEP MY LITTLE DEAD*:

"You can't put it down. It's a great book . . .a great read."
—Joan Rivers

"Crowley gives the reader a first-rate 'police procedure' story, as told in a tersely colorful style honed by long contact, and admitted fascination with Gotham's not-so-soft underbelly."
—Richard Pyle, Associated Press

"Brings us behind the scenes of the toughest case the NYPD has faced in 20 years."
—Crime author Dan Mahoney

ST. MARTIN'S PAPERBACKS
TRUE CRIME LIBRARY TITLES
BY KIERAN CROWLEY

SLEEP MY LITTLE DEAD
BURNED ALIVE

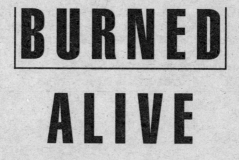

BURNED ALIVE

ALIVE

KIERAN CROWLEY

St. Martin's Paperbacks

BURNED ALIVE

Copyright © 1999 by Kieran Crowley.

Cover photograph courtesy Associated Press.

ISBN: 0-312-97030-7

Printed in the United States of America

St. Martin's Paperbacks edition / October 1999

10 9 8 7 6 5 4 3 2 1

FOR TESS AND AL

THIS BOOK IS DEDICATED TO THE MEMORY
OF KIMBERLY ANTONAKOS—MAY SHE
REST IN PEACE; AND TO HER DEVOTED
FAMILY—MAY THEY FIND PEACE.

ACKNOWLEDGMENTS

This book is based on scores of interviews and several thousand pages of police reports, confessions, court documents, and trial transcripts. I interviewed prosecutors, detectives, fire marshals, witnesses, family members, scientific experts, and one of the men involved in the crime. There are no fictional or "composite characters" in this book, although some people have been given pseudonyms, which are denoted by asterisks the first time the name appears. Some of the names have been changed, as they used to say on the "Dragnet" TV show, "to protect the innocent"—at least some of them, as well as some of the bit players. Certain events, sequences, and conversations were necessarily reconstructed from a synthesis of all the evidence, including the confessions, police reports, trial transcripts, interviews with participants, and other information.

While researching this book, I uncovered medical facts that shed new light on the last moments of the victim, Kimberly Antonakos. I also unearthed murder plots against two witnesses in the case, and against three participants in the original murder that, for various reasons, were never carried out.

First, I would like to thank my editor at St. Martin's Press—Charlie Spicer, a scholar and a gentleman—for all his help. My literary agent Jane Dystel has my gratitude for her continuing help, expertise, and cheerful guidance. I also must thank her chief editor, Miriam Goderich, for her advice and encouragement.

I wish to thank my editors at the *New York Post*, Managing Editor Stu Marques, and Metropolitan Editor Lou Lumenick without whose help it would be impossible for me to write books. I tip my hat to info-maven and *Post* Head Librarian Laura Harris and her great staff, who can find anything on ninety seconds' notice. My thanks also to Myron ''Radar'' Rushetzky at the City Desk, and Desk Assistant Christina Tam for their able assistance. Photo Editor Gretchen Viehmann, assisted by Dave Johnston, located many of the pictures for this book, and they have my gratitude. Reporter Linda Massarella was also helpful. I also acknowledge the gracious assistance of a colleague and competitor from my early days on the streets of New York— New York *Daily News* Deputy Photo Editor Michael Lipack. *Daily News* reporter Pete Donohue and *Newsday* reporter Karen Freifeld from the Queens Press Room were kind enough to share their reminiscences of the trial, and I thank them.

My thanks go to Pat Clark at Brooklyn District Attorney Charles Hynes' office, the office of Manhattan DA Robert Morgenthau, and Drew Biondo at Suffolk County District Attorney James Catterson's office. I am obliged to NYPD Police Commissioner Howard Safir, and Deputy Commissioner for Public Information, Marilyn Mode, for their invaluable help and consideration, without which this book would not have been possible. I thank Detective Phil Tricolla for his cooperation, as well as Detective Johnny Wilde, and Fire Marshal Stanley Jaremko. I am grateful to His Honor Brooklyn Supreme Court Justice Michael Gary, who was able to unseal court files to correct the public record and provide me with new insight into an important part of the case.

Detective Rich Tirelli of the Queens Homicide Squad has a talent for interrogation, and his skills were put to excellent use in this case. I thank him for all his help.

My deep thanks go to Queens DA Richard A. Brown, who was touched by the tragedy of the Antonakos case, and determined to convict the killers, despite the daunting setbacks. Prosecutor Gene Reibstein's recollections and suggestions were of great value, and he has my gratitude. I would also like to thank Julian Wise for his assistance and unique viewpoint, and Rob Ferino for his help. I would also like to tender my sincere thanks to DA Brown's spokeswoman Mary deBourbon—one of the best in the business—for all her help.

I am grateful for the expertise of Dr. Susi Vassallo, M.D., Clinical Assistant Professor of Emergency Medicine, Department of Surgery at New York University Medical Center in Manhattan, who gave me an education in the effects of hypothermia on the human body and a scientific opinion on the fate of Kim Antonakos.

Raquel "Blondie" Montalvo was very helpful, and I wish her luck in her battles for health and freedom. I am also thankful for the cooperation of Antonette Montalvo and her son. Her mother Jeanette Montalvo, and her aunt Susan Montalvo were also of assistance. My thanks also go to Luis Negron and John Cuniffe.

I am especially grateful for the frank assistance of Julio "Jay" Negron, a young man struggling to overcome a painful upbringing, fateful errors, and a brush with evil. Because he lives in fear of death, Jay tells me he is someone who lives only for today. I wish him a nice day.

Tommy Antonakos has my deep sympathy for his loss, and my gratitude for the limited help he was able to provide on such a painful subject. He has borne an unbearable burden with strength and dignity, while assisting the police like a soldier. Virtually everyone in the case has admired his courage and resolve to bring his daughter's killers to justice.

This book could not have been written without the cooperation of two master detectives—Louie Pia and Tom Shevlin of the Queens Homicide Squad. I am indebted to them for the time and effort they took to help me reconstruct a six-month roller coaster of an investigation. Both experienced investigators knew better than to become emotionally involved in a case, but they did become caught up in this one—and so did their wives. I also thank Katie Pia and Lisa Shevlin for their insights about the effects of "The Job" on the detectives who ferret out and lock up the killers among us. We all owe them a debt of gratitude.

As always, my heartfelt thanks go to Al and Tess Nemser and Kathy Nemser, for their various free services—including wisdom, legal advice, love, support, and proofreading.

My final thanks go to my toughest editor, my wife Riki, who made it all possible by lovingly sacrificing the free time she did not have to help me—when she would rather have been painting.

CHAPTER ONE

KIM

Kim's thick mane of ebony curls bounced and swayed with the pounding rhythm of the music and flashing lights on the dance floor. The floating hair framed an oval face with a cute button nose. Her large, wide mouth had smiling red lips that pointed up at high cheekbones beneath silky skin. Kim's eyes seemed to sparkle—a reflective effect caused by the blue-tinted contact lenses that she wore over her dark brown pupils. A large, ornate gold crucifix studded with garnets swung from a gold chain around her long, graceful neck, and glittering gold shell earrings sparkled from inside her hair. As the beautiful twenty-year-old danced alone, men turned their heads to watch her, their eyes following the sensuous motion of her body. Kimberly Antonakos was clothed, not in a revealing miniskirt, but in the height of dress-down fashion—as a construction worker. Brown Timberland boots that had never trod timberland added an inch or two to her lithe, 5-foot-3-inch frame, as she spun to the throbbing beat and staccato horns of the Salsa music. She wore a brown vest over a blue-and-white-striped long-sleeved blouse which was tucked into black denim pants. A message beeper was clipped to her waist. On her right hand, she wore a ring with a big, round purple gem surrounded by white stones, and a thick gold bangle bracelet. An expensive brown Giorgio designer bag, with a cellular phone inside, swayed from one shoulder.

It was a slow weeknight at "Soul Kitchen," a traveling "club" that was held in different establishments on different nights. It was, essentially, a floating disco. That night, Soul Kitchen was being held at the "S.O.B.'s," a singles night spot on Varick Street in the trendy TriBeCa section of Lower Manhattan. "S.O.B." stood for *Sounds of Brazil*, a Mecca for the Latin music scene—from Salsa to "tribal hip-hop." The décor of the club had been described as "urban tropical." The pungent smell of marijuana from the gyrating crowd wafted through the air, and mixed with the underlying odor of beer and cigarettes. For those not aroused by the stirring sounds, the bar served up a special secret potion called "roots," which, they claimed, was an old Jamaican aphrodisiac recipe. After the dance, Kim and her friend Liz each got a beer. They curled their long, pearly fingernails around the cold, dark bottles, and checked out the room. Liz Pace, 21, also had black hair and brown eyes, which she set off with heavy makeup. Liz was two inches taller and a few pounds heavier than Kim, whom she knew from her Canarsie neighborhood in Brooklyn, when Kim had attended South Shore High School.

"Is the family still there?" Liz asked.

"Yeah," said Kim.

Liz was asking Kim about her girlfriend April, who was staying in the second bedroom of Kim's apartment along with her boyfriend Josh and their two-year-old son *Timmy. Kim was kindhearted and couldn't say no to a friend. Two weeks earlier, April had asked Kim if they could stay over while the floors in their apartment two blocks away were being refinished and then painting completed.

Kim and Liz had started their night out rather late. Liz had called Kim, and the pair had agreed to go out clubbing. They often hung out together at Salsa clubs. Kim loved to dance and also loved rap music, like "Mary J" and "Notorious B.I.G." At 9:30, Kim had driven the fifteen blocks to Liz's house on East Ninety-third Street. The two young women spent a full three and a half hours chatting, applying nail polish to their long fingernails, and getting dolled up to go out dancing. They arrived at S.O.B.'s at 1:30 a.m., March 1st, 1995.

Kim looked around the club, but she didn't see anyone who interested her. It was mostly older guys. She was looking for a young, powerful, good-looking guy with wads of money, who would buy her only Moet champagne, and treat her like a goddess. She liked guys who dressed well, who wore gold, who knew how to handle themselves. Kim respected that. In the glitzy Manhattan clubs—unlike at work or at school—Kim was a star.

Kim knew she would always be the shining star of her father's life, of course, but it was time for her to find a life of her own, and she was enjoying her new independence and freedom. She had been on her own, and in her own place for more than a year, but the heady novelty of being able to stay out late and burn the candle at both ends had not yet worn off. Kim and Liz drank a few beers, but did not dance with any guys. They decided to leave at 4 a.m., when a lesbian, the only person to show interest in them, came over to the girls and made a pass at Kim.

After almost three hours of hanging out, Kim and Liz left the club and walked out into the freezing air. Kim got behind the wheel of her almost-new white Honda Civic for the trip back to Canarsie. Kim crossed a bridge above the East River toward the "City of Churches." Below, in the dark waters, the southwest wind had changed direction, and came up stronger from the west, whipping the blue-black waves up to an unquiet four-foot sea that battered against the Brooklyn shore. The streets were empty and the girls made good time.

Kim lit a Newport. As she drove, the little brown beehive deodorizer that hung from the rear-view mirror swung back and forth. Kim was a diva, a star in the clubs at night, but she wasn't an airhead. Like most young women her age, Kim was playing the field. She hadn't found the right guy, and, at twenty, she certainly wasn't ready to settle down yet.

Kim was a heartbreaker—not because she was cruel, but simply because she was sweet, beautiful, charming and sexy. When she dated a guy and it didn't click—when she realized that she wasn't in love—she would move on. Kim expected a date to treat her like a princess, and be faithful. But as soon as a guy slowed down and tried to get into a serious relationship, it would turn her off and she would break up with him. She wanted to have fun, and be in control. By not reciprocating the deep feelings of a boyfriend—simply by not falling in love with him—she could arouse powerful emotions. Some guys couldn't handle that. Kim, like most pretty girls, was learning the hard way about the male ego. Some guys would not accept rejection from a woman. They became possessive, jealous, and angry. Kim thought they were a real pain.

Kim's most recent boyfriend, Jay, was one such guy. Kim thought Jay was smooth—he was cool, and looked great. He had spent the previous night at her apartment. Kim had more or less broken up with Jay, but they had gotten together for the night. It meant a lot to Jay, but not to Kim. The next afternoon, after Kim returned home from school, she sat on the living room couch and watched music videos with Jay, their friend Josh, and Josh's little son Timmy. She also spent time alone with Jay in the bedroom again, before going out to a doctor's appointment and to do some shopping before dinner.

Josh had introduced Kim to Jay, whom he had grown up with in Bushwick, a tough neighborhood. Jay, whose full name was Julio Negron, thought Kim was beautiful, sweet, and a lot of fun. He felt that Kim treated him as an equal, even though he was unemployed and had grown up in poverty. Kim was not one to flaunt her father's wealth. That was one of the things he loved about her.

But Kim was not in love with Jay. She had already moved on. When Kim gave him the news that she felt they should "see other people," Jay reluctantly agreed. He really had no choice, and was obviously very upset. He thought that he had lost a good thing, the best thing in his life. He believed his relationship with Kim meant that he had turned a corner in his life—but then it was all over, after only a few months.

Every time Jay loved someone, something went wrong. It fell apart. It wasn't fair. He tried to be cool about it, but Jay couldn't hide his fury a few weeks later, when he twice ran into Kim and some tall black guy named Shawn in the neighborhood. Jay had recently gone to a club that he knew Kim went to, hoping to see her. He found Kim, but she was with her new boyfriend. Jay watched Kim turn her back on him and leave with Shawn.

Kim went out with Shawn Hayes and things clicked. Kim never knew exactly where he lived, just that it was somewhere on the Lower East Side—they always stayed at Kim's place. It was just as well because Shawn lived in "Alphabet City" on the Lower East Side of Manhattan, a fifty-six-square block area infamous for drugs, prostitution, violence, and other mayhem, and he supported himself by selling dope. Drug dealers lived in a very violent world, but Kim didn't give it a second thought. She didn't do drugs and felt it had nothing to do with her. After several months, Kim moved on, because Shawn refused to stop seeing other women. In the end, the break-up was easy, even though she had feelings for him.

The time that Jay saw Kim at the club with Shawn, Shawn had been with another woman, whom he immediately drove home. "Come out with me," Shawn said to Kim when he came back to the club alone. Kim agreed to go out to dinner with him, and they had a nice meal. After dinner, Shawn asked to spend the night with Kim again at her place. Kim said no. Shawn was angered at her refusal, but drove her home to Brooklyn. Because she dated guys she met in clubs, Kim kept running across men who turned out to be involved with drugs. Who else would be covered in gold, decked out in expensive threads, and flashing a wad of cash in a nightclub in the early hours of the morning on a weeknight?

*   *   *

Two months earlier, at a 1995 New Year's party in a Manhattan club called The Tunnel, Kim had met another wad-of-cash guy who went by the nickname "Psycho." He was thin and had pale, milky skin. She couldn't stand his looks. He totally turned her off, but Kim thought she might be able to bring him home to Daddy. After treating Kim to a bottle of Moet champagne, the youth asked her to go on a trip with him.

"I'm going to Florida in the next day or two, and I've got an extra ticket if you want to go," said Psycho.

Kim agreed to go with Psycho so she could visit her mother in Florida, but had no intention of sleeping with the guy. Psycho, who had seemed high, was ecstatic. Within minutes, he started professing his love for her.

"You're the one," he told Kim. "You're the girl I've always dreamed of."

Psycho later took Kim to his parents' house in Brighton Beach. He brought her home to meet his family before she could bring him to meet hers. Kim smiled and was polite. A day later, Psycho picked Kim up in a cab, but there was another guy with him. They both seemed to be stoned. At the base of Psycho's neck, Kim could see the tattooed word "TOGETHER." Around the back of his neck was the word "FOREVER." Together Forever was the name of a Canarsie street gang that the police believed were involved in weapons and drug dealing, but whose members claimed to be socially concerned rap artists. In Miami, Kim, Psycho, and his friend took a cab to a motel. She then took another cab to her mother's house, where she spent the night. The next day, Kim went back to the motel where Psycho was staying and found both guys on their beds, stoned out. Kim turned to leave, but Psycho followed her and pulled her back into the room.

"I love you so much," he told her.

He gave her a ring and said it was their engagement ring—after knowing her just those few days. He really *was*

"Psycho," she thought. It was horrendous. Kim was scared to death. She was afraid that they had come down on some kind of drug deal, and she did not want to get caught up in it.

Psycho wanted her to do drugs, but she refused. He was able to talk her into going shopping, however. Psycho bought her $2,000 worth of clothes, including a big, baggy designer jacket.

Then he took her to a tattoo parlor. Psycho already had the word "FOREVER" tattooed on the back of his neck. To demonstrate that he wanted to be together forever with her, Psycho had the tattoo artist engrave "KIM" in large letters on his calf. This made Kim nuts. It wasn't that she was against tattoos—she had two of her own: on her right hip, a scorpion, because her astrological birth sign was Scorpio; and, in the small of her back, an "infinity" tattoo—a headless, naked entwined man and woman, engaged in an act of love. No, she wasn't against tattoos, but stenciling someone's name on your body was no joke—it was permanent. She also had the feeling that Psycho thought he owned her, now that he had her name imprinted on his milky white skin.

When they got back to New York, Kim just wanted to get rid of Psycho. She returned his engagement ring, and had him drop her off, not at her own place, but at her friend April's house. She didn't think he knew where she lived, and she wanted to keep it that way. ·

"I love you. I want you to stay with me forever," Psycho told her before leaving. "We'll be together forever."

Together Forever. With Psycho. No way.

For the next few days, Psycho beeped her non-stop. He was obsessed. Her beeper would go off over and over and over. Kim thought that he was going out of his mind. She realized that taking the plane ticket and clothes from Psycho and then not staying with him was not enough. She told Liz she was going to have to "diss Psycho big-time" to get him to leave her alone. But eventually after she'd ignored Psycho's beeps for days, they stopped. She thought it was over.

A few weeks later, when Kim returned to dance at The Tunnel, a guy who resembled Psycho walked up to her.

"You're Kimberly, aren't you?"

"Yeah."

"Okay, we know you, Kimberly. I know where you are now," he said, before walking away.

Kim got the feeling that the guy was connected to Psycho. Kim was unnerved by the odd incident, but nothing seemed to come of it.

A few weeks earlier, she had brought a boyfriend home to dinner on Staten Island to meet her father and grandmother. Kim had met *Albert DeSoto, 21, in a club the previous year. After a month or so, things were not clicking, and she dropped him. But after her father had asked her several times to bring her boyfriend home, Kim brought Albert. He was a car salesman, handsome, hard-working, the kind of guy a young girl should bring home to Sunday dinner. Kim liked Albert, but she wasn't in love. She had last seen him a week earlier, and had called him at work the morning before she went out dancing with Liz. Nobody Kim was dating at the moment was really suitable to bring home to Daddy, no matter how much fun they were. She would no sooner bring home an unemployed guy like Jay than she would show her hidden tattoos to her family.

On February 28th, Kim got up early for school. She drove across the Verrazano Narrows Bridge into Staten Island to attend a morning class in business administration in a red brick building on the sprawling neo-colonial College of Staten Island campus in the Willowbrook section. Kim did not date guys from school. She thought that they were nice, but mostly nerds. The campus was just ten minutes from the gray-and-white two-story home in the suburban Arden Heights section, where her father Tommy Antonakos and her grandmother Mary lived. Kim would often stop in at home for lunch, but not that day—she had to be at work by midday at Amelia Interiors, where she did filing and bookkeeping work for the furniture firm. Kim's dad insisted that she work while she was in school, so she could contribute money toward her rent. If she wanted to have her own place, Tommy wanted her to experience the responsibility of paying at least part of her own way.

Tommy Antonakos, at fifty, was a successful businessman who had made money in insurance and real estate and was the head of a Long Island firm, Vista Systems of Ronkonkoma, that sold mainframe computers to "*Fortune* 500" companies. He was also a partner in a fire insurance business in Queens with his brother Joseph, who had shortened his name to Joey Anton. Both firms employed a total of about a hundred people. Tommy had kept his promise to a younger Kim not to re-marry after divorcing her mother, although Kim's mom Marlene had married again. It was difficult for Tommy, but he kept his promise. He never brought any of the women he dated to stay at his home while Kim lived there, because he didn't want to make her uncomfortable. Tommy was a man's man, handsome, half-Greek, half-Italian, with wavy black hair and brown eyes.

Kim came into the world at Maimonides Hospital in Brooklyn on November 15th, 1974. If Tommy spoiled Kim, or was over-protective, it may have been because he had divorced Kim's mom when his daughter was just a year old. After he moved out of their Kaufman Place apartment, Tommy spoke to Kim every day by phone. By the time she was three or four years old, he was having her over for weekends at his apartment, which was just fifteen minutes away. On Friday nights they would share Chinese food, and on Saturday morning, father and daughter would make breakfast together. Kim liked to help her dad make pancakes. Then Tommy and Kim would watch cartoons together, often her favorite—Tweety and Sylvester. For Kim's First Communion, Tommy went overboard. He threw a lavish affair at the exclusive Tavern on the Green in Central Park. It was a glittering event, and Tommy spared no expense: the kids rode in horse-drawn carriages; with Kim in the middle of the sparkling lights in her white communion dress, Tony Bennett serenaded her and her friends with his heavenly voice. "Daddy, I knew my party was going to be big, but I didn't know it was going to be this big," little Kim giggled.

Tommy threw Kim's Sweet Sixteen at the same spot. There was nothing he wouldn't do for her, and Kim grew up thinking that her Daddy could do anything. More recently, Tommy had taken Kim on a trip to Hollywood to visit a family friend, actress Alyssa Milano, on the set of the TV series "Who's the Boss?" Milano, 22, was a transplanted New Yorker and self-described "Daddy's girl," whose father was also named Tommy.

In December, 1993, sixteen months before Kim and Liz had gone dancing, Tommy finally agreed to let Kim move into her own apartment. Father and daughter went apartment-hunting together. Kim was ready to settle for any of several apartments she liked, but her dad insisted they keep looking until he found the right place. Tommy wanted an apartment that was safe, and had a second bedroom so Kim's mom Marlene would have a place to stay when she came up from Florida to visit. Tommy didn't want Kim to get too fancy too fast, even though he could have afforded to set her up in an expensive Manhattan penthouse. If Kim wanted to get a better apartment later on in life, or move into the city, he thought, then she would have to earn it. Kim's contribution to the rent from her salary wasn't that much, but it was enough to give her some responsibility, some value. Tommy felt he couldn't just give things to his daughter. Kim knew that she was going to have to work hard, but she knew she wouldn't have to struggle. She knew there was a place waiting for her in her father's company.

Tommy finally did find the perfect spot—a quiet, tree-lined block at the end of Eighty-seventh Street which ended a hundred yards to the south at Canarsie Beach Park. Tommy was concerned about parking on the block. He didn't want Kim to have to park blocks away and walk home alone at night, so he rented a basement garage right across the street. Kim would live in the ground-floor apartment of the three-story brick home. Tommy and Kim took measurements and bought furniture for the new place. Tommy was happy to see that the retired landlord, an elderly disabled veteran, sat at his upstairs window all day and looked out on the block. That made Tommy feel that Kim would be safe there. Just to make sure, he got her a message beeper and a cellular phone. That way, she wouldn't have to give her home phone number or address to guys she met. Her car had an alarm and help could be just a cellular call away. Tommy also gave her a pit bull puppy, which Kim christened with the not-so-tough name of "Sugar," and she got a cute little kitten, to which she gave the tough name "Spike." Sugar and Spike. The alarm, the beeper, the cell phone, the garage across the street, the pit bull, all allowed Tommy to sleep at night back in Staten Island, knowing that Kim was safe. After she moved into her new pad, Tommy met Kim at the Arco Diner in Bay Ridge, Brooklyn, at least once a week.

By the time Kim and Liz reached Liz's house in Canarsie, the cold wind off the water at their back had slowed to a gentle breeze. After the trip from the Manhattan club, Kim felt at ease back in her old neighborhood, where she had grown up, and where her old friends like April lived. At least she would not be going home to an empty apartment. April and Josh were still there.

"You headed straight home?" Liz asked Kim as they pulled over to the curb outside her red brick house.

"Yeah," said Kim. "I have work and school tomorrow, and my contacts are hurting. I'm really tired."

" 'Night," said Liz.

" 'Night," said Kim.

It was 3:55 a.m., March 1st, 1995—Ash Wednesday.

Kim pulled away and turned up the music on the car stereo, a new "gangsta" rap album from Arista Records called "Ready to Die." The rough, pounding song—a melange of music, drums, curses, and the Lord's Prayer—was created by a former criminal, an artist named Charles Wallace, who called himself "Biggie" Smalls, and recorded under the name of "The Notorious B-I-G". It spoke of armed robberies to finance a short, violent life filled with drugs, Rolex watches, and Q-45 Infiniti automobiles—a gangster's own obituary in 2:4 time.

The song was a fantasy about grabbing "the right bitch," and a Q-45 Infiniti automobile, as Smalls intoned to the pulsing beat: "As I lay me down to sleep, I pray the Lord, my soul to keep. If I should die before I wake, I pray the Lord my soul to take—'cause I'm ready to die . . . "

Outside the closed car, the music could be heard as an ominous bass thumping, as Kim's white Honda drove away into the pre-dawn darkness of Brooklyn.

CHAPTER TWO

MUTTS

Kim and Liz were doing their nails at 11:30 Tuesday night when the call was made. While they were manicuring, brushing their hair, and trying on clothes at Liz's place, preparing to go out for the evening, "K-Q"—a nickname which stood for "King Quality"—picked up the phone and called Nick.

"Tonight's the night," K-Q told Nick. "She went out dancing."

Nick then called his best friend and partner Joey, who soon arrived in his burgundy Maxima. Nick and Joey drove to Canarsie and parked down the block from Kim's apartment. They waited in the dark, with the car lights off, on the deserted street. They were ready.

On the seat between them was a large roll of gray duct tape and a pile of medical gauze pads. Nick and Joey were not doctors or paramedics waiting for a patient; they were small-time criminals—"mutts," in police parlance. During the night, K-Q beeped them three times on the beeper he had given them. Nick and Joey's task for the evening was not complicated or difficult, and did not call for much in the way of bravery. The two muscular men, armed with at least one loaded handgun, had to grab and subdue a woman they each outweighed by more than fifty pounds. They settled in, waiting for their quarry's white 1994 Honda Accord to arrive, waiting for an unsuspecting Kim to drive into their trap.

Cops called guys like K-Q, Nick, and Joey "mutts" because they sometimes made the police feel like frustrated dogcatchers. Mutts usually ran with a pack and could be dangerous when cornered. Detectives regularly threw nets over hounds with wild pedigrees—in the form of arrests for various crimes—but the mutts never seemed to stay in the dog pound very long. Nick was currently free on bail, and K-Q and Joey were out on probation.

Joey, a twenty-six-year-old stickup man, whose full name was José Negron, was a burly 5-foot-8-inches and 182 pounds. He sported a neatly trimmed beard that was black, but the dark hair on his head had gone prematurely gray and was an irregular salt-and-pepper. Joey, the eldest of the group, irritated the younger K-Q by referring to him as "the Kid." His nickname for himself was "N-I", which stood for "Negron Incorporated," like the famous Brooklyn-based "Murder Incorporated," icepick-killers-for-hire in the gangsters' heyday of prohibition-era New York.

Joey and Nick were kidnappers-for-hire, and their business was way off the books: kidnapping members of drug dealers' families and holding them for ransom. Joey's previous experience was pulling crimes against people who couldn't call the police; they paid up and settled out of court. A kidnapping was all in a night's work for them, but this one would be different.

He had a spot to stash the girl. Joey and Nick had used it before, a "sweet house" that was a crook's dream. If they could get this girl quickly, blindfold her, and tie her up before she saw their faces, they could get away with it. Then it was just a matter of how to spend the money they would get from her rich daddy.

Nicholas Libretti was only nineteen years old, but he was an inch taller than his buddy Joey. He had short brown hair and shifty green eyes. He may have been young, but he was trying hard to excel in his chosen profession. Five months earlier, on October 26, 1994, Nick and two other armed men had crashed into the side window of a Brooklyn home at 9:15

in the morning. The two women and the two young boys inside the house screamed as the men with guns burst in, spewing obscenities and threats. The ringleader was young Nick, who shoved his .45 automatic into one hysterical woman's mouth. Her four-year-old son watched in terror as Nick threatened to blow his mother's brains out. When he didn't like the answers about where cash and valuables might be hidden, Nick repeatedly put the muzzle of his weapon against the tot's face in an attempt to get the mother to talk.

In addition to being violent, Nick and his associates were indiscreet. Their break-in was cut short because it had been witnessed by two cops. Nick and the others fled, but they were caught on the street blocks away, handcuffed, and locked up. Police found piles of cash in the house, and Nick confessed to the crime. He and his pals were charged with robbery and weapons possession and were looking at serious time—up to twenty-five years behind bars. But the criminal justice system is not absolute and judges have discretion that can be exploited by defense attorneys. Nick and his co-defendants appeared before Brooklyn Supreme Court Justice Bernadette Bayne. A prosecutor from the Brooklyn District Attorney's office asked Bayne to impose $25,000 bail for all three bad guys. Nick's mother Helen hired defense lawyer Anthony Rendiero to argue that bail should be low because Nick would not flee; he told the judge that Nick had no criminal record and his mother was a respected community activist in their Cypress Hills neighborhood.

Bayne set Nick's bail at a low $1,000, and Nick walked out of jail the same day.

One cop was angered when he heard that Nick had been sprung, and was back out on the street. ''What are you going to do when you get him again and he has killed somebody?'' he asked a Brooklyn prosecutor.

The victims of Nick's money-making scheme became hysterical again when they learned that the man who had invaded their home and terrorized them was free. The DA's office offered to get the judge to issue an order of protection, but they declined. When they learned that he was back in the neighborhood, they fled the country. Apparently they did not think a piece of non-bulletproof paper would protect them from Nick.

Part of Nick's defense could be that years earlier, poor, sensitive Nick was scarred by the death of a nephew—Nick's sister's son. Nick and the boy, and at least one other kid, were toying with a loaded weapon, which went off. The bullet drilled a hole in Nick's cousin's head, killing him instantly. Nick blamed himself for the death.

Nick's mother, Helen Libretti, a former school crossing guard, was involved in local Democratic politics and campaigns to save a firehouse and reopen a grammar school. That same year, at a community meeting, she had questioned Police Commissioner William Bratton about police efforts against crime, specifically drug dealers. Helen often brought Nick to meetings of the local Democratic club, where they would see Congressman Edolphus Townes. The congressman's wife Gwendolyn had been Nick's teacher at PS 260. Helen appealed to Townes to write a letter to the judge chosen to hear Nick's case, Supreme Court Justice Michael Gary, asking him to go easy on Nick. Townes consented and wrote a letter to the judge on February 6th, 1995, barely a month before Nick and his new criminal partner were sitting in a car waiting to kidnap a young girl:

"I have known Nicholas Libretti since he was a small child. I have followed his development into a fine young man with enormous potential," Townes wrote. "While I certainly cannot speak specifically to this most recent incident, I feel strongly that this affair represents a clear departure from his normal behavior. It is in this light that I hope that this incident does not prove to be an indelible stain on the future of a young man that has so much to offer society. I write to ask that you afford Mr. Libretti every possible consideration."

Judge Gary went ballistic in court, and blasted the defense lawyer for submitting what he considered improper letters.

Gary was incensed over what he felt had the appearance of an attempt to influence the court. The lawyer explained that it had been the defendant's mother who had sent the letter. Despite his anger, Gary granted Nick "youthful offender" status on the recommendation of the DA's office—because Nick agreed to testify against the two other gunmen. The court record was sealed to protect Nick from retribution, resulting in no jail time—just probation for Nick. The victims of Nick's assault fled for their lives as well as from police scrutiny, but Nick was free—as long as he kept his nose clean. By comparison, Nick's accomplices did not fare so well—they went directly up the river. Bobby Hunt received a 2-to-6-year stretch in an upstate prison and John Patterson got harder time, 6-to-12 years behind bars. If Nick had been treated by the criminal justice system as the adult he was at nineteen, he would have received several years behind bars for multiple felonies of burglary, robbery, assault, and possession of a dangerous weapon. If he had received the same treatment, Nick would have been trying to sleep on the hard bunk of a prison cell on that cold Tuesday night. He would not have been lurking in a burgundy Maxima on a Canarsie street with another mutt—waiting to imprison a young girl, threaten her life, and sell her back to the family that loved her.

The plan had begun about a month earlier. K-Q was driving with his childhood friend—who had a similar, matching nickname—"B-Q," which stood for "Best Quality." K-Q was 5-foot-9-inches tall, and had short black hair and cold brown eyes. On his long, gaunt face, he wore a mustache and a wispy goatee beard—the kind once worn by magicians, or actors playing the role of Satan. The thin, bony Brooklynite was a high-school dropout, but fancied himself a criminal mastermind. K-Q was behind the wheel of a blue Nissan that belonged to his girlfriend when he first spoke about a kidnapping. He and his friend B-Q were en route from Canarsie to Bushwick, a tough neighborhood where they both had grown up. As they passed a car dealer on Cypress Avenue, K-Q stopped the car and pointed out a shining wine-red Infiniti Q-45 luxury car on the lot.

"I want that," K-Q said, pointing at the $45,000 V-8 automobile. "That's my dream car." It was absurd, of course. K-Q had no bread. Then K-Q started talking about his new plan, his pipe dream, to get his hands on his fantasy set of wheels.

"I got a scheme to make some dough," he announced. "I'm thinking about taking Kim and asking her family for ransom."

K-Q had recently gotten out of jail, and was not about to go straight. He wanted to make some money. Criminals, like people in other lines of work, evolve. Peeping Toms became burglars, burglars became rapists, rapists became murderers. They moved up the ladder, like in other professions. K-Q and B-Q were petty criminals, but K-Q was suggesting that they dare to dream, that they step up to big-time crime—with a big-time payoff. This was to be the Big Score, the Big Payday.

At just 22, K-Q was a mutt with a nasty pedigree. At 17, he had become a "Chicken Hawk." He would approach eight-year-old-boys in his Bushwick neighborhood with a business proposition:

"Hey, man, you wanna make twenty dollars?"

Not surprisingly, the answer was often yes. K-Q would then take the boys into Manhattan, where he would turn them over to adult homosexuals, who would have sex with them. The pederasts would pay K-Q $200 for pimping each kid. He turned a tidy profit until he was arrested in 1989 for promoting prostitution. He got off with only five years probation, and no jail time. The next year, he got locked up for a robbery, but the charges were dismissed. In 1991, he was busted for the rape and unlawful imprisonment of an underage girl, another sex crime. He copped a plea bargain and was rewarded with only sixty days' jail time—for saving Brooklyn taxpayers the expense of bringing him to trial. In November of 1992, a Suffolk County cop on Long Island "collared" K-Q for carrying a gun. K-Q had branched out into gun sales—another step up the criminal ladder. K-Q got only 18 months in jail and three years' probation.

His best buddy, B-Q, was the same height, but slightly more muscular and husky at 160 pounds. B-Q also had close-cropped black hair and brown eyes, but he had a rounder face and a lighter, clear complexion, boyish good looks, and a movie-star cleft chin that women liked.

B-Q's sister was married to a cop, but B-Q couldn't stay out of trouble with the law. He had also been granted "youthful offender" status for a robbery of a man who was pounced on by a "wolf pack" of teen thieves that included B-Q. He was later convicted in Queens for petty larceny, after cops nabbed him while he was trying to break into a garage to steal a car. His third conviction was for "steering"—directing drug customers to dope dealers on the street. B-Q had known Joey since he was six or seven years old, because Joey's stepfather was B-Q's stepfather's brother. B-Q had known Nick for only about a year.

On Monday, two days before Nick and Joey got the call from K-Q, the plotters had a meeting at an unlikely location—down the block from the Sixty-ninth Precinct on Foster Avenue at Rockaway Boulevard. Only a guy like K-Q, who thought he was smarter than the cops, would get a kick out of planning a major felony in view of a police station-house. The precinct was a two-story concrete bunker with small windows, and pebbles embedded in the concrete outer walls. If Kim's family reported the kidnapping, detectives in that building would investigate the crime.

"I got this thing all dreamed up," K-Q told Nick and Joey, as cop cars drove by. "Her family has money. This girl had a Lexus. It was stolen, and a few days later, she got a brand-new car."

After going over particulars, Nick and Joey left. At midnight, Joey drove Nick to another meeting with K-Q near the precinct. They got into K-Q's baby-blue Nissan Sentra hatchback. K-Q drove them to Kim's friend Liz's house, saying,

"Kimberly might come here first." Then he drove them to the two-car garage that Kim used. K-Q described her routine of going out clubbing, and coming home in the early hours of the morning, with rap music booming on her car stereo.

"She goes to clubs a lot," said K-Q. "She gets out of the car, opens the garage, pulls the car in the garage, gathers her belongings . . . When she drives her white car down the block, she'll have the music pumping," K-Q explained.

"I'll beep you the next time Kim goes out," K-Q told Joey, handing him his beeper.

They later met on a Flushing, Queens, street to work out other details. With K-Q was a light-skinned Latino kid about 16, named *Pepe.

"This is my man," K-Q said, gesturing to Pepe. "He's gonna be the guy who'll pick up the money."

K-Q's plan was simple, a throwback to the age of classical kidnapping, in which a child or adult was kidnapped and held for ransom because the bad guys believed that a father, husband, or other family member could and would pay a hefty cash ransom. For decades, the vast majority of kidnappings in the New York area and around the country had been drug snatches. Holding a member of a rich family for ransom was actually very rare—because kidnapping is a stupid crime, especially if the family calls the cops.

Kidnapping was not just stupid and vicious. It was a risky crime, because cops assumed most kidnappers had inside information, and investigated those close to the victim. To pull it off, you had to be good, you had to be smart, and you had to be ruthless. K-Q thought he was all three. In a holdup, you grab the money and run. It was an instant payoff—all you had to do was get away. You could wear a mask and gloves. In a kidnap, you have to grab and imprison a human being at a secure, secret location for an indeterminate period of time, while staying in contact with her family—with the police or the FBI listening in, recording it for voiceprint analysis, and hunting for you. Then you had to try to somehow pick up the ransom money without getting caught or followed. If the victim saw your faces, she might identify you later, so there was always the temptation to turn a kidnapping into a murder—in order to get away with it. Also, it usually required two or more bad guys—who got a cut of the ransom, but who might rat you out later when they got arrested for something else, as they always did.

One of the reasons such kidnappings were very rare was that a lot of kidnappers got caught—making it not such a good way to make a living. The finest detectives in the country, using state-of-the-art hardware, would swing into action once a ransom demand had been made—if a ransom demand was made. The NYPD's Kidnap Squad, part of the Major Case Squad working out of police headquarters in Manhattan, was a top-flight team whose prime directive was to bring the victim, "the vic," back alive, which they had done on virtually every case. They were smarter than the bad guys, and they had a bag of tricks to give them an edge: spy cameras that peeked under doors and into peepholes, through-the-wall microphones to bug rooms, scrambled radios to defeat counter-surveillance eavesdropping by perpetrators, phone tapping, and undetectable video surveillance equipment.

Nick and Joey, along with K-Q and B-Q, thought they, too, had an edge. Their advantage was witchcraft—something that placed them in a different world from the one inhabited by college student Kimberly Antonakos. All four men had been raised as Catholics, like Kim, but had become devotees of Santeria—a Caribbean pagan religion practiced by hundreds of thousands in New York. In their secret ceremonies, Santeria adherents—"Santeros"—danced, chanted, and slit the throats of goats and other animals in order to drink their blood. Under their clothes, they all wore colored beads that denoted the god that protected them. Before embarking on a dangerous criminal enterprise where there might be gunplay, K-Q, B-Q, Nick, and Joey would consult their witch doctor—"La Madrina," their spiritual Godmother. The Madrina would bless them, and arm them with "war beads." Worn under clothing, wrapped around the waist, neck, and torso like bandolero gun-belts, the war beads protected the wearers from arrest, from bullets in battle, and guaranteed success for their dirty deeds. So far, it had seemed to work pretty well. But none of them had consulted the Madrina before setting out to perform the latest kidnapping. They didn't think they needed such heavy-duty protection from a girl.

Nick and Joey had been waiting for hours by the time a pair of headlights pulled into the southern end of the block and moved up the street toward them.

CHAPTER THREE

KIDNAP

Joey watched the headlights approach in his rear-view mirror. As the white car came closer and passed their parked car, the thumping of ''gangsta'' rap music could be heard, just like K-Q said it would. The girl behind the wheel turned left and drove down the inclined concrete driveway to the basement level two-car garage, her headlights spotlighting the walnut-finished wood of the door. Kim used an automatic garage-door opener, and drove inside. She could not be seen—except from her apartment directly across the street. Nick and Joey jumped out of their car and sprinted toward the garage. As the wide door finished opening, the automatic chain motor made a clanking noise that masked the sound of two men rushing toward her from the darkened street. Kim put her car in PARK, shut off her headlights, and cut the engine. They were on her so fast she didn't have time to react, or to pick up her purse or the shopping bag with her new jeans. Joey grabbed her, one powerful arm around her shoulder pinning her right arm to her side, one hand clamped over her mouth like a vise. Her first screams could not be heard outside of the garage.

Joey threw her across the front seat. Kim fought fiercely, kicking her legs, jerking her head from side to side and clawing at the man holding her. She battled like a trapped animal fighting for survival. One of her gold shell earrings flew off and skittered across the garage floor. She gouged so savagely at Joey with her right hand that she broke some of the beautiful fingernails she had so painstakingly manicured hours earlier. The adrenaline pumping through her system killed the pain as she dug her nails into the zipper of Joey's black fatigue jacket, ripping out several metal zipper teeth and embedding them deep under one nail. Nick got busy, wrapping thick, sticky two-inch-wide duct tape tightly around the struggling girl's head. As he wrapped the living, kicking package, the loudest sound was the ripping *whoosh* as he pulled the silvery tape off the roll. He wound the tape over her mouth first—so she couldn't scream—pinching her long curls into a bulb shape. Then he wound the tape around her eyes. Joey changed his position so Nick could bind Kim's hands tightly, followed by her legs. Kim was still fighting, but it was all over. They had trussed her up like a mummy.

They used her keys to open her trunk, and then picked her up and dropped her in. They threw her pocketbook in with her and slammed the lid closed. Nick took Kim's keys and hopped in the driver's seat of the white Accord. He backed out of the garage onto the street, closed the garage, and then drove away to the north, with Joey following.

Kim hadn't given up yet, not by a long shot. She was still screaming under the tape, but not very loudly. It was unlikely that anyone could hear her outside. She was having trouble breathing, and was almost completely immobilized. For the first time in her life, she was virtually helpless, at the mercy of two men who came out of the dark and took her. She couldn't move, and couldn't see, or use her hands. Not that there was much in the trunk of the new car that would have helped her, had she been able to free her arms—only a blanket, two baseball caps, some license plate frames, and a can of rubbing compound. The tape over her eyes also covered her ears, and she couldn't hear very well, either. Kim was a prisoner entombed in her own car trunk in the dark.

Many would give up the struggle, but Kim would not

surrender. She began using her legs to kick against the metal of the trunk as hard as she could, hoping that someone would hear her. Her fashionable lumberjack boots came in handy. Every time she flexed her knees and hit the metal, it responded with a bang. She did it again and again, knocking her other earring off as she rocked back and forth in the cramped space, kicking with both feet.

Nick was not happy to hear banging coming from the trunk. If he could hear it up front, with the window closed, somebody outside might hear it, too. What if a cop pulled up next to him at a light? Nick didn't panic. The gangster reached down to the stereo and cranked up the volume of the gangsta rap song—Biggie Small's "One More Chance," a crude piece of sexual braggadoccio in which a chorus of women moaned, "Oh, Biggie, give me one more chance." Nick turned it up so loud that the rear-view mirror vibrated in time. He smirked when he realized that it completely drowned out Kim's attempt to get help. The ear-splitting racket coming from the car attracted no attention in the freezing New York pre-dawn, when apartment and car windows were closed against the cold. Just another boom-box on wheels.

Nick drove across the border into Queens, eventually turning north off Jamaica Boulevard onto a small, one-block street, then east, where he parked in front of a gray, two-story, wood-frame home. Joey pulled up behind him. About six weeks earlier, Joey had broken into a basement window of the unoccupied home at 78-08 Eighty-sixth Avenue, and stolen a key that had been conveniently left on a hook by the front door. It was a real sweet house on a quiet block, with electricity, water—and no people.

The men got out and looked around. No one was on the street, no one sitting on porches or looking out windows—no witnesses. Joey opened the trunk and picked Kim up. He left the blanket she was lying on in the trunk. He carried her quickly up the brick steps and into the dark house in both arms, like a groom carrying a bride over the threshold.

Joey carried her down into the basement, a frigid, musty, filthy mess, filled with broken furniture and piles of debris. He dropped Kim into a wooden chair. The back of the chair was up against a cylindrical metal pole in the middle of the room. Nick cut the tape on Kim's hands, and pulled them roughly around the chair. He pulled out a pair of metal handcuffs and cuffed her wrists behind her and around the metal pole, so there would be no possibility of escape—not unless she could pull the whole house down. Joey pulled off her boots and chucked them aside, leaving only Kim's dark socks to insulate her from the cold concrete floor. She wouldn't be doing any more banging or stomping.

They pulled her beeper off her waist, checked her empty pants pockets, and snatched her ring and gold bracelet. From around her neck they removed the big gold cross with red stones, which would bring the highest price at the pawn shop. They missed her watch, which Kim had left in her vest pocket. As they robbed her, Kim was still making noise under the tape. Joey lifted it, allowing Kim to speak to them for the first time. She didn't scream, or whine, or beg. She was still a gutsy Brooklyn kid, who mocked their greed in a sarcastic tone.

"What do you want, my pocket change?"

They ignored her.

"What's this all about? If you're going to mug me, why did you bring me here? Why are you going through such a big hassle?" she demanded. "Why are you going through all of this?"

Kim's eyes were still taped, so she couldn't see them smirk.

"Your father owes us money," one of them said, snidely.

"My father doesn't owe anyone money," she shot back defiantly. "My father pays his bills."

Her abductors weren't interested in anything she had to say. They didn't open the tape to have a conversation with another human being. They were worried she was making too much noise.

They still had work to do. Nick shoved a wad of gauze and a colored piece of cloth into her mouth and then put more tape over it, as Kim uttered muted protests. Nick and Joey simply walked away. She could hear them leaving, but there was no way she could know if she was really alone. Without an empty mouth to make resonant sound, the loudest noise Kim could make now was a muffled, whining murmur. She didn't know where she was or who had abducted her or why. Without a second thought, they left her alone in the dark with her nightmare.

The kidnappers got back into their cars and hit the road. Nick followed Joey onto Conduit Boulevard and then onto the Belt Parkway, which girdles the southern shore of Brooklyn and Queens. They were supposed to go west toward Staten Island to dump Kim's car, but for some reason, Joey took the eastbound entrance. They passed Kennedy Airport, and, several exits later, the Belt Parkway became Southern State Parkway when it entered Nassau County on Long Island.

Joey got off the parkway, with Nick bringing up the rear. They turned right onto a four-lane road, and then made the second right into a street of suburban homes. Joey made one more right turn and parked Kim's car at the curb in the middle of a little one-block street that looked like a dead end. Nick stopped farther up the block. Joey looked around, got out of the car, and threw his roll of silvery duct tape over a fence into someone's yard.

Nick got into the passenger seat of Joey's car, and waited. Joey noticed a shopping bag in Kim's car and grabbed it. He looked for other valuables, but didn't find any. He took Kim's purse from the trunk, and locked the car. On the way back to Queens, Nick rifled Kim's purse, taking the cash and wallet and cellular phone. He threw the brown pocketbook out the window, onto the parkway. The shopping bag contained a pair of new jeans that Kim had just bought the previous day. That, too, went out the window. Joey grabbed the cellular phone and tried to use it with one hand on the wheel.

It beeped when Joey turned it on, and when he entered a phone number, but when he hit the SEND button, he heard a recording.

"It's locked," he said.

As they neared Kennedy Airport, Nick took the phone and dialed a number. He also heard a recording that told him the fraud protection feature was engaged. It was impossible to use the phone without Kim's code, but Nick kept punching numbers anyway. The recording kept telling him to dial 611 for further assistance, so he did, hoping to get it working. As soon as he hit the SEND button, the phone transmitted a signal that was picked up and relayed by a repeater unit atop the nearby Hilton Hotel near the airport. The call was automatically relayed electronically to the customer-service department of the cellular phone company in Florida. The relay of a forty-one-second 611 call made at 5:52 a.m. from Kim's Cellular One cell phone from that rooftop repeater was recorded by a computer. In Queens, Joey stopped near his house and got out of the car to use a pay phone. He dialed K-Q's beeper, left a number, and hung up. A few minutes later, the pay phone rang, and Joey answered it.

"K-Q?" asked Joey. "The party's over." That was the code they had agreed on—the signal that they had Kim stashed away. When he returned to the car, Joey was upset.

"I don't feel right about the car."

Joey quickly drove all the way back to Long Island. It was after seven in the morning. The sun was rising and people were up and going to work. More cars were on the road, and a line of traffic was building on the opposite side of the highway, back into the city. It was rush hour. When they got back to Kim's Accord Joey took some rags and cleaning fluid from his car and began furiously wiping the outside of the driver's door and the steering wheel and console inside, trying to obliterate his fingerprints—something he should have done earlier.

An hour later, Joey dropped Nick off at his Brooklyn home, and then went home himself. They were both tired from their work. As the sun rose into a cold, gray sky, they went to sleep in warm, comfortable beds.

CHAPTER FOUR

ASH WEDNESDAY

The morning sky was ashen, and a frigid, drizzling rain was falling. Later in the day, the clouds broke up and let through some sun, which warmed the winter air above freezing to forty degrees. At 10:30 a.m., K-Q called B-Q, who was staying at his sister's house. K-Q told the sister who was married to the cop that it was important. She woke B-Q up and put him on the phone.

"You know, Kim is gone," said K-Q.

B-Q remembered K-Q saying he wanted to kidnap Kim, but he did not think K-Q was serious. K-Q described how Nick and Joey had taped her eyes, mouth, hands, and legs; how Joey had had to turn up the music because she was banging the trunk. Before he hung up, he told B-Q that they would let Kim go when they got the money. Later in the day, after calling Joey, K-Q went to a pay phone and dialed Tommy Antonakos' phone number in Staten Island. At the Antonakos household, a telephone answering machine in Tommy's home office clicked on.

"Hi," a man's voice said, and then paused. K-Q took the phone away from his ear. He then held a small microcassette tape recorder up to the mouthpiece, and pushed the PLAY button. A strange, high-pitched voice, like a cartoon chipmunk, came out of the hand-held tape recorder. It was a speeded-up tape that had been recorded at a slower speed.

Under normal circumstances, it would have been a funny voice, but if your daughter's life was at stake, it would have been terrifying.

"Hugged your daughter lately?" the voice chirped sarcastically into the phone. "Seventy-five thousand dollars— Your money or your daughter."

After a pause, Tommy's answering machine message had continued to play, at the same time as K-Q's taped ransom demanded. K-Q, the mastermind of the gang, was playing a tape to a tape. He stopped the machine, put his ear back to the phone, and listened, waiting to hear what the father had to say, waiting to move to the next step. Of course, he heard nothing. After a while, he hung up. In Staten Island, Tommy's answering machine clicked off.

Confused, K-Q redialed and tried it again—with the same results.

Why wasn't the father saying anything?

In Woodhaven, Queens, as soon as Jeanette let her schnauzer "Baby" out into her back yard, the dog started going crazy. Baby began running around and barking in the direction of the fence separating the small grass yard from the rear of the house around the corner. Jeanette Montalvo knew no one was living inside that house on Eighty-seventh Road, even though it didn't look abandoned.

"Baby! Be quiet! Baby, come here!" she scolded. Jeanette was perplexed. Baby was a quiet dog. Why was she acting like that?

On Long Island, Joanne noticed a white Honda Accord parked across from her house. Joanne Scully lived on Tucker Place in Malverne. She often saw cars parked there during the day because the quiet suburban street was right off the Southern State Parkway, and commuters who were carpooling into the city often left vehicles there. She went about her business, assuming it would be gone that night, as the cars always were.

*   *   *

At 3 o'clock, Tommy's beeper went off while he was at his
desk at his computer company, Vista Systems in Ronkonkoma. It was his friend *Gina Cuozzo calling from Brooklyn.
Gina and Tommy were dating, and Kim worked for Gina
part-time at Amelia Interiors, where Gina was the office man-
ager. Tommy dialed her number.

"Tommy, is Kim with you?"

"No, Kim is not with me. Isn't she working?"

"Kim never came to work. I got a call from April that
Kim never came home last night." Kim had been scheduled
to work from noon to 4:30 in the afternoon. Gina had an
appointment in Manhattan and could not leave until Kim
arrived. At 12:30, Gina beeped Kim, but there was no response. She didn't call Tommy until several hours had gone
by because she didn't want to get Kim into trouble.

Tommy immediately had a terrible feeling in the pit of
his stomach that something was wrong. He was very concerned, and knew Kim would not just disappear without calling him or telling him that she was departing from her
normal routine. He and Kim were very close and spoke every
day. Tommy dropped everything. He hung up the phone, and
headed toward Canarsie in his Ford Taurus.

As he drove, Tommy became more and more alarmed,
driving faster and faster. He was startled to suddenly see
flashing lights in his rear-view mirror. It was a traffic cop,
who pulled him over to the side of the road. When Tommy
told the officer that he was rushing into Brooklyn because
his daughter was missing, the cop let him go with a warning:

"Take it easy."

Tommy couldn't take it easy. He arrived at 1437 East
Eighty-seventh Street just after four o'clock. The door to
Kim's apartment was opened by Josh, who introduced himself. In his hand was Kim's address book and daily appointment book, the one Tommy had given her. It was the first
time the two had met, but Kim had told her father about

Joshua Torres and April Dedely being her house guests. April, a secretary in a Brooklyn law firm, was at work. Josh, who was not working, was taking care of their cute son, Timmy. Tommy certainly didn't mind when he had heard Kim was having company. It meant she wasn't alone.

"Where's Kimberly?" Tommy asked, as he stepped inside. "Do you know anything about what's been going on here?"

"Kim hasn't been home," Josh replied.

"When did you hear from her last?"

"She called last night to say she was going out, and we haven't heard from her since then," Josh explained. "I've been making calls to all her friends to find out if anybody heard from Kim. I made, like, forty or fifty calls, and everybody is calling back except for a fellow named Psycho."

Tommy was taken aback by the name. When Tommy asked Josh if he knew anything about the guy with the scary nickname, Josh said yes.

"Psycho is a really bad guy. He's crazy about Kim. She was scared of him."

This was all news to Tommy. His daughter was being stalked by some guy named Psycho? Kim hadn't told him—and now she's missing? It was like living in a bad dream. Josh said that Kim had been out dancing with a friend named Liz, whom Kim drove home. Tommy asked Josh to call Liz. He wanted to talk to her. In the meantime, Tommy had another idea. "Do we know if her car is in the garage?" he asked, stepping outside.

Tommy didn't hear an answer. Josh stood on the front steps of the red brick home, and watched as Tommy crossed the street and tried the garage door handle. It was locked. Tommy knocked on the door of the family from whom he had rented the garage. He asked the woman to check and see if Kim's car was inside. It wasn't. Tommy had seen enough. He got in his car and drove to the Sixty-ninth Precinct. He walked past several blue-and-white patrol cars and rushed into the stationhouse.

The desk officer told Tommy to wait, and he soon spoke to a woman officer, who listened to his story and wrote it down. But this cop seemed to be treating it as routine. She did not understand how urgent this was. She explained that NYPD guidelines called for twenty-four hours to pass before they would act on a report of an adult missing person—because so many people simply ran off, got drunk, or shacked up somewhere. The only exceptions were for kids under sixteen years of age, the mentally or physically handicapped, those in need of medication, or any who might be a danger to themselves or others. Kim did not fit into any of those categories.

Tommy was a businessman, a man of action. He wasn't used to doing nothing. He wanted to speak to someone else. He wanted to speak to a detective. Tommy would not leave. He would keep telling his story until someone understood.

Detective Phil Tricolla was busy doing paperwork on a case in the second-floor Squad Room, when an anti-crime sergeant from downstairs walked into the room.

"Listen there's a guy downstairs. His daughter's missing. Maybe you want to talk to him?"

Phil didn't have to talk to the guy, but the paperwork could wait. Phil had heavy experience working "cold" cases, old unsolved homicides. A few minutes later, a prosperous-looking man wearing glasses and dressed in an expensive suit and tie walked in. He held out his right hand for Phil to shake, a firm grip. In his other hand, the man held an address book.

"My daughter's missing," Tommy said. "I know what you're going to tell me—she ran off with some guy . . . I'm telling you . . . she calls me at least once a day. I know my daughter well enough that there is something that has to be wrong." Tommy talked about Kim and what had happened. Listening, Phil got the impression that this guy and his daughter were really close. He had a feeling for the guy. Phil felt that somehow, she had been taken against her will.

Phil had been on "The Job," as cops call it, for twelve

years, and had been a detective for five. He had learned to go with his gut instinct whenever he could. "Things just don't fit," Phil thought. "I'm taking this case. Rules are made to be bent."

Phil fed a Missing Person Report form into his typewriter. He began asking Tommy questions and typing the answers into little boxes on the long, triplicate form until it was finished. Slightly relieved that, at last, something would be done, Tommy gave Phil Liz Pace's name and address out of Kim's book—the last person who had seen Kim. After Tommy left, Phil called Liz, who told him about the night of dancing.

"We hung out. We danced, we talked to a couple of guys," said Liz. Phil asked her if they had been drinking.

"We had a couple of beers, but we didn't get hammered," Liz replied. She said she and Kim liked to hang out in Salsa clubs and dance. When Phil asked about distinguishing marks, she told him about Kim's tattoos, the scorpion and the naked couple. Women were great witnesses. Liz was also able to describe every single article of Kim's clothing and jewelry, from head to toe.

By the time Tommy left the precinct, it was already nighttime. Things seemed worse in the dark. He stopped by Liz's house and asked her if she and Kim had been followed from the club. Liz did not think they had been. When he arrived back at Kim's place with Liz, his friend Gina was there, along with Josh and April and their child. Tommy had known Kim's friend April, a pretty girl with blonde hair, for years. He also knew her parents from the neighborhood.

"Everybody has called in except this guy Psycho," Josh told Tommy again. "He's the guy we should check out." Josh said the guy was some kind of gangster. "Everybody's cool, but Psycho."

While Tommy was there, Josh made some phone calls to Kim's friends, like Jay, her most recent boyfriend. Josh and April had introduced Jay to Kim.

"Have you seen Kim, have you heard from Kim?" Josh

asked Jay. "She's missing. She didn't come home." He hung up and told Tommy that Jay had no idea where Kim was, but would come over to help.

April beeped Shawn, a former boyfriend of Kim's, and asked if he had seen Kim. He hadn't, but he also volunteered to come out and help look for her. Josh told Tommy that he knew a lot of hidden places where car thieves stashed stolen cars.

"I could show you around—to look for her," Josh volunteered.

Tommy, Josh, and Gina went out in Tommy's Taurus, looking for Kim's car. Josh took them to various back streets and wooded lots around Canarsie. They drove through parking lots and shopping centers where Kim might have gone. They checked out abandoned car hulks in weeded lots. Their heads turned toward every dark-haired girl that might be Kim, every white car that might be hers. Then they left the neighborhood and Josh directed them onto the Eastbound Belt Parkway and over a drawbridge.

"Pull onto the service road," Josh told Tommy, who parked in the desolate spot. Gina stayed in the car. The younger man took Tommy's flashlight and led the way, as they waded through dead weeds and garbage. They descended along a dank, sandy path that led down under the shadowy bridge to a pitch-black garbage dump frequented by denizens of the criminal underworld. The stark landscape was in the borough of Queens, but, in the darkness, in Tommy's anguished state, it may as well have been on a cold shore of Hell.

"Watch out for the rats," Josh warned.

How could Kim just vanish? Tommy had not yet told his mother or his ex-wife in Florida that Kim was missing. That morning, he had been on the planet Earth, but he was now on a planet called Wednesday, where time seemed endless, where the geography was pain. Kim was his whole life, his whole world. Wednesday. Today was Ash Wednesday.

"I don't like the way this looks, Joshua," Tommy said,

as they drove back to Canarsie. "I'm scared."

Instead of going back to Kim's place, Tommy drove to his old parish church, Our Lady of Miracles on East Eighty-sixth Street, so they could get ashes and pray for Kim's safe return. Tommy parked right in front of the church, and he and Gina got out of the car.

"Do you want to come in and get ashes with me, Josh?" asked Tommy.

"No, I'll wait here in the car," Josh replied.

Our Lady of Miracles was a small white church built out of wood, with a simple white cross atop its triangular roof. It was built in 1936 and dedicated to an ancient Madonna and Child shrine in Sicily that was uncovered in the year 1547. The religious painting and covering arch were discovered on a Sicilian hillside during a police search inspired by falling rocks and an apparition of a little boy and a beautiful lady dressed in white. Tommy was looking for a miracle, and wanted to ask God for some help.

Inside the church, a center aisle between rows of dark, wooden pews led to a simple white altar and a large crucifix under a trussed-beam A-frame ceiling. A nave in the center of the left wall contained the shrine of Our Lady of Miracles—a green-robed Virgin Mother and Child, adorned with crowns and flanked by flowers, and rows of flickering blue glass memorial candles for the dead. Ash Wednesday is the first day of Lent and customarily a time of public penance. During the traditional annual Ash Wednesday service, ashes are placed in an urn on the altar and consecrated before a High Mass. A priest then dips his thumb into the ashes and daubs a sign of the cross on the foreheads of parishioners. While he applies the ashes—made by burning the palm fronds from the Palm Sunday service the previous spring—the priest utters a Latin prayer.

"*Memento, homo, quia pulvis es, et in pulverem revertens*"—Remember, man, that thou art dust, and unto dust thou shalt return.

Tommy and Gina said their prayers and received their

ashes, the mark of the penitent faithful. Back at the apartment, Tara, Kim's friend since the seventh grade, had arrived. A beautiful girl with short blonde hair and pretty hazel eyes, Tara was very upset. She brought her fiancé Steven to help search for Kim, but there was no news. Tara was worried sick about her friend. Everyone in the apartment was talking about Kim and looking at her pictures in an album in the living room. Tommy called his lawyer and the FBI, but could not sit still. He would not rest until he knew Kim was safe. At 8:30, he asked Josh if there was a spare key to Kim's garage.

"Do we have Kim's keys?" Tommy asked Josh. "Do we have a set of Kim's keys around here? What keys do you use? Did Kim give you a set of keys to come in and out?" Josh handed over a set of keys and Tommy took them across the street. One of the keys opened the big door, revealing a darkened, empty garage. Tommy found a light switch and flipped it. He noticed a small glint on the floor.

"What's that?" he asked, walking toward it. Josh rushed over and picked the object up before Tommy could get to it. It was a gold seashell earring, the only thing in the garage. Tommy was sure it belonged to Kim. That meant she had made it home, and then she and her car had vanished. Liz Pace arrived and told Tommy it was Kim's earring, and that she had been wearing it the night before. She had already described it to the detective. Tommy rushed back into the house to call Phil Tricolla.

"Don't go back in the garage, don't do anything," Phil told Tommy over the phone. "I'm coming over."

Josh suddenly told Tommy that he was going to his old neighborhood, Bushwick, to hunt for Kim's car, because he knew a lot of "chop shops" there. Car thieves took hot cars to chop shops, where they were quickly chopped up into valuable parts for resale. Phil rushed over. Tommy, who was very upset, showed the earring and the garage to Phil, who tried to calm the worried father until they had more facts.

"You know what, Tommy? This could be an earring she

lost months ago." Phil showed the piece of jewelry to Liz.
"Do you recognize this earring?"

"Yeah, it's the earring Kim was wearing last night."

"Positive?"

"Positive."

"How positive are you?"

"She was wearing those earrings last night," said Liz.

Tommy told Phil about Psycho. Liz also said that Kim
was afraid of him, and that Psycho was some kind of gangster who had fallen totally in love with Kim and was obsessed with her. Phil realized he had a problem. First, he
canvassed the block. He rang every doorbell and spoke to
all the neighbors, but they had all been asleep. Not one had
heard or seen anything suspicious. He took Kim's address
book and told Tommy he had to get back to the stationhouse
and pull out the stops. He said he would put out a stolen car
bulletin on Kim's Accord. The GLA—grand larceny, auto—
alarm would go out to cops all over the city. They would
have Kim's license plate on their "Hot Sheet" by the next
shift, and the stolen car description would go out to all fifty
states. "Here's my home number, call any time," Phil told
Tommy before he left.

What had happened? Did this Psycho grab her, or was she
the victim of a carjacking or some other jealous boyfriend?
Phil contacted the city Department of Sanitation, and the Department of Transportation—but Kim's car had not been
towed away anywhere in the city. Phil alerted Kim's college
security department, who said they would also investigate.
The detective called American Express, and the emergency
number for the bank that had issued Kim her ATM card. Phil
drew a blank. No one had been using Kim's plastic. Morgues
and hospital emergency rooms would be checked. He asked
the NYPD Aviation unit to send a helicopter to look for the
car, since cars are usually easier to find than people. He
called the Port Authority Police at the airports and asked
them to check their parking lots, since many car thieves
stashed stolen cars there.

After putting out the alarms on Kim's vehicle, and arranging for a helicopter to search in daylight, Phil thumbed through Kim's phone book. Some names and numbers had been scribbled on the inside of Newport cigarette boxes, one on a lipstick-stained card from a Manhattan club. He ran across listings for relatives, like "Uncle Joey," and "Daddy," hairdressers, school, and girlfriends. There were also more than a dozen males listed. Were they friends, schoolmates, cousins, or boyfriends? One listing just had a beeper number for "Psycho"—the next order of business was to find him. There were lots of other names, lots of potential suspects. Phil had a lot of work to do. On the way home to Long Island in the early hours of the morning, he did not take the parkway, but detoured through the rough neighborhood of East New York, looking for Kim's car.

Rather than sit around waiting for something to happen, Tommy decided to do his own detective work. Calls were made to Psycho's number, without success. He knew only that Psycho lived in Brighton Beach. April told him she thought Psycho lived in an apartment building across from a Chinese restaurant with a red awning.

"We're all afraid of him," she said.

Tommy drove to the Russian community of Brighton Beach, also home of the Russian Mafia, and, amazingly, located a Chinese restaurant with a red awning. First he checked around for Kim's car, looking on the street and in the garage of Psycho's building. It wasn't there. Then the well-dressed man in gold-rimmed glasses with ashes on his forehead began asking people on the street for help.

"Do you know Psycho? Have you seen him around?" Tommy implored, over and over again. "My daughter is missing."

Some of the people seemed frightened of the polite, but desperate, man. He went into a pool hall. He stopped anybody still walking the street in the middle of the night. Tommy couldn't sleep with Kim missing. He knew that if

Kim was in danger, she was waiting for him to come get her, to find her—to bring her home.

The clouds were gone. The sky was clear but the temperature had dropped to the freezing point. Alone in the dark, Tommy searched all through the endless night.

CHAPTER FIVE

PSYCHO

Tommy gave up his search about five in the morning on Thursday. He drove back to Kim's place to check one more time. After he let himself in, he found a guy asleep on the couch in the dark living room. Tommy woke him up, and the groggy young man introduced himself:

"I'm Jay," he said. Jay, the guy Kim had been dating, one of the kids helping with the search, thought an exhausted Tommy.

"I'm Tommy. Any news?"

"No."

"Go back to sleep."

After the darkest day of his life, Tommy drove home to Staten Island, more miserable and tired than he had ever been. He checked his answering machine, hoping to hear some good news, but there was none. He collapsed into a fitful sleep for a few hours, and then shaved, showered, and changed his clothes. He was back at Kim's apartment by noon. Kim's friends began arriving and leaving—fanning out to look for her or her car again, with Tommy directing the search. A distraught Tara told Jay she feared something really bad had happened to her childhood friend. Kim had been like a sister to her.

"I know Kim's gonna be OK," Jay told her. She wanted to believe him.

Tommy's brother Joseph, who ran the family fire insurance business in Woodhaven, arrived with a group of his friends to help in the search. Out of their hearing, Jay joked that the men looked like mob "gorillas." Joseph, who had simplified his name to Joe Anton for business reasons, ran the insurance agency that was a block away from mobster John Gotti's social club headquarters—the Bergin Hunt & Fish Club at 98-07 101st Avenue. The buzz on the street was that nobody could buy or rent in the neighborhood unless they were mobbed up, because the Gambino Family were paranoid about outsiders—especially FBI agents who wanted to find apartments to set up their cameras and bugging equipment. Suddenly, talk of assistance from "heavy hitters" from the old neighborhood began to circulate among the searchers. After all, what worried father wouldn't do anything he could to get his child back safely? Most parents—if they had grown up with wiseguys in the neighborhood—would grasp at any straw, any help, to get their kid home safe and sound.

Josh and Jay discussed it and convinced each other that Tommy and his brother were members of the Mafia, of Gotti's crew. Everybody knew the story about the guy who had lived across the street from Gotti in Howard Beach. On March 18, 1979, the neighbor was driving down the block when he struck twelve-year-old Frank Gotti with his car. The poor kid was killed, but it didn't end there. Four months later, while Dapper Don John Gotti was on vacation in Florida, the neighbor was last seen being ushered by several men into a van. He vanished, and was presumed murdered. No corpse was ever found and no one was ever charged in the case. And that was for an accident. Josh and Jay felt that whoever had taken Kim had better watch his ass. The boys from the Bergin Hunt & Fish Club would hunt them down, and take them fishing—as bait.

Phil Tricolla was thinking carjacking, and when Cellular One told him that Kim's cellular phone had been used near the JFK Hilton Hotel after she disappeared, it reinforced his suspicion. The problem was that carjackers would also have stolen Kim's credit cards and put them on the street immediately, before they could be cancelled. No one had used Kim's American Express card to buy anything, or withdrawn money with her ATM bankcard. Carjackers often drove victims straight to a cash machine.

A sex crime or a kidnapping were possibilities, but most snatches were to extort drugs, or money, or both, from drug dealers. In one Bronx case, the ruthless rip-off artists did not kidnap the newborn baby of their target. They simply held the family at gunpoint and placed the screaming infant inside a microwave oven. They set the radar range to HIGH and threatened to hit the START button unless they were told the location of the loot. Not surprisingly, the bad guys got what they wanted. But, since no ransom demand had been made for Kim, Tricolla had no reason to believe she had been kidnapped.

"Psycho's got my daughter," Tommy told Phil when the detective arrived at the apartment. Tommy gave him a picture of Psycho that he'd found among Kim's possessions. It showed Psycho with his strawberry-blond hair almost completely trimmed off his round head, exposing prominent ears. He had pale skin, blue eyes, and a scraggly mustache and beard. He had a goofy smile, and was holding up a huge fan of green one-hundred-dollar bills. The kid had thousands of dollars in his hands. Phil took Psycho's picture to the Sixtieth Precinct in Brighton Beach. He showed the picture to a detective he knew.

"Psycho? Yeah, I know him," the detective replied. Psycho was a mutt, he said.

Within minutes, Phil had Psycho's pedigree—a Bureau of Criminal Identification computer printout of arrest information, with his photo, height, weight, eye color, Social Security number and home address. Psycho, 23, had been born in Odessa, Russia, and later came to the U.S. with his parents. He was out on $5000 bail, after being charged just the previous month with the statutory rape of a twelve-year-old girl. Psycho was a reputed member of a street gang called Together Forever, a loose confederation of Russian and Hispanic youths who hung out on the Coney Island boardwalk. Together Forever was suspected of drug dealing, extortion and gun running.

Phil went out with his partner Jimmy Tierney to find Psycho. He was hopeful. Maybe Psycho had refused to take no for an answer, and had Kim tied to a bed somewhere. In police work, mysteries are rare. If investigators could find out what people around the victim knew, the perp was usually the most obvious guy. It was then just a matter of getting enough evidence to brace the mutt, and get him to give it up. Everybody was pointing to Psycho. Was it that easy?

Guns on their hips, Phil and his partner sat outside Psycho's place in an unmarked car. They preferred to grab bad guys in the open, unexpectedly. If Psycho was the right guy, it wouldn't help if he barricaded himself inside his apartment—particularly if Kim was there. At 1 o'clock, Psycho came waltzing around the corner. The detectives casually got out of the car and stopped him in his tracks.

"Hey, Psycho, what's up?" said Phil. "We got to talk to you."

They put Psycho in the back seat of the car, and carefully watched his face for the genuineness of his reaction. Experienced detectives had an essential piece of equipment that Ernest Hemingway called "a good crap detector." If Psycho betrayed guilty knowledge about Kim, or lied, it would show in his face. Phil asked about Kim.

"Tell me who she is again?" responded Psycho in a Russian accent. He may have been evasive, but he seemed far too cool for someone who was supposed to have kidnapped someone. He also seemed high. Kim was the girl you took to Florida two months ago, Phil reminded him, the one whose name you have tattooed on your calf.

"I met her at a club. We talked on the phone a couple of times," said Psycho.

He did not seem nervous at all. Psycho claimed that the

body art was in honor of a friend of his named Mike, who kicked drugs. The letters did not stand for a girl's name, but for "Kick It, Mike." He pulled up his pants leg and showed them the periods after each of the letters—dots that could have been added late—making it an acronym. Psycho claimed he was a stockbroker and that he never bought Kim a ticket, she had paid her own way. He said Kim stayed with her mother, and he never saw her and never bought her anything, just talked on the phone. When they asked Psycho where he had been on Wednesday night, he gave them a vague story. He didn't have an alibi, but Phil didn't think he knew anything about Kim. Of course, he never asked why they were asking about Kim. He never asked what had happened to her. Obviously he was concealing something, but Phil thought Psycho did not act like a guy who had a girl tied up somewhere, or a murderer.

"I may not be done with you," said Phil, handing Psycho his card. "Call me at noon tomorrow."

Phil's crap detector had not gone off.

"What happened?" Tommy asked, when Phil arrived at Kim's apartment.

"Tommy, this isn't the guy," Phil replied. "I don't think this guy is involved. I think we're chasing our tails here." Phil said he would continue to check Psycho out. If he called the next day, if he didn't bolt, Phil was sure that Psycho—despite his nickname—was not involved. It was somebody else. It was time to go through the list of all the people Kim had known, everyone she had ever dated, and check them out. Tommy was crestfallen. It had seemed so simple. Psycho had to be the one. Phil went back to Kim's book, and the elimination process began. That night, after a long day on the case, Phil took a different route through East New York, still looking for Kim's car on his way home to Malverne.

Tommy felt good that Kim's friends were willing to pitch in, and stay up all night searching for her and her car, and calling everyone they could think of. When Josh got back from looking, Tommy told him what had happened with Psycho. If Psycho did not call Phil back the next day, that might change things. If Psycho took off, it would mean he was the guy.

"We're not going after Psycho," Tommy told Josh. The beleaguered dad could not believe Psycho was not involved, and Josh agreed. Who else could it be? Josh told Tommy that a friend of his had seen a carload of cursing Russian guys driving down Kim's block the night she disappeared. Did the cops know about that? No, they didn't, said Tommy, but he would tell them right away. Tommy got Josh's friend's name and phone number. Josh then said he and Jay were going back out to look for Kim's car, and check out more chop shops in Bushwick. As Josh and Jay were leaving, Tara's fiancé Steven asked to go along.

"No," said Josh immediately.

It was better, he said, that Steven go in his own car. That way, they could cover more ground.

Jeanette Montalvo was sick of hearing Baby bark at the house around the corner. It was after 9:30 at night and the animal had been barking around the clock for two days. She kept barking and running around, like someone was there. Jeanette complained to her husband about it.

"Something's going on. Baby's going crazy." Then, suddenly, Baby stopped barking. When Jeanette called Baby, she didn't come in. Jeanette went out and found Baby on her back, senseless and silent, her legs in the air. It looked like someone had "pinched her down" by pulling the skin on the back of her neck. Jeanette looked around, but saw no one. She went inside and called her daughter.

"Antonette, tell Joey to come over and see what's wrong with Baby. I think somebody pinched her down."

Joey got on the phone. "Ma, I'll be right there." He arrived very quickly. Baby seemed to be fine by the time he got there. Joey walked around the back yard, put Baby inside the house, and left.

* * *

K-Q and B-Q drove to "Weedgate" to score some "weed," or "chronic"—as in chronic user—as marijuana was called on the street. They passed cash through a metal gate, and a hand passed out a small bag of dope—and they got high. Later, at a pay phone, K-Q dialed Tommy Antonakos' number in Staten Island. Again, he played his ransom tape into the phone after he heard a guy answer, but the guy didn't say anything.

K-Q lived with a girlfriend who had a job, an apartment, and a car—an inexpensive Japanese compact, which he was driving. She was willing to support him, no questions asked, as long as he did not cheat on her. But, in addition to being a criminal genius, K-Q was a ladies' man. He was currently seeing several other women on the sly, including his last girlfriend. If he had a Q-45 Infiniti the color of fine wine, with luxurious leather upholstery and deluxe appointments, then he could really impress the girls. To K-Q, Kim was a hot set of wheels. To the others, who had no specific use for the money yet, Kim was simply livestock, money on-the-hoof.

K-Q and B-Q were on their way to a meeting of conspirators, arranged by beeper. It should have been time for the ransom drop and the payoff, but there was a snag.

"We've got her," said Nick, when they met on a Canarsie street. "Now it's your part now, it's your turn to contact the parents."

"I did it already, and it didn't work," said K-Q. "The father didn't say anything." He explained how he called the house, someone said hello and he made the ransom demand. Joey returned K-Q's beeper, and demanded to know why they didn't have the money yet.

"I'll try it again. I can't figure out why this isn't happening yet, but he's playing it close to the vest. He hasn't even told his mother she's missing yet. This is just like a drug dealer's child. He loves her," K-Q said, trying to put a positive spin on things.

"Everything's going good here," K-Q told them, despite all the evidence to the contrary. "They don't know nuthin'. I got 'em pointed the wrong way, I got 'em looking at Psycho. They rolled up on Psycho, and he bitched-up, he started crying," K-Q chuckled. It wasn't true that Psycho had cried when questioned by detectives, but K-Q was trying to cheer up his gang.

"Yo, we got the D-Ts fooled—they're going after Psycho," K-Q exulted.

But B-Q was not so proud. He said he "felt creepy" about the whole business. K-Q did not respond. Instead, he did a mocking imitation of Tommy Antonakos, sobbing about his missing only child:

"I don't want to know how this happened, I just want her to be OK," K-Q intoned in a boo-hoo voice, before reverting to his own. "So it seems like he would pay the dough for his daughter."

B-Q asked Joey if he was taking care of Kim.

"Is she okay?" B-Q asked. "Where is she? Is she warm? Did you feed her? Yo, we gotta put a blanket on her or she'll die."

"She's okay," said Joey. "She's close. She's safe."

He assured B-Q that he took care of her every day. It was a lie. Joey did brief scouting expeditions to make sure Kim was still there, but he had not put a blanket on her, or given her any food or drink since they left her in the basement. Joey was afraid of being seen, of drawing too much attention to the house.

"Show me the house," K-Q told Joey. "I could find her and be a hero." K-Q had not told Joey and Nick about his fear that the mob might be after them.

Joey shook his head and rejected K-Q's latest scheme. He declined to tell K-Q where Kim was. Instead, he listened as K-Q did most of the talking. K-Q liked talking, liked to be in charge. As K-Q made fun of Tommy's misery, and laughed at the cops, a small microcassette tape recorder was silently turning in Joey's pocket, its red light blinking—recording everything they said. The voices were a little muffled through the material, but still audible. With things going wrong, Joey had decided that he wanted some insurance. It was just business. What if the kid, K-Q, decided to stiff him and his buddy Nick on the payoff? What if he got jammed up on something else, or this thing blew up?

Insurance was a good thing.

Dark clouds scudded over Queens, and the temperature dropped to 25 degrees. It was a lot quieter at Jeanette's house, now that Baby was inside and had stopped barking. From her kitchen window in the rear of the house, Jeanette could see the side windows of the abandoned house as she washed the dinner dishes in the sink. A flickering light caught her eye. She thought it might be a flashlight or a candle on the first floor. She ignored it. She also heard a faint sound coming from the direction of the house. When she heard it again, she listened from the window:

"Hmmm . . . Hmmm . . ."

She had no idea what it was, but there were a lot of old people on the block who might make such a whimpering noise, and she didn't think anything of it. Also, people sometimes hung out behind the abandoned house to drink and take drugs. It wasn't any of her business. She did nothing. She went to bed. Sometime during the night she heard the gate to the abandoned house open, but, again, she did nothing.

Phil was in bed by midnight, when the phone rang. It was Tommy Antonakos. He had a new lead. *Bob Murphy, a friend of one of Kim's friends, had seen a car full of rowdy Russian punks in the neighborhood on the night Kim went missing. Tommy relayed the information, and Phil dialed the Sixty-ninth Precinct detective Squad Room, a twenty-four-hour operation. Detective Alex Malpica answered, and Phil asked him to do him a favor on his missing persons case. Alex was busy, but this had a higher priority—a possible witness in an abduction.

"Alex, drop what you're doing and interview this guy," Phil asked. He said he would pick it up in the morning. Malpica called Phil back later to say that the witness, Josh's friend, had seen Psycho's picture—and they got a hit.

"I think he was in the car," the youth told detectives.

Phil had to go back and look at Psycho and his friends. Had he been wrong about Psycho? They were back to square one.

CHAPTER SIX

ALONE

Kim was helplessly, completely alone for the first time in her life. She had been given an undeserved sentence of physical and mental torture, like a maid consigned to a medieval "oubliette"—a French word meaning a place of confinement to oblivion, a place of forgetting. An *oubliette* was the sunless solitary confinement pit of a dungeon. Those cast there were condemned to perpetual imprisonment, or to perish secretly, without food or water, and be forgotten.

An oubliette had only one hole at the top to admit air, and Kim could only breathe through the small space that left her nostrils exposed between her blindfold and her gag. Her mouth was filled with gauze, and taped shut with sticky duct tape that pinched the skin of her face. She could not see because her eyes were wrapped with windings of tape that also covered her ears, and muffled her hearing. Her shoeless stockinged feet rested on cold cement.

At first, being seated—even taped to a chair with both wrists bound with cold metal handcuffs behind her back around a steel pole—was better than being banged around inside a car trunk. The pain-dulling adrenaline rush that had accompanied her struggle with her abductors, and her attempt to attract help, eventually wore off, leaving a host of aches, pains, and discomforts in its wake. Her contact lenses again began to smart, an itchy soreness that would have been eliminated if she could have simply removed them. One finger throbbed with pain where zipper teeth remained embedded under her fingernail, which was akin to another type of ancient torture. When she tested her bonds, they were heartbreakingly solid. When she flexed the muscles in her arms and pulled at the cuffs, the metal did not give, but simply dug painfully into the skin of her wrists until it met the unyielding bones of her hands. If she could get only one hand free, she could pull the tape off her eyes and mouth, and scream her lungs out. But, after pulling, and twisting, and squirming every way she could, she was still stuck. The loudest noise she could make with her stifled mouth was a whining cry at the back of her throat. She could also make a louder whining hum inside her nose. If she exhaled forcefully at the same time as she made the nasal hum, it would create an even louder sound, a kind of human yelp:

"Hmm! Hmm!"

Why didn't anybody hear her? Her efforts to free herself and call for help were tiring. Muscles began to ache. But even resting had a price in bondage—her muscles and joints began to tingle with pins-and-needles, from being in the same position for so long. She began to feel the raw cold embracing her. Without a jacket or blanket from her car, she quickly lost body heat. Cold air also dehydrated the nasal passages and the body's response was to produce mucus that made breathing even more difficult.

Soon, all she could feel was the biting cold. Slowly, her hands and feet became icy, and then numb. Her body automatically began a process of self-protection called vasoconstriction—the restricting of blood flow to the extremities, in order to defend the vital internal organs and the brain from the bitter cold. Under her clothes, Kim's skin broke out in goose bumps. Later, she began to tremble. Her skin turned pale, numb, and waxy.

Kim had probably experienced such a chill at some time in her life. It was the first stage of hypothermia—the effects of low temperature on the body. The gooseflesh occurred when the body's defenses against cold ordered the hair follicles to stand up, in an effort to provide some insulation.

When her core body temperature dropped from a normal 98.6 degrees, to below 95—a mere 4 degrees—Kim's body entered the next phase, mild hypothermia. She began to shiver, intermittently at first, and then intensely, uncontrollably, painfully. She was powerless to stop the shuddering and shaking, the chattering of her teeth. Her body was sending electrical impulses to her muscles, causing them to quiver spasmodically and generate heat, in an effort to ward off the deadly, piercing cold. The long, shivering night seemed endless, but was actually short, since Kim had not been kidnapped until almost dawn. She slumped into one or more exhausted, fitful sleeps, only to be awakened by insistent pains and more ceaseless shaking. Nightmares are normal during such unrestful naps, but other dreams came—dreams of rescue, of escape. Yet always Kim was a prisoner, awakening inside the cell of her trembling body, her screaming mind. Each return to consciousness would bring the same horrible realization that her nightmare was not a nightmare, but reality—a waking fright she could not escape.

As the hours passed, it became more and more difficult to keep track of time. Wednesday morning became afternoon, as Kim's absence was noticed, and her father investigated and went to the police. Wednesday became Thursday, as Kim's dad, family, and friends searched for her. By Thursday at sunrise, Kim had been imprisoned for a full, endless day. The sense of measured time and continuity is one of the things that separates reality from dreams. In the perpetual dark, without the normal cues of day and night, the reinforcement of clocks, the companionship of other people, and daily routines, time begins to lose its authority. Kim was still wrapped in pain inside her stone-cold basement vault, an unreal place that she had never seen. Her eyes burned from contact lenses grating on her eyeballs. An unquenchable thirst arrived with wakefulness, as did pangs from her empty stomach. The need to relieve the bladder was first an annoying twinge, then a frustrating, urgent ache, and, finally, a humiliating release.

Kim experienced a lessening of her constant quivering as the temperature outside climbed to 40 degrees on Thursday, which warmed Kim's subterranean prison, and her body, somewhat. From time to time, a furnace in another part of the basement came to life when the temperature in the upper part of the house fell below 55 degrees; she could faintly hear the thermostat click on the warming equipment, creaks and groans of pipes filling with warm water above her, bringing heat everywhere in the house—except to Kim, quaking and chattering in the chair.

Kim was desperate, but there was only one thing she could do. She renewed her feeble cries for help, trying over, and over, and over. Through her pain and confusion, through the tape tight over her ears, Kim could hear a dog barking somewhere outside. Maybe the dog could hear Kim's noises and was barking in response. Her abductors had not driven long enough to be out of the city. If there was a dog, there should be people. When the dog yelped, Kim yelped back, a faint echo. She yelped until her strength gave out. She never knew that a woman next door, the owner of the dog, had heard her wordless cries for help, and gone about her business.

After sunset on Thursday, Kim had been exposed to sub-freezing temperatures for a brutal thirty-six hours, and she entered the final stages of hypothermia. At the setting of the un-warming sun which Kim could not see, the merciless thermometer dropped again. The strange condition of hypothermia usually affected hapless climbers on Mount Everest, or polar explorers. It was an affliction of unfortunate souls trapped in the eternal snows—not college students, hidden less than fifty feet from a city street, where dozens of people lived. Her body temperature dropped below 90 degrees, marking the onset of mental confusion and apathy. Kim's thoughts, and her breathing and pulse, slowed down. She felt drunk, and begun to hallucinate, to converse with relatives or friends who were not there. Kim thought of her family—her beloved father, mother, uncle, and grandmother, and she prayed.

Thursday night or Friday morning, almost suddenly, as if in answer to a prayer, Kim's shivering lessened, and the palsy lifted. Mercifully, Kim did not feel cold anymore. She may have suddenly felt warm. All her frustration, her pain, and her terror, vanished with the shuddering. A feeling of blessed calm descended on her, like moonlight glittering off a silent snow bank. Her body temperature had fallen further, and she gradually began to lose consciousness, as if she were pleasantly falling asleep. Under her silvery blindfold, the pupils of her eyes became fixed and dilated, even though there was no light. Kim's brain was numbed by cold, frosted with forgetfulness. Her skin became colder, and turned bluish-gray. Her muscles gradually stiffened, and her body became rigid, like a seated statue. Her heartbeat and breathing seemed to have ceased, but she was still alive.

Doctors with experience in hypothermia know that a frozen victim of the cold was not to be considered dead until she was warm and dead. One hypothermia victim who had been taken to a morgue had recovered completely after being warmed up. Kim was in a cold-induced coma, a dangerous state of suspended animation, but she was only three or four hours away from revival, if found in time. Hypothermia victims were metabolic iceboxes, and had to be thawed slowly. Sudden thawing could be disastrous to the cardiovascular system. Care had to be taken to keep the deadly cold blood away from the heart, lest its frigid touch induce ventricular fibrillation—a heart attack. Warming fluids injected into abdominal spaces, along with a heart–lung bypass machine, could slowly heat her body by thawing her chilled blood, and bring her back to life. Kim looked and felt like a frozen corpse, but she was a Sleeping Beauty—who could only be rescued by the warming kiss of doctors.

Kim did not notice when Wayne McCook walked up the brick front steps of his mother's house at 78-08 Eighty-sixth

Avenue on Friday morning. She never heard his key in the lock, or his footsteps above her head. He had no idea that anyone was in the house. Wayne, 51, an inspector of underground telephone lines, only stopped by the house on the first Friday of the month to pick up his mother Ruth's Social Security check which arrived in the mail that day. His mom, a widow, had had to leave the home in 1991, when illness forced doctors to amputate her leg, and she went to live with relatives on Long Island. Every month, Wayne would ask his mother to sell the empty house, but she refused—for sentimental reasons. She insisted that the electricity be kept on, and the thermostat be kept at 55 degrees, no matter how wasteful it seemed to her son. A month or two earlier, Wayne had noticed that a basement window had been broken, and a house key on the rack by the front door was missing, but he was not very concerned. There was furniture, but nothing of real value in the house, and nothing seemed disturbed. Besides, he was not interested in taking the time and expense to change the locks. He picked up the mail and glanced around the living room. Wayne was unaware that the derelict house, the house he had grown up in, was the prison of a twenty-year-old girl who was tied to a chair in the room beneath his feet. He would not have been able to see Kim unless he went into the kitchen and descended the basement stairs. But Wayne had no reason to go into the basement. He had not been there for years.

In a hurry to get back to work, Wayne took a quick look to confirm that his mom's check was in the pile of envelopes, and bundled up the remaining mail under his arm. He turned and walked out without a second thought.

The door locked behind him with a final slam.

CHAPTER SEVEN

PSYCHIC

Phil came in to work on Friday morning, and the interview with Bob Murphy was waiting on his desk for him, in the form of a DD-5 detective report that said that Psycho may have been in a car a block away from where Kim had disappeared. If Psycho was on Kim's block that night, it would explain why his alibi sounded so phony. Did Psycho and his gang grab Kimberly? Every detective instinct that Phil had was telling him that Psycho, who didn't act like a psycho, knew nothing about Kim. If he called back, as instructed, Phil's opinion would be further reinforced.

When Phil told Tommy that the latest witness had seen a picture of Psycho, and said he might have been in the car, Tommy was convinced anew that Kim was being held by Psycho.

"You gotta pick him up again," said Tommy.

While Josh and Jay were out on the street, driving around, Josh was beeped by Tommy Antonakos. Josh called from a pay phone and told Tommy that he was looking for some guy named Tito, who had been seen driving a new white Honda on Jamaica Avenue. Tommy asked Josh and Jay to go to Psycho's neighborhood and talk to Russian guys about the latest development.

"We gotta go to Coney Island," Josh told Jay after he hung up the phone.

At noon, the phone rang in the Six-Nine Precinct Squad Room.

"Hello?" said Phil.

"Yeah, hello," said Psycho. "You told me to call?"

Psycho had dutifully followed instructions. He was not acting like a bad guy. Phil asked him to come in to the precinct the next morning, without telling him that he hoped to have a witness place him in the area where Kim had vanished. Phil wondered again if he could be wrong about Psycho. He would bring Psycho in, and Murphy could look at him through the one-way mirror, to be sure. Phil was still looking for Kim's car. Calls were made to Port Authority police at the airports, who were scouring the parking lots for the snow-colored Honda. They had come up empty. A police chopper searched Brooklyn and Queens on Wednesday night and Thursday morning, but was unable to locate the missing girl's car. Was it in a garage? Had it been chopped up already? Where the hell was it?

In Malverne, Joanne Scully had been looking at the white Accord parked across from her Malverne home for three days. It obviously wasn't a commuter's car-pool vehicle. She picked up the phone and dialed 911. Later, two Nassau County cops arrived in a squad car, and Joanne's husband Dennis, a plumbing contractor, went out to speak to them. The cops called the plate in, waited a few minutes, and then received a radio call back. They told Dennis and Joanne that everything was OK, the car was not stolen or anything and they left.

Tommy asked April and Josh to move back to their apartment, because Marlene, Kim's mother was arriving that afternoon on a flight from Florida. Tommy hoped to find Kim, so he would not have to tell her mom that she was a missing person, but after two days he gave her the news, and she insisted on coming to New York. Tommy picked Marlene up at Kennedy Airport and brought her back to Kim's apartment.

After seeing and hearing firsthand what was being done, it was obvious to Marlene that everything humanly possible that could be done was already being done, without success. The powers of this world had not found her daughter, so Marlene decided to enlist a psychic in the hunt for Kim. Tara went with Marlene to consult a clairvoyant named *Claire Day. The women went to the Bay Ridge, Brooklyn, home of the spiritualist, a dark-haired woman in her mid-forties. Tara and Marlene told her their dilemma. The medium clutched some possessions of Kim's and then went into a trance. Marlene took out a small tape recorder and set it to RECORD:

"She's not in Brooklyn anymore," the seer intoned with her eyes darting about, as if she had journeyed to a distant place in her mind, and was describing a misty image to those without eyes to see.

"She's OK . . . She's alive but tied up . . . She's tied to a bed . . . She's in a home, it's not really a vacant house . . . She's in a basement . . . She's in a cold place . . . She's not wearing any shoes . . ."

Marlene and Tara pressed for more details, a location where rescuers could search.

"You are not going to find her . . . She will find her own way out . . . Kimberly is going to find her own way out of there . . ."

The answer was frustrating and confusing. They had to find her. How could Kim find her own way out, if she was tied up? When the medium was asked who was responsible for Kim's abduction, she concentrated, and spoke again:

"I feel a 'J,' I'm getting a big 'J' . . . I keep seeing the letter 'J.' "

Marlene paid for Claire's services, and Tara drove her back to Kim's place. Tara and Marlene gathered everyone in the living room and played back the tape of the psychic for Tommy, Gina, Steven, April, Josh, and Jay. Everyone lis-

tened calmly—except Josh and Jay. They acted as if a neu-
tron bomb had gone off in the living room. Silently, they
locked eyes without anyone else noticing. When Marlene
said that Kim was tied up in a basement, and was in a cold
place, without her shoes on, Josh's eyes widened. A look of
panic flashed through his eyes at the news that Kim was
going to find her own way out. She was going to escape?
Both men fought to keep their cool, as they heard Marlene
ask the psychic who had done this to her daughter.

"She said she got a 'J' a big 'J' " Marlene repeated after
the tape ended. She said she might go to the psychic again.

Josh and Jay glared at each other, their thoughts racing.
Josh turned as white as a ghost. Joshua's name began with
J. Jay's name began with a J. Joey's name also began with
a J. Everyone's name but Nick's began with a J. No one in
the room mentioned this obvious fact, but Josh and Jay were
bugging out, completely paranoid. First, they can't make the
ransom demand. Then they think the father knows Mafia
guys, who are looking for them. Now, some psychic is telling
her family where Kim is, and the initials of the people who
had her kidnapped. Were they playing with them? How could
her father keep hearing the ransom demand on the phone and
not say anything? Did he know? Were they about to get
whacked? Were they about to get arrested? The whole
scheme wasn't just falling apart—it had blown up in their
faces. Josh and Jay felt like they were radioactive, like their
pants were on fire. They couldn't wait to get the hell out of
there. After making a hurried announcement that they were
going to go to the store, they rushed out the door to beep
Nick and Joey. They had to have a meeting that night—as
soon as possible.

Later, Phil arrived and Tommy introduced him to Marlene.

"My wife went to a psychic," who said that Kim was
okay—alive, but tied to a bed somewhere, Tommy told Phil.

Marlene told Phil that the woman had some interesting
things to say that might help him. Phil listened politely to

what Marlene had to say about the fortune-teller, but he was a detective—not a believer in psychic phenomena.

"Tommy, the worst thing you can do is go to a psychic," Phil said later.

Phil told Tommy that he would pick up Psycho on Saturday morning and bring him into the precinct. He asked Tommy if he wanted to watch the second interview with Psycho from behind the one-way mirror. Tommy said yes. He would be there.

Tara went home, unnerved by the experience with the psychic. She was troubled by Kim's disappearance and also troubled by the friends Kim had surrounded herself with in recent years. She didn't like some of them and she didn't know what the hell Kim was doing with some of those people. She hoped that what the psychic had said was true, that Kim would find her own way out. But she was still agitated and restless. Tara tossed and turned in her bed, but could not find sleep.

CHAPTER EIGHT

HELL

Josh and Jay were in a panic—scared and confused. They thought of themselves as tough street guys, but the odds against them had just gone through the roof. Josh had felt that the cops were no problem—he was in the perfect spot to learn exactly what they knew, and to keep them chasing false leads—Psycho or somebody else. Josh had never even met Phil Tricolla, but, through an unwitting Tommy, he was giving the detective his marching orders. It was sweet. Even with their fears of mob involvement, it could still have worked if they had kept their nerve. But Josh could not understand why the father would not talk back on the phone after he heard the taped ransom demand. Tommy loved his daughter, that wasn't it—was he stupid? The psychic thing tore it. They were willing to kidnap a girl, risk arrest by the cops, even risk getting blown away by the Mafia—but they couldn't fight the spirits.

"It's all falling apart," Josh lamented, as he drove April's car to the meeting. Josh would have to keep driving April's car—there would be no free, top-of-the-line Infiniti Q-45 for him. He would not be getting his dream car.

"We have to let her go," said Jay.

Josh agreed. It was all too much. Both men were very superstitious, and they felt they were tempting fate. Jay got the impression that Josh believed Kim knew he had arranged her kidnapping—even though it seemed impossible. On the way to the one a.m. meeting, Josh made a stop at the apartment of a friend named *George. He told Jay he needed a change of clothes to go into the filthy basement, because he was going to go back to Kim's place afterwards. Josh parked and they entered the Bayview Projects housing complex.

It was Friday night. When they arrived at George's apartment, a party was in progress. The bumping sound of rap music could be heard through the apartment door. Inside, the sharp smell of crack assaulted the nostrils. George, his girlfriend, and about a dozen friends were drinking and doing drugs.

Josh borrowed a pair of black, army-style fatigue pants, and slipped them on over the pants he was wearing. Then he put on a matching jacket. That might have seemed odd to many people, but in Brooklyn, felons embarking on "a mission" routinely donned a second pair of pants and another shirt or jacket. Once the crime had been committed, the strange fashion choice came in very handy. Criminals knew enough about cops to know that the descriptions of thieves, or gunmen, or killers that police broadcast over their radios were very basic—gender, race, and clothing. A fleeing felon could not change his sex, or his race—but he could change his clothes, provided they were sufficiently baggy, and of a different color. Once he had shuffled off the portly coil of clothing, the bad guy had, essentially, laundered himself. In a crowd, he was the Invisible Man. The cops would continue looking for a guy in red pants and a purple jacket, or whatever. Reversible jackets were also popular. In fact, baggy-pants bad guys had inspired a clownish craze for beltless, falling-down trousers—a look previously seen sported only by arrestees at Rikers Island, whose belts had been taken by authorities to prevent suicides. One stickup man in baggy pants was literally tripped up by his too-loose trousers. He fell flat on his face and narrowly avoided capture by cops wearing pants that fit. No one at the party thought it unusual that some guy came in, put on someone else's clothes over his own, and left.

Jay did not layer-up. He had no intention of going down in the basement. Josh could not stay away, he had to be in charge. Things had been going wrong, one after another, but now it was time to fix them. If they let Kim go, there was no proof, no case. Once she was home, the cops and the Mafia goons would lose interest—hopefully.

The gang met at a neon and fluorescent–lit Dunkin' Donuts on Woodhaven Boulevard. Josh and Jay quickly communicated their dread and their bewilderment to Joey and Nick. Hearing about the mob and the psychic for the first time, Joey and Nick immediately agreed that they should cut Kim loose. Like Josh and Jay, they were also very superstitious, and were freaked out over what the psychic seemed to know. They were not happy. They had committed crimes that could send them all to prison for a long time, but now there wouldn't be any big payoff—no money.

"It's gotta be done," Josh ordered. "We've got to let her go."

That meant that the girl would have to be removed from Joey's "sweet house" and taken somewhere else, as they would have done after collecting a bag full of ransom cash. It meant exposure, with no reward. What if the cops stopped them this time, while she was in the trunk? Joey had guarded the location of his sweet house from Josh, but now he was willing to share it. He wanted to share the risk with the guy who thought the whole thing up, the guy who screwed up the ransom, the guy he thought had made them mob targets.

"You fucked up," Joey told Josh, pointing an accusatory finger at the younger man.

"Excuse me?" Josh shot back. Josh, like many street people, did not take being "dissed"—disrespected—lightly. Their urgent business prevented the men from tangling further. It could wait. For now, they both needed each other. Joey drove, with Josh seated next to him. Jay sat behind Josh, Nick behind Joey, like seconds en route to a duel. Joey drove to Jamaica Avenue, turned north on Seventy-Ninth Street, and parked his car in the middle of the block. Just down the street on the left, in the first wooden two-story home from the corner, lived Jeanette Montalvo, Joey's common-law mother-in-law. His girlfriend Antonette and her son were inside. The four men debated who would go inside the nearby sweet house and bring Kim out. They discussed letting her go in a park. Finally, Joey, Josh, and Nick got out and quietly walked to the corner under a dark cloudy, sky, their breath fogging as they exhaled in the 25-degree air. They turned left on Eighty-Sixth Avenue, and up the steps of the first house on the left. Joey opened the front door of number 78-08, and entered the dark home, with Nick using a flashlight to light the way. Josh and Nick went down the basement steps. As soon as they had descended the stairs to the basement, and Nick threw the flashlight on Kim, they knew something was wrong. Although Kim was still handcuffed she seemed to have gotten off some of the tape around her wrists—but that was not the problem. Her head was thrown back, tilted upwards, toward the ceiling. She wasn't breathing at all.

"I think she's dead," said Nick.

Jeanette emerged from her first-floor apartment, and walked out the glass front door and down the wooden steps with her daughter. Videotapes in hand, Jeanette and Antonette Montalvo turned left on the sidewalk, and then left again, on Eighty-sixth Avenue. They were on the way to the video store on Jamaica Avenue to return movies and look for others. As they passed 78-08, Jeanette noticed some kind of light, like a bulb, in the basement of the abandoned home. Again, she decided to mind her own business, and she mentioned it to no one. The women turned left at the corner, toward the store. Later, they returned home by a different way, and did not pass the house again that night.

*   *   *

Josh kicked Kim hard in the shins, so hard you could hear the impact of his boot against her leg. She did not react at all. Kim was like a frozen, lifeless statue. Nick got out his knife, and hurriedly cut the duct tape around Kim's face. He slipped, and the knife sliced into Kim's cheek. She did not scream. The pair looked at each other. With rising fear, Josh went behind Kim's back and felt for her pulse. Nothing. She seemed to be frozen solid. Josh and Nick went upstairs to give Joey the news, which hit him hard.

"What are we going to do?" asked Nick.

"Pick her up, take her outside, and dump her somewhere," said Josh.

Josh and Nick went back down into the basement. They grabbed Kim. When they touched her, it did not feel like touching warm, soft, living flesh. It was like trying to lift more than 100 pounds of frozen meat. They pulled and grunted and cursed, but she was stuck—frozen to the chair. The fearful men then hurried through the shadows to the car.

"She's dead," blurted Josh as soon as the car doors closed.

"She's dead," echoed Nick.

"What do you mean, she's dead?" asked Jay, wide-eyed. "Are you sure?"

"I'm sure. Positive," said Josh.

"How do you know she's dead, for sure? How do you know she's dead?" Jay demanded, his voice rising.

"I checked her," said Josh. "She just looked froze. I walked up to her and kicked her in the leg."

"What happened?" asked Jay.

"Nothing. She didn't move, she didn't respond. She didn't do anything," Josh said. "Then I checked her for a pulse, to see if she had a pulse. When she didn't have one, I thought she was dead."

"When I went to cut the duct tape off her eyes, to see if she would open her eyes, or something," Nick said, "the knife punctured her head and she didn't move."

Josh expressed anger at Joey for not feeding and taking

care of Kim. He felt that Joey had put them all "in deep shit." Again, came the urgent question:

"What're we gonna do?" Nick asked. Could she be carried out with the chair and dumped somewhere?

"No," said Josh. "Fuck it! Burn the whole place—this way there will be no fingerprints. Just burn the house with her in it. It gets rid of all the evidence. We should burn the house down, so there's no fingerprints, anything that will come back to me. We can't get caught."

The motion was quickly carried. Josh was in charge again.

"Let's go to the gas station," Josh commanded. Joey obeyed, stopping at a station on Forest Avenue. Pretending to have a car that had run out of gas, Josh bought a gasoline container and filled it up. When they returned to the same spot, all four men went back into the dark house. Joey refused to go downstairs.

"You pussy!" sneered Josh, as he lugged the sloshing gas can toward the basement.

Joey and Jay stayed upstairs in the kitchen, while Nick and Josh descended the stairs. They agreed that Josh and Nick would set the fire, and the other two would be ready to block the door to the basement with the kitchen refrigerator, to prevent firemen from dousing the blaze. Downstairs, Nick used a little key to remove his pair of handcuffs from Kim's wrists. Josh then pulled off a piece of the charred duct tape that had bound Kim, and put it in his pocket—as a souvenir. Nick kept the flashlight on Kim, starkly illuminating a beautiful, dark-haired girl with her eyes Heavenward. Joshua walked over to Kim and spoke to her: "I'm sorry it has to end this way, but life sucks," he said sarcastically. "Shit happens." Kim could not hear her friend consigning her to the flames with a cruel joke.

Joshua Torres then kissed Kim's cold forehead—not the magical, waking kiss of a prince, but a sardonic kiss of death. He stepped back and doused her with gasoline, pouring the flammable liquid on her face and head, soaking her hair, drenching her clothes. Some of the fuel splashed onto Josh's borrowed pants, and dripped in sheets onto the concrete floor. Nick backed up to the stairway, but kept the shaky flashlight trained on Kim. Both men prepared to run, as Josh took out a matchbook and lit a match. He tossed the flaming match at the motionless figure, and was running toward the stairs when the gas ignited.

The gasoline detonated, brightly lighting the trash-filled cellar with a hellish orange glow. The flames from the burning figure rose from the fiery pit and mushroomed obscenely onto the ceiling above. They ate away at the wood beams, burning a hole and filling the house with black smoke.

Joshua's words had not reached Kim. She had not felt his boot slam into her shin, and felt no pain when Nick cut her head. She did not feel the terrible flames that enveloped her upper body. Mercifully, though Kim's body was in the flaming chair, Kim herself was gone. She was still alive, but in a deep, dreamless sleep. Her brain was too cold to feel any pain. The last acts of her frozen body lasted only seconds. Smoke was inhaled into her lungs, and her skin began to blister—and then her body quickly died. Kimberly Antonakos was not in the flames—she was already at rest in a cool place, beyond suffering and the wickedness of men. She had escaped from the oubliette. She was free.

In a way, Kim had found her own way out.

"Okay, we lit up!" said Josh, reeking of gas fumes, as he and Nick emerged from the basement. The four men quickly shoved the refrigerator against the basement door, dashed outside, and jumped in the car. They were in such a frenzy to get away that Joey forgot to lock the door behind him.

"Let's go!" ordered Josh.

Joey quickly drove away. The four young men were quiet for a time. The magnitude of what they had done silenced even Josh, the man who called himself King Quality. The heavy stench of gasoline from Josh and the gas container filled the small car and stung their eyes—as if the fumes might explode and consume them all at any second. Joey floored his Maxima to the end of the block and turned right. He hung a left into Forest Park, and got on the Interborough Parkway. They were all lost in deep thought, as Joey took the Grand Central Parkway north to the Long Island Expressway, where he headed east. He got off the L.I.E. at Exit 25, Utopia Parkway, made a few turns, and stopped in front of a house with garbage cans near the street. After looking around, Josh got out with the empty gas container and deposited it inside one of the cans. He got back in the car and Joey took off again.

"We messed it up," Jay said, after a while. "This wasn't supposed to happen at all. She was supposed to be all right."

Even that simple statement carried an implied criticism of Josh, the mastermind. No one responded out loud. As he was driving, Joey took out the key to his sweet house. He pressed it on the console, broke it in two, and threw the pieces of metal out the window. Then he pulled over to a curb. Nick got out and threw his handcuffs into a storm-drain sewer. Joey drove back to the Dunkin' Donuts, where they had met earlier in the evening, and put the car in PARK.

"I think it's a good idea for us to stay away from each other for a while," Joey said.

Everyone thought about it and agreed. Josh and Jay got into Josh's blue Nissan and drove away, toward Kim's apartment. The sudden beeping of Josh's pager startled them. Josh picked up the beeper and stopped the noise. He looked at the familiar phone number, and pulled over to a pay phone. Josh dropped a quarter into the coin slot, and dialed the number.

"Hello?" said Tommy Antonakos.

"Hi, it's Josh." Tommy had a job for Josh and Jay: he wanted them to check out a motel by the airport, and see if Kim's car—or Kim—was there. Tommy gave Josh the name and address of the place, while Josh pretended to write it down. He told Tommy they would check it out, and hung up. Josh got back in the car and headed, not for the motel, but for his friend George's place. When they arrived, Josh honked the horn, and George came to the window.

Inside, upstairs, Josh stripped off the fatigue jacket and pants, which stank of gasoline. "These have to be washed," he told George, as he stepped out of the trousers. He gave his friend some phony story about how he had gotten gas all over himself.

"Let me go to the bathroom," said Josh, taking the bundle of smelly clothes with him. In the bathroom, Josh covered the pants with soapy water and left them to soak in the sink. Then he stepped into the bathtub in his boots, and ran water over them to wash off the gas.

Back at Kim's place, April, Liz, and Tara greeted Josh and Jay when they returned just before 3 a.m. The guys said they had had no luck looking for Kim or her car, and they were tired after a long night of searching. It was time to drop Liz off at home, and for Josh, April, the baby, and Jay to go back to Josh and April's apartment two blocks away. Before they left, Josh picked up Kim's phone and dialed the number of his Aunt *Maria's place on Avenue L. He was only on the phone for fifteen seconds, and then everyone walked out the door. It was 2:48 a.m., on March 4th.

In the early hours of the morning, Joey, Jay, Josh, and Nick fell asleep, thinking, not of Kim, or of her family, but of how death had changed everything, how their asses were now on the line. They were thinking about alibis, and the legal consequences of a death committed during a felony. They were thinking about murder, and how to avoid paying for nature's worst crime. They wanted to avoid prison, but most of all, they wanted to avoid the feared mob vengeance: a bullet in the head, or maybe even being set on fire, like Kim. With the house burned down around her and the gas can, handcuffs, and house key gone, there was nothing to connect them to Kim, or to the spot. They had left the evidence in flames behind them, and no one knew who had done it. Except them—all four of them.

The CIA had a saying for such paranoid moments: "Two men can keep a secret—providing one of them is dead."

The four were now bound tightly together by their secret—too tightly. For the first time, they had killed, and for the first time, all four had a reason to kill the other three. Each one had something on the others—forever. The rest of their lives would be spent looking over their shoulders, wondering when or whether someone would rat them out when they got jammed up, as they probably would.

Yeah, thought Joey, but he was the only one of the four who had insurance.

CHAPTER NINE

TORCHED

John was sitting at his dining room table, filling out form for mail-order clothes when he smelled smoke. It was almost 2 a.m., not a time for people to be cooking or burning dinner. John thought that his home of more than twenty years was on fire. He walked into the kitchen. The smell was stronger there. Alarmed, he rushed around, checking appliances, searching for the fire. He checked the whole house, including the basement, but could not find the source. John Cuniffe was not about to ignore it. He had just three years previously retired from his city job as a subway carman. He was trained to respond to emergency situations, and his experience told him something was on fire nearby. He went outside and down the front steps of his home at the corner of Seventy-ninth Street and Eighty-sixth Avenue. The night was quiet, and a light, downy snow was gently falling from a cold sky. John detected the same burning odor in the air outside, but he couldn't see any fire, or any column of smoke. He was the only soul on the street.

He peered south, at the elevated subway line on Jamaica Avenue at the end of the block, but saw no problem there. He followed his nose around the corner, onto Eighty-sixth Avenue, where the scent was stronger. He walked through the flurrying white flakes past 78-08 and other houses to the corner of Seventy-eighth Street, and still could not find the fire. He decided to give up, and turned back toward home. But, as he approached 78-08 again, his eye caught a wisp of smoke puffing from the first-floor window to the right of the front door. John walked into the driveway of Ruth McCook's house, which had been empty for more than four years, and saw more puffs coming out of the second-floor rear window. He quickly walked into his house and dialed 911. Then he went back outside and waited for the fire trucks to arrive.

John's neighbors, Jeanette and her husband Carlos, were awakened by the sound of sirens and bleating fire-truck horns converging on the block. As they got out of bed, red lights were flashing through the windows. Jeanette Montalvo looked out her rear bedroom window and saw a big, red flame, like a torch, burning behind a basement window in the empty home behind her house. She heard violent crashing, and glass breaking, as shadowy figures in capes and helmets attacked the blazing house, smashing windows with their large axes. Jeanette was scared, very nervous, for some reason, filled with emotion—maybe because the scene looked like the death, the *murder* of a home, even if no one was living there. She began to cry.

Jeanette picked up the phone and, with tears running down her face, called her daughter, Antonette, who had a young son. Antonette was alone in her bed, sound asleep.

"Antonette," Jeanette said tearfully, "you know that abandoned home next door to me?"

"Yeah?" Antonette answered sleepily.

"There's a big fire, and a lot of smoke. They're breaking up the whole house."

"You okay?" Antonette asked her tearful mom.

"Yeah, we're okay."

"Okay, call me in the morning."

The teleprinter in Engine Company 236 in East New York, Brooklyn, clattered to life and printed out an alarm of a fire at 78-08 Eighty-sixth Avenue in Woodhaven. Fire Lieutenant

Fred Reich and five other firefighters manned a tiller truck—
the kind with the long, motorized ladder, and the second
steering wheel in the back—and raced with lights and sirens
to the address. As they pulled up to the scene of the fire,
smoke was pouring out of the windows, doorways, and from
under the roof of the two-story wood-frame home.

Other firefighters had arrived before them, and were already in the house. The first fireman to approach had found
the front door closed, but unlocked. They were proceeding,
according to Fire Department procedures, with Ventilation
and Search, in which they removed windows and doors, and
punctured the roof to allow the smoke and heat out. Neighbors said that the house was empty, but firefighters still had
to risk their lives to search for anyone who might be trapped
inside. Many firemen had been injured, and some had been
killed in such searches. Often, they found squatters in abandoned buildings. Homeless people sometimes accidentally
set places alight, when fires they started for warmth got out
of hand. Sometimes, in the blinding smoke, firefighters ran
into booby traps set by drug dealers for cops. They had to
be ready for anything.

Fred walked down the side alley of the house, also searching for the origin of the blaze. When he peered into a small
cellar window at ground level, Fred saw an orange glow. He
informed the chief on the scene, and the firefighters, that the
fire was in the basement. He ordered a hose brought around
the back and down a basement entrance there. It was a storm-
cellar entrance with a padlock on it. Fred ordered a truck
company at the scene to bring a bolt cutter and a Hallgan
tool—a huge crowbar—and the door was forced open. The
firefighters, all wearing self-contained breathing masks,
dragged the hose down the stairs and into the acrid, black
smoke for about ten feet.

The tower of flames was visible ahead. They blasted, not
the flames, but the ceiling above the fire with high-pressure
water. They knew that if they turned the hose on the source
of the fire it could push the flames around—sometimes with

disastrous results. The torrent of water cascaded down and quickly knocked over and extinguished the single fire source in the middle of the room.

At that moment, the production of black smoke by the fire ceased. The cold water expanded into steam, turning the basement air from a thick black to an even thicker white. The change in smoke color signaled their victory over the fire. Often, firefighters outside a fire, seeing charcoal smoke turn snowy, would joke: "We have a Pope," referring to the ritual smoke signals sent up from the Vatican in Rome by Catholic Cardinals after the selection of a new Pontiff. In the basement, visibility was practically zero, and Fred did not want his men to get hurt.

"Stay put," he yelled, loud enough to be heard through the mask.

He got a flashlight, and found the stairway leading upstairs to the first floor of the house. He climbed the stairway and tried to open the door at the top, but it wouldn't budge. He put some muscle into it and the door slowly opened enough to let him into the kitchen. Smoke from the basement poured up and out the broken first-floor windows, clearing the basement. The obstruction, Fred saw, had been a refrigerator that had been pushed against the door to block the entrance.

He told the firemen upstairs that the door was the way down to the basement. The firefighters, going by touch in the still-smoky house, felt their way around by touching the kitchen cabinets, working their way around the refrigerator, and down the stairs. Fred went back down. It was much clearer in the cellar, which he saw was a Collyer's Mansion—but the fire had been confined to one area.

A Collyer's Mansion was a fireman's term for a firetrap, a home filled with junk and debris. The phrase dated to March, 1947, when Manhattan police were called to the Collyer Mansion on upper Fifth Avenue, and found two dead brothers inside. All entrances had been blocked and the home was filthy, rat-infested maze, filled with tons of old newspapers and junk. One of the booby traps that the brothers had rigged to trap intruders had snared the concert-pianist brother, Langley Collyer. He died of heart failure after a mountain of suitcases, breadboxes, and newspapers fell on him. His brother Homer, a lawyer, died of starvation several days later.

In the clearing air, Fred was startled to see a shocking sight, like something out of a horror movie—a charred figure slumped in a chair, burned from the waist up. It was the worst thing he had ever seen in five years on the job. It was upsetting to see a human being dead in a fire, but it was more upsetting to realize it had been a woman. The body, whose face was unrecognizable, had been gagged. The arms were behind the back, as if they had been tied. The fire had apparently burned away some of the restraints. As the air in the basement cleared, Fred removed his mask. He smelled gasoline. It was obviously some kind of foul play. This was a case for fire marshals and detectives. Lieutenant Fred Reich picked up his radio:

"We found a victim. Ten forty-five, code one," he announced, radio code for a dead body. The message squawked out of every radio at the scene. One of the firefighters rushed over to the figure and grabbed the head, in an attempt to administer mouth-to-mouth resuscitation. The blackened chair collapsed in pieces and the body fell on the floor. The firefighter's heart was in the right place, but nothing could be done for the victim. He was just messing up a crime scene.

"Back off," Fred told the fireman. "We'll leave everything as it is."

When the chief outside heard that they had "a torch job," an arson-murder, he notified police and fire marshals, who found no sign of forced entry. The first floor was in complete disarray, but there was food in the refrigerator. The second floor showed signs of habitation, including toilet paper and towels in the bathroom. Paramedics from the Emergency Medical Service arrived, and, as a formality, the victim was pronounced dead at 3:14 a.m. The call would also bring to the scene people from the Medical Examiner's office, an assistant district attorney, Nightwatch detectives, the police Crime Scene Unit, and, in the morning, the detectives who would "catch" the case and investigate the apparent homicide.

Julian awoke to the sharp sound of his bleating beeper inside the dark bedroom of his Manhattan apartment. A sleepy-eyed glance at the clock told him it was just after 2 a.m. He remembered it was early Saturday morning, and he was the ADA assigned to beeper duty that night, a rotating responsibility shared by the prosecutors who worked for Queens District Attorney Richard A. Brown.

Assistant District Attorney Julian Wise, 27, had that morning been interviewing a surviving victim in the "College Point Massacre" case in his small office in Kew Gardens, behind the court building on Queens Boulevard. It was difficult to think about what that poor young woman had been through. She had been shot in the face and her throat had been cut from ear to ear by a gang of drug thieves. Their greed for drugs and cash had turned a second-floor apartment in a "nice," quiet neighborhood into a slaughterhouse. Six people—including a pregnant woman—were shot and stabbed to death over a $15,000 drug debt. A seventh victim, Julian's witness, had survived a bullet to the head and a slashed throat. The young woman had jumped out a second-story window, staggered to a neighbor's home, and knocked on the door with blood-soaked hands. She was about to testify against the drug killers who had left her for dead—men who valued life at less than $2000 a head.

Saturday was the last day Julian was going to be on beeper duty, because of the upcoming College Point Massacre trial. Beeper duty meant that he was on call and had to report to any murder in Queens County. It didn't necessarily mean that he would be assigned the case, but he had to "catch it" and represent the Homicide Bureau at least until the morning, when his boss—Homicide Bureau Chief Greg Lasak—would decide who would prosecute the case.

Julian had no intention of taking on any new cases; he was too busy with the massacre trial.

Julian dialed the homicide hotline number and was told that a girl was found burned to death in the basement of a home in Woodhaven. He wrote down the address. For some inexplicable reason, as he showered and dressed quickly, the call about yet another female victim struck a chord. He had a feeling about this one. On the way to the scene, Julian picked up his cellular phone, and called Rob, a young lawyer who had just started in the Homicide Bureau. Rob was scheduled to go on the beeper the following night, but Julian thought the rookie's education in murder should start early.

Rob Ferino, 27, was very much asleep, and very unhappy to hear the sound in the dark. He picked up the phone and made a noise into it. A voice that was very much awake came out of the phone.

"Rob, Rob, get up, get up. It's Julian. There's a body, and it's big—at least, I think it's big."

Rob made some more noise into the phone, about how he wasn't supposed to be working now, not until the next night.

"Rob, forget about tomorrow. Come to this scene—I've got a feeling about this."

Rob sighed, and reluctantly agreed. He turned on the light, wrote down the address of the murder scene, and agreed to meet Julian there as soon as possible. After a very fast shower, Rob threw on his clothes and went out the door. Just to complete his perfect evening, he briefly got lost on the way.

Rob Ferino had wanted to be a cop when he was in high school, but his mother kept throwing away his Police Department applications when they arrived in the mail, afraid that he would get killed. So Rob did the next best thing— he became a prosecutor. After getting a law degree from St. John's University, he had joined the Queens DA's office as an Assistant District Attorney only a year earlier.

Rob had dreamt for years about fighting crime and getting into a courtroom. In his first year, he was in court every day, but he was not sure who was winning the battle with evil-doers. The problem was that crime fought back. Crooks without cash were given lawyers, and crooks with money—because crime did pay—hired even better lawyers. They all knew more than a neophyte A.D.A. struggling to learn the ropes and master courtroom maneuvers.

Rob started doing "intake work," real grunt work with long hours. He worked the graveyard shift at night in the arraignment court, prosecuting small-time thieves, small-time drug dealers, small-time prostitutes, and other criminals. An arraignment court is the fast-food part of the legal system, where short-order justice is served. The major purpose is to bring the charges before a judge, who determines whether bail may be set or not, and how much. It was routine. There was no testimony, no witness, little drama, but the motley, often bizarre assemblage of arrested men and women was an education in itself. One night, a man's name was called on a charge of common prostitution, and the most beautiful woman Rob had ever seen was ushered in handcuffs before the judge. The paperwork in front of him said this was a guy, but he couldn't take his eyes off the incredible, buxom woman's body and face that were attached to this man's name. It was a classic "she-male" hooker, altered by surgery. The defendant noticed that Rob, who had led a relatively sheltered life, was staring. After bail was set by the judge, the "woman" turned around and blew Rob a kiss on the way out.

After seven months doing arraignments, Rob himself "made bail." He was sent to Family Court. There, he was able to conduct informal versions of hearings and trials. It was good experience, but it was ugly—all the violent, dirty secrets of dysfunctional families, including wife-beating, child abuse, molestation, alcoholism, and drugs. It was the most depressing place he had ever been. Several times, Rob had to prosecute some bad kids—juveniles arrested for armed robbery. The parents yelled at Rob, the judge, even the cops who had made the arrest, as if they were to blame.

Rob learned that the unpunished juvenile delinquents often appeared later in adult arraignment court. That was the low point. Fortunately, after he served his sentence in Family Court, Rob was promoted to the Homicide Bureau. At last he would be fighting crime, prosecuting real, adult bad guys. And that night, Rob was on the way to the scene of an actual murder—his first.

When Julian arrived at 78-08 Eighty-sixth Avenue he saw all the familiar sights associated with a fire scene. Several fire engines, their red lights still flashing, were parked at odd angles in the middle of the icy two-lane side street, connected by a network of snaking hoses, each as thick as a man's arm. There was a sharp smell of smoke in the cold air as he approached a group of firefighters clad in heavy black coats and boots near the front of the house. The night was cold, the kind of damp, New York cold that sucks the heat from your body. He had rummaged briefly through his Jeep, trying to find a sweater to pull on over his suit jacket, but couldn't find it. He introduced himself and one fireman said that he would lead him to the crime scene.

As soon as he entered the darkened home, Julian detected the pungent aroma of gasoline. He followed the fireman, who used a large flashlight to guide their way through the house, accompanied by the sound of dripping water and the squawking of firemen's portable radios. Suddenly, just as they neared the kitchen in the rear of the home, the floor under Julian caved in. One of his feet crashed through the fire-weakened timbers. He cried out in surprise, but the fireman turned around with the light and yanked his foot out of the hole as if it were something he did every day, which it probably was.

Walking carefully, Julian followed his guide into the kitchen and down a stairway to the freezing basement. A new, powerful smell assaulted his nostrils. It got worse and worse as he descended the dark stairway, until it became so revolting that he thought he might be sick. In the light of several flashlights, which reflected strangely off the water on the basement floor, he saw a shocking scene—a half-scorched form lying on its side in the center of the unfinished basement. Julian realized with a start that the disgusting odor turning his stomach was the smell of burnt human flesh. He had seen more than 200 dead bodies during his career, but he had never seen anything like this.

"This is the most disgusting job," Julian thought, as he examined the victim. "I gotta get outta here." He walked back through the house and out into the fresh air.

Julian was outside when Rob arrived to begin his on-the-job training.

"This is a little different," Julian warned.

"Why is it different?" asked Rob.

"There's a girl burned in the basement," Julian answered. Rob followed Julian inside the gloomy house.

"Rob! Be careful!" yelled Julian, warning Rob not to step into the same hole that Julian had earlier.

Rob smelled the acrid smoke and some other wretched odor that he could not identify. As they descended a dark stairway and saw a prone, blackened body, Rob also realized that the smell was burned flesh.

Julian explained the crime scene to Rob, pointing without touching anything. "See her ligature marks, that's probably where she was tied up," he told Rob indicating the wrists. He pointed to an exposed section of unburned skin. "She's white, maybe Hispanic . . . maybe those are her boots."

Rob listened carefully, but this was not just another day at the office for him. He was shaken by the presence of the body. The first sight of death reaches inside and grabs your guts. The mind reels, but the body itself reacts with visceral fear. He wanted to appear professional, even if he didn't feel that way.

"Do you know who she is?"

"Who knows?" asked Julian, listing various possibilities. The smart money would have been on a drug killing. Drug bandits often tortured recalcitrant victims who stubbornly refused to reveal the location of caches of dope and cash.

Once their examination was done, Julian and a sick-looking Rob retreated outside into the lightly falling snow for some fresh air. Rob reached for a cigarette and lit up. As the lighter flame ignited the white tube of tobacco, and Rob inhaled the smoke, he began to retch. He was struck with involuntary dry heaves of nausea.

"Is it always going to be like this?" Rob asked Julian after a few minutes.

"No. You've just seen the worst thing you will ever see in your life," Julian assured him.

Maintaining the part of seasoned veteran, Julian concealed his own revulsion—which was beginning to harden into a commitment to himself to find another line of work. He had seen enough.

"OK, that's all we have, there's nothing for us to do," said Julian. "Go home."

The police knocked on Jeanette's door before seven in the morning. When she heard that a body had been found in the fire, she told them about Baby—how she had been barking for days. She also told them about the lights she had seen in the house. But Jeanette Montalvo did not mention the whimpering sound she had heard coming from the direction of the house. After the detectives left, Jeanette called her daughter again.

"Antonette, you know they found a body in there, in the house."

"Mommy, I don't believe that, that's not true."

"That's true, they found a body in there, a female," Jeanette insisted. "Whoever did that knew that house was empty."

When Antonette hung up, she relayed the information her mother had just given her to Joey, who had arrived home and was lying next to her in bed. But Joey Negron was very tired. He had been out late, working. He rolled over and went back to sleep.

CHAPTER TEN

FOUND

Louie arrived at work for a "Day Tour" shift at the One-Oh-Two Precinct, in the Richmond Hill section of Queens, just before eight o'clock Saturday morning. Chugging on a Marlboro cigarette, the handsome thirty-four-year-old man with wavy black hair and a neat mustache strode up the steps of the old stone stationhouse, which had been constructed the year before the First World War began. The entire structure had recently been refurbished inside and out, but some traditions continued—horses for mounted units were still stabled in the basement. Detective Louie Pia was also part of a long NYPD tradition. He was a second-generation detective, with a dozen years on The Job, half of them as a detective. Louie's dad, Louis, Sr., had been an NYPD detective for more than a quarter of a century—until the day he logged his son in for a court appearance for one of his cases and decided that he had been on The Job long enough.

"You know when you punch your son into court—it's time to check out," the elder Pia laughed, and put in for retirement to make room for the new generation.

"It's a great job," he always told Louie.

And it was. Louie absorbed police work from his father, but he actually learned how to be a detective from his partner Tom Shevlin, whom Louie considered the best detective in the county. The previous year, Tom had become a member of the elite Homicide Squad—the guys who worked all the heavy cases. Louie was a natural detective, and was getting a reputation for winning the confidence of "perps"—perpetrators—and convincing them to do the right thing, to confess. Louie had a quick smile, and friendly brown eyes—he was everybody's buddy. One of his heart-to-heart talks with one murder suspect led Louie to hug the killer, as a way of getting him to end his unbelievable denials and confess.

"I know you did it," Louie told him in his gravelly voice, as he embraced the suspect.

The bad guy cracked, and told his friend Louie how he did the killing.

There had been three murders committed overnight in Queens, which was a normal amount of mayhem for the weather and that time of year. One homicide had occurred in the 106th precinct, the second in the 110th precinct, and the third was in the confines of Louie's precinct.

"Are you going to the fire scene?" the desk sergeant asked Louie, as he passed the high front desk.

"What fire scene?" Louie asked.

"The fire scene in the basement . . . the body in the fire."

Louie went upstairs, and was assigned to the case, a girl burned in a Woodhaven cellar. The phone rang a few minutes later and Louie picked it up. It was Tom Shevlin. He wanted Louie to meet him at the scene, and work with him again.

"This is the one," Tom informed Louie. "This is a heavy."

Tom had been doing The Job almost twice as long as Louie, for twenty-two years, and he had been a detective longer than Louie had been on the force. Louie was impressed with how knowledgeable, calm, and confident Tom was. Tom could "read" a crime scene like a book. He would silently walk around the scenes of killings or multiple murders, looking at every body, bullet hole, and bloodstain, and then describe what had happened, as if he had been there when the crime was committed. Louie was happy to be working with Tom again. They still considered each other partners, and they were good friends. After work, the detectives and their families socialized together on Long Island, away from the death and crime of the city.

It was freezing cold in the basement. Whoever had set the girl ablaze had wanted to make sure she was dead, beyond rescue. Why else had they shoved a refrigerator up against the cellar door? The objective, Tom thought, had been to obliterate her, as well as any evidence. The two detectives had seen death in many forms, and had become hardened to the sight, for their own mental health—like doctors. But still the image of the burned victim, accompanied by the smell of fire and flesh, was sickening. Both men had daughters. They kept their human outrage and anger in check because they had work to do. The best way they could help the victim and her family was to do that job well and lock up the scumbags responsible.

Tom could tell it was a homicide from across the room. People who burned up in accidental fires were found in a fetal position called a "pugilistic stance"—because they looked like boxers with their dukes up. But this girl was on her right side, and her hands were stretched behind her back. Tom saw remnants of burned tape on her wrists and forearms, which obviously had bound her to the destroyed chair, blackened pieces of which lay underneath her prone form. Tom noticed that the long, carefully manicured fingernails on her blistered hands were bent and melted from the heat of the fire. Most of what had been her vest lay in ashes behind her. In a pocket of the vest he found a seared watch, its leather band burned away. The victim's head lay against another partially burned wooden chair. Obviously she could not have set herself on fire if she was tied up. It was definitely not a suicide. Her legs were bent at the knees, so she had died while sitting in the chair, which had crumbled beneath her. Tape that had been on the wrists and forearms had protected the skin underneath from the flames.

Tom observed a halo effect burned into the concrete floor where the chair had been. The space under the chair had not been burned. It didn't take a Sherlock Holmes to figure out that some brave lad had poured gasoline on top of the woman while she was restrained in an upright position, and then simply set her on fire. Was she dead before the fire or did she die in it? Tom hoped the poor girl was dead before they torched her. There were no obvious indications of torture, or of gunshot or stab wounds, but the fire may have obliterated any such telltale external signs. An autopsy and X-rays would, hopefully, settle the issue. Why did they remove her boots and place them six feet away? Tom wondered.

Tom and Louie did not touch the body. Louie carefully jotted down its position, its condition, and the clothing of the victim in his notebook. Louie then sent another detective, Rich Van Houten, out to a *bodega* to buy paper bags and masking tape to bag the victim's hands. Tying bags around the hands of murder victims was standard procedure, and might preserve vital evidence. Often a victim struggled with her assailant, and some clawed at their killers with their fingernails, under which could often be found traces of blood and skin from the killer, who could then be identified by DNA comparison tests.

The Crime Scene detective made measurements, drew a diagram of the basement, and took photographs of the body and the scene. Using little brushes, they dusted smooth surfaces, looking for latent fingerprints, a difficult and painstaking task. They dusted any surfaces someone might have touched—even the blackened and melted duct tape. All of the victim's clothing would be checked at the police lab for the presence of hairs and fibers that might link a bad guy to the scene. The soles of her boots would be scraped, and any dirt found subjected to soil analysis. One detective even dusted a piece of a broken light bulb on the floor for prints. Another found a single strand of black hair near the bald victim. A white or Hispanic woman with black hair in New York—that narrowed it down to several million. Pieces of charred clothing and duct tape were bagged for analysis.

They found no fingerprints, which seemed odd to Louie. Had they been wiped off?

When the Crime Scene detectives were done, Tom and Louie had a closer look at the body. Beneath the carbonized waistband of the pants, Louie found two tattoos: a scorpion on the right hip, and two naked figures in the small of the back. They took several Polaroid pictures of the skin art. Detectives liked tattoos. Without the possibility of facial or other identification, tattoos were helpful, although only dental records could confirm identity officially.

When the gruesome task was finished, Tom, a man of few words, took one last look at the victim, and shook his head sadly. "What a way to go," he thought.

They went outside, into the wet snow, and began knocking on doors, canvassing the block. Other detectives helped in the door-to-door operation. One detective wrote down all the license plates of all the cars on the block, but it was unlikely that any of them belonged to the killer. John Cuniffe told Louie and Tom that the house had been empty for years. It didn't look abandoned, and the neighbors helped keep up the appearance by picking up junk-mail circulars from the front stoop—one man even put out some of his garbage for collection in front of the house—to discourage squatters or break-ins. He told them about the woman who owned the house, how she was sick and lived on Long Island with her son. They asked him if he had seen or heard anything suspicious recently.

"I really didn't hear anything, see anything . . ." Cuniffe said apologetically. He wasn't an eyewitness, he wasn't even an ear-witness—he was just a nose-witness, who had smelled smoke.

"Does anyone check on the house?" Louie asked.

"Yeah," said John. "Her son Wayne. He's an ex-Marine. He was . . . in Vietnam."

Tom and Louie looked at each other. They had possible suspect number one. Slowly, along with other investigators, they worked their way around the neighborhood, knocking on doors, interviewing everyone, and handing out cards. They were looking for a handle on the case—a witness, the name of the victim, a description of a car or a person seen at the house. Louie and Tom had the responsibility of bringing the killers to justice, and they needed a break—but the others on the block knew less than John. The investigators had just begun the Golden Forty-Eight—the vital two-day period after a murder, during which the leads that solved most homicides were uncovered. So far, they had a murdered girl without a name. Worse than that, they had found no murder weapon, no fingerprints, no witnesses—no case.

So far, so good.

With nothing to go on from the scene, they headed back to the precinct, where they would stoke up on detective fuel—coffee and cigarettes—and get to work.

The clock was ticking.

When Phil arrived at Psycho's house in Brighton Beach, to pick him up and bring him back to the precinct for further questioning, he saw Tommy Antonakos sitting in his car down the block. There was no harm if Tommy did a little detective work on his own. It might even help—as long as that was all he did.

Julian had gotten home around 5 A.M., but despite his full day ahead, after what he had seen, he could not sleep. Later that morning, he met Rob in the Queens DA's office and showed him how to fill out a "Body Found" report. At 7:30, Julian called the 102nd Precinct and asked the commander of the Detective Squad to assign Lou Pia to the case. Julian felt there were no better detectives in Queens than Pia and his partner, Tom Shevlin. This one wasn't going to solve itself. It looked like a "mystery" case and Julian wanted the best. Julian prized Shevlin's experience and Pia's ability to win the trust of fearful witnesses and elicit confessions from the murderers themselves, as he had done in the College Point Massacre case. The lieutenant in the One-Oh-Two told

Julian that he had already assigned Shevlin and Pia to the case. Later, Julian called the precinct, and got Louie on the phone.

"Louie, I've got a strange feeling about this case," Julian said. "There's something wrong about it."

"Yeah, there's something different about this case," Louie agreed—the question was, what? Louie poured himself a cup of coffee from the perpetually boiling pot in the detective Squad Room, and lit a Marlboro. He removed his jacket, exposing his loaded .38-caliber pistol in a holster on his left hip, and sat down at his desk. Tom Shevlin picked up the phone and dialed the Missing Persons Squad at Police Headquarters in Manhattan. Tom described their "Jane Doe," and was told that, of recent disappearances, the most likely possibility was a missing college student in the Sixty-ninth Precinct in Brooklyn—because she had tattoos. A detective named Phil Tricolla had the case.

"They got something that looks good in the Six-Nine," Tom told Louie.

Louie dialed the Six-Nine squad. At the Foster Avenue stationhouse, Phil still had Psycho cooling his heels in the interview room, and Tommy Antonakos watching from behind the one-way glass. Phil was trying to locate Bob Murphy and get him in for an identification, but the guy had suddenly refused to come in and see if Psycho was one of the guys in the car near Kim's house. When the phone rang, Phil picked it up. It was a Detective Louie Pia, from the One-Oh-Two in Queens. He said he had a body and wanted to see if his body and Phil's missing person were one and the same. It was a routine request. Phil had already eliminated several bodies in his investigation.

"Whaddya got?" Phil asked, picking up a pen to copy the description of the murder victim.

"We got a female, white or Hispanic, in her twenties, black hair . . . scorpion tattoo on her hip . . ."

Phil slammed down the phone. Damn. It was the worst news he had heard in twelve years as a cop. On his desk was a photo of a smiling Kim in a bikini. The little scorpion tattoo adorning her hip was clearly visible. It was unprofessional to hang-up, but Phil had lived the case for a week, doing everything he could to get this girl back to Tommy. He had never gotten emotionally involved in a case—until now. Phil sighed, picked the phone back up, and called the Queens precinct.

"Run this by me again," Phil asked Louie, who described the age, height, tattoos, clothing, and boots of Kimberly Antonakos.

After a few minutes, Phil agreed there was a strong likelihood that Kim was Louie's torched victim.

"Coincidentally, the father is here," said Phil. "I got this scumbag Psycho here," he said, explaining briefly what was going on.

Louie told Phil to keep the father and his possible suspect there, and they would come right over. Phil had to tell Tommy the news. It was the hardest thing he had ever done.

"Tommy, you've got to prepare yourself, if something happens," Phil warned, after telling him that other detectives were on the way to see if a dead girl they had found was Kim.

When Louie and Tom arrived, Phil was talking to Psycho, while Tommy Antonakos waited in the Squad Room. When they walked in, Louie and Tom thought Tommy was a detective, and asked him where Phil was. Tommy got an eerie feeling. As soon as he saw the detectives walk into the room, Tommy knew that Kim was dead. Phil returned and spoke to Louie and Tom in another room. When they came back, Tommy was numb with dread over what he knew they were about to tell him.

"We want to talk to you about your daughter," said Louie.

"We've found a girl that possibly could be your daughter," Tom said.

Tommy began to explain how Kim had disappeared, and pulled out pictures of a beautiful, smiling brunette. He held the happy pictures out to Louie Pia, who tried to explain the unexplainable.

"No, we can't use them," Louie told Tommy gently.

"Why can't you use them?" a confused Tommy asked, holding the snapshots in his outstretched hand. He didn't understand.

Louie tried to be as gentle as possible, but there was no nice way to say it.

"Because your daughter has been burned. The girl we found, we can't identify her from pictures."

To be sure, Kim's dental records would be needed, he said. It would take a few days. How could Tommy understand? It went way beyond a parent's nightmare. No parent could even imagine such a fate for their kid. It was impossible for Tommy to imagine that his beautiful only child—who'd sat on his knee and laughed at Tweety and Sylvester cartoons—would be kidnapped by heartless men and burned alive. Tommy was a strong man, but he couldn't stop the tears. After a while, he was able to tell the detectives what they needed to know about himself and Kim. Gina was also briefly interviewed.

"I have to go home and tell Marlene," the despondent father told the detectives.

Tommy left with Gina, to inform Kim's mother that her daughter was dead.

Phil was dejected. He beat himself up emotionally for not saving Kim. He felt that he had had four days to find her when she was alive, and he had failed. Phil asked Louie and Tom if they wanted to question Psycho, who was still in an interview room. Tom Shevlin spoke briefly to Psycho, their second suspect—but had no intention of questioning him yet. They had no idea who was who in the case, or what the hell was going on yet.

"Howya doin'?" Tom asked Psycho.

He gave the pale young man his card and told him that he might need Psycho's help in regard to Kim's disappearance. Psycho was polite, said he was a stockbroker, but seemed very nervous. Tom told him he could go. Tom felt you only could go at a guy hard once before he lawyered-up, and this was not the time. He and Louie had homework to do. The dental records would probably confirm Kim's identity, but they needed to find out everything they could about the father, the family, and the friends of Kim. Tommy had told them about Kim, her work and school, himself and his business, and everything up to that point. They needed to speak to Kim's friends. It was a murder investigation, and everyone would have to be re-interviewed. A call was made to Kim's apartment, and April, Josh, Liz, and Jay were asked to come to the precinct—but they were not told why. Homicide detectives preferred to watch people's faces when they learned the bad news, in order to gauge whether the reaction was genuine, or an acting job by someone who already knew. At 5:40 in the evening, April was asked into a room with Phil, Louie, and Tom Shevlin, while Josh, Timmy and Jay waited outside in the hall on a bench.

"We found Kimberly," Louie told Kim's friend. "Someone burned her. She's dead."

"You motherfuckers," the pretty blonde spat at the surprised detectives. "Why didn't you tell me on the phone? Why did I have to come down here? You could've told me over the phone."

People sometimes reacted in different ways to tragedy, but Louie thought this was pretty odd. Her best friend was dead, murdered horribly, and all she could think of was, why did she have to make the ten-minute drive to the precinct, where the grieving father of her good friend needed comforting?

"I want to leave," said April, who then began crying.

Then she asked for Josh. She wanted him with her. Louie went out in the hall to get him. He saw two Latino guys sitting on a bench with another young woman and a kid. The guy sitting next to the little boy, playing with him, was scrawny, with a scraggly beard and mustache. Louie thought he looked like a weasel.

"Which one of you is Joshua?" Louie asked.

"I am," said the thin guy.

"We're going to need you in the room."

"Why?" Josh asked.

"April's requesting that you come into the room. We did find Kimberly," Louie continued. "She's dead. We informed [April] of it and she became quite emotional."

"Well, yeah," Josh responded. "She is like a sister to me, and she is like a sister to April. We're very tight, we're very close."

"Well, are you going to come into the room?" Louie asked.

"Yeah," said Josh, standing up, and making a little speech. "I will do anything to help to assist in this, because I am looking to find the people that did this."

With Josh sitting beside her, April told Louie and Tom that she worked long hours as a paralegal. She and Josh had been kicked out of her mother's apartment because of bad blood between her mom and Josh. Kim had let them stay at her place until they could fix up the floors and paint their new apartment. April had met Kim years earlier because her brother Michael, who had since married, had been Kim's first boyfriend. After they broke up, Kim and April had remained friends.

Louie and Tom exchanged a look. They were interested. April said that Kim had dumped Michael. The investigators made a note to check him out—he was their third suspect. It was part of the process of eliminating people, removing them from suspicion, until you couldn't eliminate the killer. What if, deep down in his heart, Kim was his first love? Had he tried to rekindle the old flame, and been rebuffed? Did he make the decision that if he could not have Kim, nobody could? Burning a girl alive did not seem like the act of a stranger—more like an ultimate act of hatred, destruction, obliteration. They would be speaking to Michael Dedely soon.

April said that she and Kim often went to clubs and Kim

met a lot of men because she was so pretty. She said she had introduced Kim to Josh and his friend Jay, whom Kim had dated. That was suspect number four. Jay was the only guy Kim dated who did not have money or a fancy car, said April. She said that she and Josh were together in Kim's apartment with the baby the night her friend vanished. She and Josh had gone to bed, and heard Kim's phone ring about 1:30 in the morning. Josh was going to answer it but decided to let the answering machine get it. When April woke on Wednesday morning to go to work, Kim had not come home, and her bed had not been slept in.

"Kim was a sweet girl, who had all the toys and money," said April, but "she was not stingy, and would share what she had."

Louie and Tom turned to Josh, and asked him a routine question that they had already asked April—his date of birth. He sat up straight in his chair, highly offended.

"What do you need that for?" asked Josh, who knew perfectly well why—the detectives were going to check for arrest records of everyone they came in contact with.

Josh was upset because he knew what they would find. When they told him that everybody else had given their birthdays, Josh reluctantly told them that he was born on June 9th, 1973. They asked Josh if he had any nicknames, and he told them everybody called him K-Q. Josh told the same simple story as April—they were each other's alibi. He said that he woke up later than April on Wednesday, and did not even know that Kim had not come home. "I woke up the next day and I didn't even realize anything was wrong."

He said it wasn't until 1 o'clock that April called and told him that Kim had not come home that morning, and had not shown up for work.

"I beeped every one of her boyfriends," using Kim's address book, Josh explained. "The only one that didn't call back was this guy Psycho, this Russian guy. They went to Miami together. He's, like, obsessed with her."

April echoed Kim's problems with her eager suitor.

"Psycho scared her. She felt he was obsessed with her and had a tattoo of her name put on his leg after knowing her only a couple of days," and even tried to give her an engagement ring, said April.

She also related the story that Kim told about some friend of Psycho's coming up to her in a club, and telling her, "We know who you are."

"Who would do this?" Louie asked her, meaning the murder.

"That guy Psycho," April said, without hesitation.

When asked for his alibi on the night Kim was killed, Josh said that he was out with his friend Jay, looking for Kim. Tommy Antonakos had beeped him at one point, and they had checked out some motel on Cross Bay Boulevard, Josh said. He said they had returned to Kim's apartment about one in the morning—before she was killed.

They next spoke to Liz, who told them about her night out with Kim, about how she was afraid of Psycho, and the trip Kim took to Florida with him. Liz described in detail the clothing and jewelry Kim wore that night, including a unique cross with red stones. After Liz left the room, Louie and Tom decided that the cross would be one of their secret "holdbacks," or "vest cards." Holdbacks were used to eliminate false leads, or phony confessions—and to incriminate the real bad guys.

Jay was next. He had no problem giving Louie and Tom his date of birth, and said that his nickname was B-Q. He said he had dated Kim for a while, and then they had agreed to see other people. They were still friends, still "hung out together," he said. Jay told them he had spent the night before Kim disappeared with her at her apartment, and had slept over. The night she went missing, he said, he slept at his sister's place, the one who was married to a cop.

It sounded like a gold-plated, bulletproof alibi to Louie and Tom, but, of course, they would still check it out.

Jay then told them how he and Josh had searched for Kim, by going to chop shops, and looking for her car. Tom asked him the address of the chop shop in his old neighborhood. He shrugged, and said he couldn't remember. Josh had been driving. That morning, when Kim was burned, Jay said he had been out with Josh, searching for Kim until one in the morning. Suddenly, Jay looked around leaned forward helpfully, and dropped a bomb:

"Tommy is Mafia," he announced.

"How do you know that?" Tom asked, a bit surprised.

Jay replied that Tommy's brother had his office next to Gotti's headquarters, where only connected people could rent or buy. The brother had also showed up at Kim's place with a carload of mob "gorillas" to look for Kim, he said.

This was new. It certainly gave the detectives pause. Of course, it didn't matter if the victim was John Gotti's daughter—they still had to find her killer. But it didn't make sense. Louie and Tom had never heard of anything like it. Italian gangsters did not kidnap each others daughters and set them on fire. If Tommy Antonakos had offended wiseguys, they might break his legs, but they would not grab his daughter. If he had stolen from the mob, they were much more likely to tuck a couple of slugs behind his ear, and dump his lifeless body in the street, than to torch Kim. Either something very strange was going on, Tom thought, or this kid Jay was full of shit.

After they were done, Louie and Tom drove Jay back to Kim's apartment. Outside, there were, indeed, several beefy guys in expensive clothes—friends of Kim's uncle. They might have looked like hoods to some, but that didn't mean they were. A lot of heavies didn't look like movie gangsters—they looked like anybody else.

"Didn't I tell you they were Mafia?" asked Jay. "They look like gorillas." He seemed scared.

After Jay left the car, Louie and Tom discussed the new development. Was Tommy Antonakos, or his brother, connected? Were they associated with mobsters? After all, Kim had been found in Woodhaven. The name Woodhaven conjure up images of a peaceful glade, but there were no woods in Woodhaven, peaceful or otherwise. It was a busy commercial area under a noisy, rusted elevated subway line, and the only haven there that came to the detectives' minds was mobster John Gotti's social club. Was Kim killed in retaliation for some slight to members of organized crime? Anything was possible, but made guys were all Italian, and Tommy was only half-Italian. If La Cosa Nostra had a serious problem with Tommy, they wouldn't need permission from anyone to put a hole in his head, and leave him in the weeds along the Belt, like in *The Godfather*—a 'leave the gun, take the cannoli' situation. But it made zero sense, Tom thought. If it was a kidnapping to get Tommy's money—or to get mob money back—why hadn't anybody made a ransom demand? Mobsters didn't call cops in the first place, like Tommy had. One thing seemed certain—the girl was his whole life. Tommy would have paid any price to get her back. If he had paid someone, and not told police, why was she torched? Tom and Louie decided to confront Tommy with what Jay had said, and took him for a ride. Either the investigation was about to go down a new, strange road, or they were about to offend a man who had just lost his daughter. It couldn't be helped. They had to know.

"Listen," Tom Shevlin said to Tommy, broaching the subject of the Mafia. "Are you involved in anything yourself? Because if you are involved, we need to know."

"I have nothing to do with the mob," a surprised and confused Tommy responded. "My daughter was barbarically killed . . ." He trailed off, in frustration. "I was never in the mob, but I do know some people to say hello to."

Tommy said that he and his brother had a fire insurance business about a block away from Gotti's headquarters, but denied any involvement in organized crime. Tommy's denial was believable, but, they told him, they would check him out anyway, to make sure. Tommy said that was fine—but he asked them to "hurry up" and investigate him quickly, so they could get to the ones who killed Kim.

Back at the stationhouse, Phil had finally gotten Bob Murphy in to look at Psycho through the one-way mirror.

"That's not the guy," Murphy said, as soon as he saw Psycho.

Phil was relieved that his instincts had not been wrong, but he was in a personal and professional turmoil. He was out of the case because it was a homicide in another precinct. He had told Louie and Tom that he didn't believe Psycho was involved, and they seemed to agree—but was he wrong about Psycho? He had to find out if he was right, had to know if he had failed to arrest the guy who had destroyed Kim. He had one more test for Psycho—he would bring him to the scene of the crime. If Psycho was the killer, he had to react. He would jump out of his skin. Phil told Psycho that he was going to drive him home. He and his partner put Psycho in the back of an unmarked car and drove toward Woodhaven almost the opposite direction from Psycho's home in Brighton Beach. The two detectives up front were silent. It didn't take long for Psycho to notice that they were not headed for his house.

"Where're we going?" asked Psycho.

"I gotta drop something off in Queens," said Phil.

When they arrived on Eighty-sixth Avenue, they parked three houses away from the burned home. Wide yellow tape with "CRIME SCENE—DO NOT PASS" printed on it in black letters was stretched across the sidewalk in front of the house, and wrapped around a tree and a NO PARKING sign. Phil looked at Psycho. Nothing—he betrayed no reaction at all, no guilty knowledge of what had been done there. Phil got out of the car. The charcoal smell of the gutted house filled the air. The detective walked under the tape and down the driveway of a home, waited a while, and returned to the car. Psycho was not scared or nervous. He was only impatient to get home.

"If he did this, he'd be bugging out, he'd be shitting," Phil thought as he looked at the calm but impatient Psycho.

"You done?" asked Psycho. "We going now?"

Phil was convinced he had been right about Psycho all

along: He wasn't involved in Kim's death. Although Phil had not found Kim alive, at least he had not been wrong about Psycho. It would have been unbearable if Psycho had killed Kim after Phil had left him walking around.

"Yeah. I'm done," said Phil. "We're going now."

The next day was a full one for Louie and Tom. After a night of beginning the massive task of eliminating all of Kim's friends and associates, they went to the Sixtieth Precinct and checked out Psycho. His nonchalance with Phil the night before seemed to let him off the hook—but what if he had his gang do it for him? What if they had burned her without his knowledge? They got printouts of the rap sheets of all the Together Forever gang buddies of Psycho, along with Intelligence Division reports on the gang's activities.

While Tom read the files on the gang, Louie drove to the Queens Morgue, the office of the city Medical Examiner, on the grounds of the Queens Hospital Center, to witness the autopsy of their victim. This was the moment when Kim's silent body could still speak. Not only could her damaged remains mutely give testimony to the terrible drama that was her abduction and destruction, but it might still incriminate her killers.

When he walked into the autopsy room, Pathologist Dr. Kari Reiber, a veteran of some three thousand autopsies, had already arranged Kim's clothes on a separate table from the body. Louie could smell gas fumes emanating from the blackened clothing.

As she worked, Dr. Reiber, clad in a green surgical gown and pale rubber gloves, spoke into a microphone dangling over the stainless-steel table, describing every step, every organ, every finding. She administered a "rape kit" that tested for semen in or on the body. The test would prove to be negative. Kim had apparently not been raped or sexually assaulted. That was one motive down, thought Louie. If an enraged jilted lover had killed her, he reasoned, could he have resisted the chance to molest her? Dr. Reiber took the paper bags off, and examined the burned and blistered backs of Kim's hands closely.

"Before I open her up, I'm pretty sure she was alive, when set on fire," she told Louie, with growing anger—pointing out blisters surrounded by red skin on Kim's right hand. She explained that it was a "vital reaction," and that only a living body could send blood to a burn area like that. She asked Louie if there were any particular examinations that he needed in the case. Louie asked her for scrapings from under the fingernails, preservation of the tape around the hands and mouth for lab tests, hair and fiber examination, estimated time and cause of death, and the contents of the victim's stomach.

Dr. Reiber began to take scrapings from underneath the melted fingernails and placed them into evidence envelopes. She found something stuck under a nail on the left hand and reached for a tweezer to extract it. Louie watched her pull out four metal zipper teeth, apparently ripped from a zipper by a desperately clawing hand. Would the bad guy keep the jacket with the broken zipper? Louie wondered. From Kim's eyes, the pathologist removed two contact lenses that had been baked from blue to gray by the heat. Dr. Reiber picked up a scalpel and opened the throat of the victim. The inside of the windpipe was as black as coal. That meant that the dead girl had been breathing during the fire, which had seared and blackened her trachea, Reiber explained. The stomach was completely empty, except for a tiny amount of brown fluid—not surprising for someone tied to a chair for four days. Louie decided that that was their second holdback: the fact that Kim's stomach was empty. Who else but the killer would know she had not been fed?

"I certainly hope you get the guys responsible for this," an outraged Dr. Reiber told Louie when she was done. "She was still alive when she was set on fire—they burned this girl alive."

CHAPTER ELEVEN

"LET'S GO FOR A RIDE"

Josh knocked on the apartment door, which was opened by George's girlfriend *Judy Collins. Judy was not particularly happy to be awakened by Josh, who would stop by whenever he felt like it, at any hour of the day or night—sometimes at two or three in the morning—looking for George. Sometimes Josh even called Judy at her job, asking for George. Josh was always asking for favors of some kind. He would ask to have his laundry done, ask them to do shopping for him, or to babysit Timmy, so he could go somewhere while April was at work. Just the previous night, Josh had borrowed some of George's clothes and returned them in the middle of the night.

"Kimberly's dead," Josh announced. "They found her. Somebody burned her."

George and Judy knew Kim, but they were not as close to her as Josh, who was her good friend. Josh wanted them to get up and go somewhere, but George, after partying from 5 p.m. Friday night until 4 a.m. Saturday, was still asleep. Josh returned about 3 o'clock in the afternoon, just as George and Judy were getting ready to leave to pay their respects to Kim's father.

"Let's go for a ride," Josh said. "Do you want to see the house where she was?"

Judy and George did not want to go to the scene of the crime, and told Josh so.

"I want to go and see what's going on," Josh insisted.

Since Kim had been such a good friend of Josh's, the couple felt bad about refusing. They agreed to go, and went downstairs to Josh's car. Josh slid behind the wheel and began driving. No one noticed that he did not refer to a map, or a written set of directions. He never stopped to ask directions. For almost five miles Josh did not even glance at the passing street signs; he just drove directly there, eventually turning onto a small street and pulling up in front of a house with police tape around it.

"This is where she was held at," Josh told them, like a tour guide.

Later, Josh went back to Kim's apartment, where he found April, Jay, and Shawn. Josh suggested to Kim's grieving friends that they go to the house where Kim had been killed. Josh got behind the wheel of April's car and again drove straight to the Woodhaven house. No one got out of the car. After looking at the crime scene for a while, Josh drove everyone back to Kim's place, where Shawn met Tommy Antonakos for the first time.

That night, when Jay decided to go home, Josh offered to drive him. When they were alone in the car, Jay again began to lament what had happened.

"How did it all go wrong?" Jay asked. "Why did it happen?"

Josh's eyes narrowed at talk that he considered a sign of weakness. He fixed Jay with a hard look.

"Hold your own, or you know you'll get it," Josh threatened.

On Sunday, Tara and April were helping Kim's family set things in order. They went to the cleaners, to see if any of Kim's clothes were there. Tara, out of curiosity, told April that she, too, wanted to go past the house where Kim was found, to see where it had happened. April told Tara that she didn't know how to get there. When the two young women returned to April's apartment, Josh was there. April asked Josh for directions. Rather than explain, Josh said he would take them there—and he had a strange request. He asked Tara if he could borrow her video camera. He said he wanted to use it to videotape the murder scene. Tara turned down the ghoulish request, and refused to lend her camera to Josh. They looked at the house and went home.

Later that night, Josh drove alone to the death house and sneaked inside. After having been to the scene twice with other people, other witnesses, he thought he could safely enter the house without fear of consequences, should he get caught. He carefully made his way to the basement and surveyed his handiwork. He was not pleased. The fire had burned a hole in the first floor, but had not consumed the body and the entire house, which had been the whole idea. Once again his plan had failed, but he was still in the clear.

Josh pulled out a beer can and opened it, making a *schpritz* sound in the quiet cellar. He raised his drink in a mock toast to the empty space that had once held Kimberly Antonakos, and declared—in both sarcastic tribute, and sincere triumph:

"Sorry, Kim."

CHAPTER TWELVE

ANGUISH

Kim's murder received light press coverage at first—because both police and news editors did not yet know what they had. Police Headquarters in Manhattan issued a press notice, and reporters were assigned to the case. Newspapers, television, and radio ran the first of many stories about a young girl who had been burned alive. The crime was so savage, so primitive, that it inspired revulsion and anger, and actually sent shivers up the spines of many New Yorkers who read it or saw it on television.

Kim's murder shocked a tough town that many thought could not be shocked.

On Sunday, the *Daily News* ran a twelve-paragraph story headlined "SLAY VICTIM FOUND AFTER BLAZE." The victim was not identified.

"We assume something was holding her in the chair, but we can't say how she was tied," Detective Sergeant William Rhone told the paper. A few television stations also ran stories about the woman who had been set on fire in Queens. Viewers who watched the report reacted with revulsion— except for four men who knew exactly what had held the victim in the chair.

They reacted with fear.

Josh, Jay, Joey, and Nick called each other and got together for a quick meeting on the street. Josh bought a copy of the local weekly paper which carried a big story about the murder—his first clipping.

"Look, it's all in the paper," Josh told them.

The meeting was a rehash of their arguments and finger-pointing of only a day earlier—who "fucked up" and how—but now it seemed like the whole police force was after them. Joey and Jay also seemed upset that Kim was dead, although it did not seem to trouble Josh or Nick very much. They were all confused about how they had become killers. Josh did not like the way Joey was talking to him. Joey felt that Josh had screwed up getting the money. If he had gotten the ransom quickly, she wouldn't have died. Josh felt that Joey was supposed to keep Kim alive, and had "fucked it up." Josh kept his cool, and explained again that Kim's death "shouldn't have happened in the first place," but that setting the place on fire "was the only alternative we had." The squabbling continued until Josh surprised them by telling them that he had been to the torched house several times to check it out. Nick and Joey had been afraid to go near the place, but not Josh. You had to give it to the guy—he had *cojones*. He had a set.

"We messed up," Josh said, explaining that the house was still there, with only a hole in the basement ceiling. He told them the cops had nothing to go on, and warned his cohorts to keep their mouths shut.

"They got shit. Hold your own," Josh ordered, glaring at Joey. "If you snitch, you go! Keep it real. *Asta la muerte*—we're gonna take it to the grave."

The message was clear—he was still the head gangster and anyone who talked would get it.

Joey thought about his secret insurance, the tape he had made of one of their meetings. He could nail this kid Josh, and Jay, with it—but he would also implicate himself, and his best friend Nick. If the cops ever figured it out, he could make a deal. Joey felt bad about the dead girl. Raised a Catholic, he felt blackened by a mortal sin, and he wanted to get clean.

On Monday morning, while Tommy's brother Joseph made final funeral arrangements for his niece, *Newsday* published a small story—"FIRE KILLED QUEENS MYSTERY WOMAN"—that identified her as a New York college student, whose dental records were being compared in an effort to confirm her identity.

That afternoon, in the state capitol in Albany, State senators began debating the new death-penalty bill. Governor George Pataki had made passage of such a bill the biggest plank in his campaign platform, and the debate was virtually moot—because the Republican-controlled senate already had the votes lined up for passage. The talking went on until 8 o'clock that night, when the measure was put to a vote. It carried overwhelmingly, by a 38–19 majority. The legislature had passed death-penalty bills every year since 1977, only to have them vetoed by Democratic governors. The bill called for capital punishment, via lethal injection, for those found guilty of about ten kinds of serious crimes—including murders committed during another violent crime, like rape, robbery, or kidnapping. Also facing death would be serial killers, hit men committing contract killings, anyone who killed a judge, cop, or prison guard—and anyone who tortured their victims. Experts estimated that as many as twenty per cent of New York State's 2,400 annual murders might be classified as capital crimes. Senator Dale Volker, an upstate Republican and former cop, said the law would be a deterrent, and would "send a message" to criminals that New York had gotten tough on crime. "There are people who are dead today who would be alive if we had a death penalty," the legislator said.

While the passage of the bill meant that future killers might face death for heinous offenses, the measure would not take effect for six months, until September 1st. If Kim's killers were found, they would never face the death penalty.

On Tuesday, The *New York Post* ran a full story across the top of page ten that revealed Kim's name, and the fact that she had been alive when set on fire, possibly by a carjacker—"BOUND BEAUTY WAS BURNED ALIVE."

"Whoever did this didn't want anyone to identify her," one investigator said.

"There was everything sweet about her," Kim's friend Liz Pace told a reporter. "She was a beautiful, sweet girl. I'm in a lot of pain right now. I don't know why anyone would do anything like this to her. She was everything to anybody who knew her."

The last paragraph of the story featured a phone number for anyone with information about the crime to call detectives.

Tommy, shouldering the unbearable burden of Kim's murder, as well as the method of it, concealed from his ex-wife how Kim had died. To protect Marlene from the truth, Tommy told her that there would be a closed white casket, because Kim was killed in a car crash trying to escape from her abductors. The wake was held at a funeral home a few miles from Tommy's home on Staten Island. Dozens of bouquets and floral tributes surrounded the casket, and lined the walls of the room. Sheltered from a cold, drizzly sky outside, the room was filled with tears, but smelled like a garden. Suspicion was also in the air. Kim's relatives, friends, and classmates filed past the pale casket. Many stopped to kneel and pray next to her body. As they said their goodbyes, they looked at a large photo display—pictures of Kim as a kid growing up, her high-school graduation picture, and other happy pictures of her smiling her big smile.

"The killer is still out there, and nobody knows who did it," one young man who had gone to high school with Kim told a *New York Post* reporter outside the funeral home.

"The cops told me it was way too vicious," one angry family member said. "It's gotta be somebody she knows. Who is it? We have to find out!"

"She was a great girl," another high school classmate said. "I have this videotape of her from a picnic last summer, and I was playing it over and over all night, and there's this part where we zoom in to her face, and someone says 'Smile,

Kim!' and she smiles her beautiful smile. I've just been looking at that all morning.''

"I saw her just three days ago," said Rosa Luciamo. "I
still can't believe it.''

As the mourners came and went, a police cameraman videotaped them, and zoomed in on their faces. Louie Pia and
Tom Shevlin had arranged for an undercover police van op-
erated by the TARU unit—the secret Technical Assistance
Response Unit—to record anyone who attended.

On Wednesday, the *Daily News* featured a story that said
police believed hatred to be the motive for the murder—
"SLAY VICTIM BURNED ALIVE."

"Obviously, this crime is a crime of hate," said one cop.
"Somebody hated her enough to make her suffer in the worst
kind of way. He had to know the house was empty. There
had to be a reason he took her there.''

Investigators said they were going to talk to several of the
dead girl's boyfriends.

"Oh, what a doll," said Kim's landlord, Nat Sanders.
"She was a very kind person. She took in a cat and a dog,
and she's clean, and nice. You couldn't have asked for anybody better as a tenant.''

Before the 10 a.m. service, Jay arrived at the funeral home
in Staten Island, and walked into the crowded, hushed room
where Kim's closed casket lay. He saw Tommy, and a lot
of Kim's friends, many people he didn't know. He didn't
want to go up to the casket at first.

"Here I am coming to the funeral, and I'm going to have
to face the family, being a piece of shit," Jay reflected.

His guilty thoughts were interrupted by Kim's red-eyed
mother. Despite her grief, Marlene saw Jay and hugged him,
trying to comfort her daughter's friend.

"Jay, you know it's going to be all right," Marlene told
him.

"Yeah. I'm sorry, Marlene. I offer you my condolences,"
Jay replied.

What a hypocrite he was. Jay was sorry that she was

dead, but he was acting like he knew nothing about what
had happened. Finally, Jay worked up enough nerve to approach Kim's coffin. He stood next to Shawn, looking at the
photos of her. Both young men started crying. Tommy saw
the boys sobbing at the casket and walked between them. He
put his arms around them both and tried to make them feel
better:

"Don't worry about it, it's going to be all right, I promise
you," said Tommy, who had already vowed to his dead
daughter that her killers would be brought to justice. "Now,
we'll get these guys, we're going to get them."

"Yes we will," said Jay, in an angry voice. "And when
we do, I want a crack at them."

From the funeral parlor, the memorial moved to the
Church of Our Lady Star of the Sea, Kim's parish church, a
modern, red brick church set back from the road atop a
grassy rise not far from Tommy's home. The hearse pulled
into the driveway and alongside the church, in front of two
hundred crying mourners, including Jay, Tara, Liz, and April.
Josh's eyes were dry. Louie Pia and Tom Shevlin were there
to pay their respects—and also to see who attended Kim's
last rites, and how they acted, and who did not show up.
They all followed the casket into the house of worship,
through glass entrance doors flanked by evergreen trees.
Marlene sobbed pitifully, as her husband and Tommy supported her and led her inside. The family's tears were wails
of anguish. A robed priest, Father Jeff Conway, and two altar
boys greeted Kim's remains in the vestibule. One altar boy
held a staff topped by a cross. The other swung a smoking
incense burner back and forth on the end of a chain, which
clicked as the sweet-smelling smoke wafted Heavenward.
The casket was blessed by the priest, and a white silk pall
was placed atop it before it was rolled down the center aisle
and placed before the simple altar. The grieving company
followed the casket down the aisle. The side walls of the
church admitted multicolored light through vertical stained-

glass windows, each one depicting an image of a saint staring down on the wooden pews.

"There is no rhyme or reason why she had to leave this world at such a young age," Father Conway told the assemblage from the wooden pulpit in front of a huge crucifix.

Jay sat under the shimmering glare of all those saintly eyes, and sobbed. No fingers pointed out his guilt, no bolt of lightning forked out at him from above. Everyone around him knew he was crying for Kim, just as they were. Only Jay—and the unblinking eyes above him—knew that he was also crying for himself.

After the Mass of Christian Burial, Kim was taken to the Moravian Cemetery, a beautiful 255-year-old burial place, whose grounds feature ponds filled with fish and ducks, grassy hillocks, stately old trees, and peaceful meadows. The cemetery was established in 1740, and the first Moravian church was built in 1763. During Colonial times, the island was occupied by British troops, and served as a place of burial for Redcoats who perished in the New World. Beginning in 1865, Commodore Cornelius Vanderbilt and his family donated additional land to complete the necropolis.

Kim was interred with further prayers and painful tears in a stone building behind a pink granite slab in a mausoleum site, alongside her grandfather William Antonakos, who had died a decade earlier. Beneath the visceral agony of farewell was the enduring fury that a beautiful young girl who left her home in Staten Island to move into her first apartment would return so soon to live forever in that restful place of death. It had never occurred to Tommy that he would live to bury Kim. He had assumed that the next service for Kim at their parish church would be her wedding, not her funeral. To Tommy, Kim could never be gone. He spoke to her as if she were there. He vowed to his daughter that he would see justice done. They would find her killer and see that he was punished.

They would do it together.

CHAPTER THIRTEEN

KIM'S CAR

Louie Pia and Tom Shevlin were doing everything they could to locate Kim's car. If it no longer existed, that would point toward a carjacking that had ended in murder. In that case, the Honda would have already been disassembled in a chop shop. Tom checked to find out if Kim's car had been towed, and was sitting in a pound somewhere. It wasn't. He had also checked parking tickets, hoping that an abandoned car might have received a summons from a dutiful cop, but Kim had not been issued a ticket in months.

The fact that Kim's cell phone had been used after she was last seen was interesting. While she was in the dark trunk, did Kim bang buttons on the phone, trying to call for help? Louie contacted Cellular One, and was told that no one in customer service had had a conversation with anyone that night on the victim's phone. It was possible that someone who did not know the security code was trying to use the phone. Louie and Tom drove over to the Hilton Hotel near JFK Airport in Queens, because whoever had tried to use the phone had done so within a fifteen-block radius of the building—right after she'd vanished. Louie and Tom wanted to make sure that Kim's car was not in the Hilton parking lot, or on the streets nearby. It wasn't, and no one at the hotel had seen her.

The day after Kim disappeared, Cellular One records also

showed a hit on an electronic "repeater" relay on Liberty
Avenue in East New York, Brooklyn. Louie and Tom also
checked that neighborhood, with the same frustrating results.
But Tom still did not think it was a carjacking. His gut told
him it was a kidnap that had gone sour—but where the hell
was the car?

Joanne Scully and her husband Dennis had been wondering
about the white car parked across from their house in Malverne for a week. When they awoke on Wednesday morning,
March 8th—the day of Kim's funeral—the car was still
there. The day before, a woman neighbor from around the
corner, who was also convinced it had been stolen, had tried
to open the car door. It was locked. Even after the rain, it
was obvious that someone had rubbed dirt off part of the car.
The glass, door, and parts of the body were smeared, probably with a cloth, where someone had done a very bad job
of car washing—or a good job of wiping away fingerprints.
Inside, a red alarm light blinked constantly. A beehive-
shaped air freshener dangled from the rear-view mirror, and
a woman's purple hairbrush was on the passenger seat. A
folder and a piece of paper with scribbled directions sat atop
the dashboard. When a friend arrived at the house, Dennis
complained to him about how the cops were not doing anything about the Honda, and that they were sure it had been
stolen. His friend took one look at Kim's Accord and said:

"Dennis, did you see the news? They're looking for this
car."

He explained that the car belonged to some girl who had
been murdered in the city. They had even given out the
license-plate number on television, and it seemed to be the
same. Joanne immediately picked up the phone and dialed
911. A Nassau County police dispatcher said a car was on
the way. At 8:40, when no one had arrived for a full hour,
Joanne dialed the Malverne police, who arrived within
minutes. They "ran the plate" and it came up stolen, with
a warning to contact NYPD and safeguard the auto for prints.

Some kind of glitch had apparently allowed Kim's car to remain hidden for a full week. The county police arrived ten minutes after the locals, and took charge. Following the instructions on the stolen car "hot sheet," a Nassau County police officer called the Six-Nine Precinct in Brooklyn and asked for Phil Tricolla.

"You have an alarm out on a white Honda?" the Long Island cop asked the city detective.

"Yeah, I do." said Phil.

The cop described the white Accord, and gave the correct plate number. Phil reminded them to safeguard it for a fingerprint team.

"Where is it?" Phil asked eagerly, ready to copy down the address.

"You know where Malverne is?"

"Yeah," said a stunned Phil. "I live in Malverne."

He couldn't believe it. Kim's car was in his town, two blocks off Southern State Parkway, one block south of the Hempstead Avenue exit. He had passed that damn car twice a day, maybe a hundred yards away. A stand of trees prevented it from being seen from the parkway, and it was hidden from sight on the tiny side street. Phil was upbraiding himself for not being psychic, for not knowing the car was there. It was an irrational reaction, further proof that he had become emotionally involved in the case.

He hung up the phone, and he and his partner sped out there. Louie and Tom, who had been in Staten Island at the funeral, were also notified, and rushed out. When they arrived, there were at least forty cops, detectives, and bosses from three different departments. Crime-scene photographers were taking pictures of the position of the vehicle on the block, and crawling around in the street, looking for clues. Groups of curious neighbors gathered to watch the proceedings, and detectives began going from house to house, looking for anyone who had seen or heard anything. No one had. The only people who had any information were Joanne and Dennis Scully, who could only say that the car had appeared 'on the morning Kim went missing and had been sitting there ever since. Their neighbors had not seen who left the car, and had heard nothing, except for one resident—who had seen a small red car, with a lone man inside, slowly circle the block several times that week. Was it someone checking on the car? She had not gotten a plate number.

While canvassing neighbors' houses around the corner, on Gerard Street, Louie asked a woman if he could look in her yard. Just inside a fence, he spotted a roll of gray duct tape on the grass. He was excited because he was sure it had been thrown there by a bad guy. It was the same type of tape that had been used to bind Kim. Louie alerted a Crime Scene detective, who picked up the tape with hands covered by surgical gloves. He dusted the tape roll for prints—but found none. Small fibers that had stuck to the tape were collected and put in plastic evidence bags.

After the canvass was complete, a rookie detective walked over to the car and looked underneath. As he leaned over, the inexperienced investigator placed his bare hand squarely on the glass of the driver's side window. He was contaminating the car with his own handprint, and possibly wiping away crucial fingerprint evidence. A booming voice belonging to a detective captain who could not believe what he was seeing could be heard a block away:

"Get your hand off of that car or I'll slap the shit out of you!"

The rookie pulled his hand off the hot car as if it were on fire. He was embarrassed, and sheepishly sought out an experienced Queens Homicide detective, Rich Tirelli.

"I fucked up big-time, didn't I?" asked the neophyte detective.

"Yeah," agreed Rich, with a smile.

Kim's car was towed to the Six-Nine Precinct garage, where the Crime Scene detectives would examine it for hours. Tom felt that finding the car in one piece gave strength to either the bungled kidnap, or the revenge theory. If it had been a carjacking, why was the car not chopped up? If it had been a snatch, that explained why she had been held for days before being killed. But what went wrong? Did they just chicken out? Maybe that was why she had no food in her stomach—they were too scared to go feed her. What were they scared of? Had they also heard the rumors that Tommy was mobbed-up? That might have done it. Tom was keeping his fingers crossed. Now that the car had been found at last, he hoped it was going to give them something to go on.

Back in Brooklyn, the Crime Scene detectives dusted for fingerprints, but found nothing on the outside of the car— other than a large handprint. They disabled the alarm. As soon as they opened the trunk, they immediately found the glittering mate of Kim's gold earring that Tommy had found in the garage. It was near the back of the car, resting on the trunk upholstery, next to a gold license-plate cover. They took flash pictures, also documenting the baseball caps, a white power cord, a navy-and-red plaid tartan wool blanket, and other items in the relatively neat trunk. The earring did not yield any fingerprints, nor could it identify the killer, but it told one thing very clearly: Whoever had done this had thrown Kim into the trunk, probably already tied up.

The evidence gatherers bagged and cataloged the earring in a plastic baggie. They also bagged samples of hair from Kim's hairbrush, and other hairs of the same color from the seats, trunk, and inside the caps—presumably belonging to Kim. Other individual hairs were found on the seats, floor- mats, and other areas—including light brown, reddish- brown, and dyed reddish-orange hairs that did not match Kim's hair color. Three brown-and-white hairs that looked like animal hair were also collected. All were saved for pos- sible comparison to suspect hairs. Tiny fibers sticking to the duct tape found in Malverne were compared to fiber samples from the trunk lining and floor mats, but they did not match. One fingerprint was lifted from the inside passenger's side. Cigarette butts were carefully collected from the ashtray. The filters that had come into contact with the smokers' mouths would be removed and tested for DNA.

Louie and Tom were not happy. There seemed to be nothing useful from the car. They were now certain that Kim had been stuffed in the trunk alive and driven to the Woodhaven house. Perhaps the mysterious stray print would turn out to be useful. Of course, it wouldn't incriminate anyone who had ever had a legitimate reason to be in Kim's car—which let most of her friends, family, and boyfriends off the hook. Fingerprints scientifically proved that a certain person had left them, but did not come along with a date certifying when they had been made. In short, they still had nothing. The next step would be the phone dumps—subpoenas for telephone records.

Back in Malverne, the press had heard about the development in the Antonakos case, and were interviewing everyone who would talk.

A *Daily News* reporter knocked on the Scullys' door and asked if they had seen anything.

"Not really," said Dennis. "My son said he saw somebody walking by."

"We saw him wiping the car. You could see ... where, like, somebody wiped something off," said nine-year-old Danny, describing the smudges on the car observed by all the neighbors.

"You saw the killer? You saw the killer?" the excited reporter asked the child.

Joanne swept her son inside the house.

The next day, the *Daily News* reported on page three, in a story entitled "BOY SAW TORCH KILLER," that the killer of Kim Antonakos "was later spotted by residents when he returned to wipe it clean of fingerprints, sources said yesterday." One source, quoted as saying, "We saw him wiping the car," was identified only as "one little boy who lives on Tucker Lane." When Joanne and Dennis read the story, they were terrified. Theirs was the only house on Tucker Lane, and Danny was the only boy on the block. A furious Dennis called the *Daily News* and complained, but there would be no retraction. The paper stood by the story.

"Do you realize what you've done? If this guy did come back, you've set up my little son!"

"Mister Scully, do you know how many kids live on Tucker Lane?"

"This isn't Brooklyn. This is Long Island, and he's the only kid on the street!"

Rich Tirelli called the Scullys to ask them about the newspaper report, but they denied that their son had seen the killer. They asked for protection, and the Nassau County police assigned twenty-four-hour police presence, in case the killer decided to re-visit Tucker Lane. Once, it had been rare for killers to go after a witness, but it had become far more common. The penalty for two murders was often the same as for one. Dennis and Joanne, also the parents of fifteen-year-old Dennis, Jr., would not draw a free breath until the killer was locked up—if he ever was.

To at least one interested party who read the *Daily News* story, it looked like Joey had messed up the disposal of Kim's car. Why dump it in the suburbs? If it had been left on the street in Bushwick or East New York, the vehicle would have been stolen or stripped to the bones in no time. The cops would have had nothing. If Joey had left prints or had been seen, he might get caught—and anyone under arrest would be motivated to cut a deal.

Several days after the news about Kim's car was on television and in the papers, Joey was at the wheel of his car on Bushwick Avenue in Brooklyn, and Nick was sitting next to him. Joey took Kim's car keys out of his jacket pocket and tossed them out the open window. Joey was forced to give up any idea of retrieving Kim's valuable new car. The keys were of no use to him anymore, and could only be used as evidence against him.

Like Josh, Joey would not be getting any free dream car, either.

CHAPTER FOURTEEN

AN OFFER HE CAN'T REFUSE

Tom Shevlin answered the ringing phone in the Queens Homicide Squad. It was Kim's friend Jay.

"A black Caddy went by again," a breathless Jay said. "It went by slow, with Italian guys looking at me."

It was the second time Kim's young boyfriend had called. He was convinced that Mafia goons in long black Cadillacs were watching him. He said he was afraid that, in their zeal to find Kim's killer, they might come after him, and hurt him—by mistake.

"Listen," Tom replied, "If that is the case, and the mob is involved, you're better off coming to us—they'll pull your limbs off."

Jay protested that he didn't know anything about Kim's death. For someone who was not involved, Tom thought Jay was a very paranoid guy, very nervous. Obviously the threat of Mafia vengeance beyond the law scared the hell out of him. It would probably scare anyone who had been involved. Later, Tom and Louie discussed the matter. They were under pressure from their superiors to question Psycho again, despite the fact that they believed he had nothing to do with it. This kid Jay was scared, but they had nothing on him except his minor arrest record for drugs and attempted car theft. He had a confirmed alibi for the night Kim was taken— he had been asleep in the home of a police officer. The first order of business was to get everyone's pedigree, their criminal record, if any. The next step was to "dump" the phones—subpoena phone records, which took weeks.

Because they had no real evidence of any kind, Tom and Louie decided to use what the bad guys probably had—rumors and fear. It couldn't hurt for the word to get out on the street that wiseguys were roaming the streets, hunting for the killer. It might help. If the detectives did nothing to dispel these rumors, it would seem to confirm them. No one could possibly have any moral qualms about fibbing to a killer. If the murderers were not afraid of the law, but they were afraid of mobsters—so be it. Tom informed Tommy Antonakos about Jay and his fear of Italians in dark cars—and about the ruse he hoped might break the case.

"I think that's a good sign, Tommy," the detective said. "If he's paranoid, he's cracking. We're going to run with this, we're going to use this. One of them is going to crack and tell us. The first guy who comes in, that's who we'll deal with most."

"Do whatever you think is going to solve this," Tommy replied.

The grieving father felt that finding Kim's killers was far more important than what a few people said about him.

Tom and Louie still thought Psycho was not involved, but the New York City Police Department ran on paper and hard evidence—not intuition. The slaying had all the earmarks of a crime of passion, and the spurned Psycho fit the bill, right down to his nickname. One boss did not agree that Psycho should be ruled out, and wanted him brought in again. Tom argued that if Psycho had abducted a girl because she would not have sex with him—why wasn't she raped?

"Then what was the motive?" the boss demanded.

"It looks like a kidnapping," Tom suggested.

"How come there was no ransom?" his boss shot back.

"Something went wrong," Tom shrugged.

"Okay, we go your way—for now—but get a profile from Ray Pierce."

Detective Ray Pierce was the NYPD's shrink, whose specialty was putting bad guys on the couch before they had been caught. He produced "psychological profiles" of bad guys, based on their words and deeds. The profiles were used to include or exclude people as suspects. The boss wanted an official report from the forensic psychologist at headquarters to back up Tom and Louie's gut feelings. Tom got the assessment for the file and went back to work.

Although Psycho seemed to be in the clear, that did not mean his gang, Together Forever, was. What if they had decided to punish Kim for dissing Psycho? A stack of rap sheets of gang members, and police Intelligence Division reports on the group told a story of a loose-knit band of young toughs who started out on the Boardwalk at Coney Island, and graduated to drug trafficking, gun-running, and extortion of local merchants. Together Forever members were tough, but they claimed to be a gang with a heart and a soul. They claimed to be, not thugs, but rap music stars. They had made several albums, and also sold t-shirts and baseball caps bearing their logo.

According to police reports, Together Forever was led by a gentleman named Paul Rivera, also known as "Zance," who was on probation after arrests for robbery, attempted murder, and assault. The main headquarters was on West Thirty-fifth Street at the end of the Boardwalk, in a bad neighborhood. The Brighton Beach crew hung out at an all-night newsstand near the other end of the Boardwalk, a few blocks from Psycho's home. Investigators believed that some members were involved in drug dealing in Coney Island and the housing projects. They wore their calligraphic gang symbol—a combination of the letters T and F into one letter, inside a circle—"surgically implanted" as a tattoo on their right shoulders, as well as on hats, t-shirts, or medallions. The TF sign had been stenciled on walls, street signs, and members' cars. Stores that paid protection money to the gang were emblazoned with the TF sign on the front of the shop. Enterprising gang members even put a large TF flag atop the old defunct Parachute Jump at the nearby Coney Island amusement park.

Cops believed the group had ties to the Coney Island mob and Russian gangsters in Brighton Beach, for whom they were rumored to run errands. The band obtained guns by driving to Virginia in rented cars, buying weapons, and transporting them back to the city. They had allegedly amassed an arsenal of pistols and machine guns. Uniformed cops said they had seen one member firing a machine gun into the ocean, apparently for fun. Together Forever did not discriminate—it was an equal-opportunity gang. They imposed no ethnic, racial, or religious barriers, and the group had Latinos, Blacks, and assorted Caucasians, like Psycho.

Louie Pia leafed through a booklet produced by the gang. TF member Michael Garrett, Zance's second cousin, had authored a pamphlet entitled "Beauty and the Beast," by the "T.F. Foundation," in which he claimed that Together Forever—via rap music and good deeds—was saving young men from the crime, drugs, and violence of the mean streets. One member who had been a street criminal, "is now a successful disc jockey." Two others became successful stockbrokers, as Psycho claimed to be.

"TF members Paul Rivera and Michael Garrett, once two street thugs," the pamphlet said, "are now sensational rap artists in an up-and-coming rap group called Beauty and the Beast." The self-promotional material claimed they had "given back to the community that raised them" by starting a Little League team called the Falcons, and sponsoring low-admission dance parties for the underprivileged teens. The values espoused by TF, Garrett wrote, were "unity, peace, and most of all, love," which could be achieved "through the beauty of music, that calms the savage beast within."

But in the back of the booklet was a page listing "The Law" and another entitled "Punishment." For theft, the first offense was punishable by loss of a finger, and a $500 fine. A second offense would cost the guilty party another finger, and "any property that the victim asks for." For informing, the first offense was punishable by "DEATH. Alone, like the animal you are." Disrespect to the organization, to TF, defined as "badmouthing, lying about, interfering with the good public image," would merit "loss of your front teeth, and $1000 fine." The second offense required no less than "DEATH ALONE LIKE THE ANIMAL YOU ARE."

Had the gang branched out into kidnapping? Louie wondered if Kim, by badmouthing the insistent Psycho, had committed a capital crime in the unified, peaceful, loving world of Together Forever. Was that the reason for the apparent threat in the disco? Had Kim been sentenced to die like an animal?

One week after Kim's death, the *New York Post* ran a piece by police reporter Larry Celona—"POLICE EYE EX-BOYFRIEND IN CO-ED TORCHING"—that said a young man nicknamed "Psycho" was a suspect in her murder. The story mentioned the statutory rape charge against Psycho, his Together Forever connection, and the trip to Florida, but did not use his real name. Two days later, after filtering up and down the police department chain of command, and around the street, the mob rumors also emerged in print. *Daily News* columnist Mike McAlary's piece on Monday, March 13th was headlined "KILLER BETTER OFF IF COPS GRAB HIM." The column said that everyone in the search believed Psycho "put a match to the daughter of a friend of wiseguys . . ." Mafioso hoods were out looking for "the two-bit Russian gangster named Psycho" on the weekend, so they could administer the death penalty—while detectives had been sent home, due to the budget crisis. Interestingly, the last sentence of the column read:

"It is just another New York fable."

Two days later, *The News* ran a slightly different story in the news pages, that said several boyfriends were under suspicion—and included Psycho's claims of innocence.

"We went out three times," Psycho said. "I have no idea who did this to her, but the police know who I am, and where

I am. When they find out who did this sick thing to her, you'll know I'm telling you the truth.''

Psycho's dad said he and his wife were terrified that someone was going to kill their son without benefit of trial.

"Everybody's convicting my son—I almost wish he would get arrested. His mother and I are afraid for him to go out in the street, where somebody could shoot him for this horrible crime.''

The column certainly had an effect on Psycho and his family, but he did not crack. He did not come running into the precinct babbling a confession, and demanding sanctuary. It just confirmed what Tom Shevlin and Louie Pia already felt—Psycho was not the guy.

The question Louie wanted answered was, had the real bad guys gotten the word? Would one of those who had killed Kim be so afraid of the mob that the offer of a deal would be one he could not refuse?

Four other *Daily News* readers had also seen the column. The cops still appeared to be pointing at Psycho, but the worst fear of the small-time gangsters seemed to have been confirmed. It had acquired the authority of the printed word: Gambino goons were ready and eager to whack them—for free—as soon as anybody squealed.

To them, it now seemed like a matter of life and death.

CHAPTER FIFTEEN

MYSTERY

Tom Shevlin was obviously affected by the crime. For the first time in his professional life as a detective, he had brought a case home with him. On the first night, he had told his wife Lisa about the girl who had been burned, that he was awaiting autopsy results that would tell him whether she was dead or alive when she was set on fire. "Maybe it won't be that she was alive," Tom said hopefully when he called home. A day later, when Tom found out Kim had been alive, he was disgusted and enraged. "Can you believe what they did?" Tom asked his wife by phone. "She was fucking alive!"

Louie felt the same way. From that point on, they were both obsessed. They had to solve the case. Every night, it seemed to Lisa, Louie Pia or Tommy Antonakos would call and discuss something with Tom. Often, Lisa, who was pregnant with her second daughter, could tell that the dead girl's father was in tears on the phone, and Tom was trying to comfort him.

Tom and Louie went over and over details, trying to come up with new ways to go at it. One night, Louie and his wife Katie came over for dinner, and the men talked about the case until four a.m. Once, while at the wheel of the family car, Tom pointed to a man on the street.

"That looks like Joshua," said Tom.

"Who?" asked Lisa.

Tom explained that Joshua was a guy he liked for Kim's murder—his gut told him that right from the beginning, but he had no evidence.

Lisa, who was in the final month of her pregnancy, and Katie Pia joked about their obsessed husbands, but they, too, were becoming involved. It was not possible to avoid feeling some of the anger, frustration, and determination—especially when Louie and Tom lost sleep and skipped meals. They were either away working on the case, or at home—but not completely there. Lisa and Katie got used to that far-away look in their eyes that meant they were thinking about the case. Louie was smoking Marlboros like a chimney, and was on his way toward losing twenty pounds. He would toss and turn in his sleep, worrying about the case. Sometimes he woke up, walked over to the dresser where there was a pen and paper, and wrote an idea down before going back to bed. Tom also sometimes could not sleep at night. The case was taking control of their lives.

"Money doesn't buy you everything," Louie told Katie one night. "Here was a girl who had everything, and her life had to end like this."

Louie told Tom that it was still early in the case, but "so far, you might as well throw the fucking thing in the Dumpster."

He and Tom had the duty, and responsibility, to find Kim's killer—something they both took very personally—but they had zip. There was no evidence—like prints, hair, or DNA—to link a suspect to the murder scene. If they had a suspect. There were no witnesses to the abduction or the torching who might identify a suspect or a getaway car. There was no clear motive—only questions.

The first order of business had been to check out Tommy Antonakos, who came up clean. He and his brother were half-Italian, but that was not a crime. Tommy was not a "made guy" or a mob associate. Tommy had said he knew some people from the neighborhood in Woodhaven, but that was not surprising. The wiseguys were very paranoid about who moved in or did business in their neighborhood. The FBI and NYPD were always trying to infiltrate the area with cameras and microphones, and the gentlemen of the LCN—"La Cosa Nostra"—were very suspicious of everyone around them. At one point, mobsters had located hidden FBI surveillance equipment on a train trestle at the end of the block—aimed at John Gotti's social club. Needless to say, it was torn down by persons unknown. In short, in order for Tommy and his brother to do business even a block away, the Goodfellas had to know who they were, and where they came from—to ensure they were not Feds or cops. Julian in the DA's office also checked with a friend at the FBI, and got the same answers. As far as Louie and Tom were concerned, that ruled out any mob involvement in the case, and they moved on. Of course, they would continue to use the mob rumors to goad suspects.

Was the murder simply what it looked like on the surface—a crime of passion by some guy who couldn't have Kim, and wanted to burn her off the face of the Earth? The male ego was a dangerous thing. Each year, hundreds of homicides, called "domestics," were committed by jealous, rejected men. Enraged at being dumped by a wife or lover they either loved, or felt they owned, or both, some men snapped, and became vicious, merciless killers. No judge's Order of Protection—unless it was printed on bulletproof paper—could save a woman from the wrath of such a man, because he did not fear the law. Many avoided jail by turning the murder weapon on themselves, and committing suicide. But, so far, no other bodies had turned up in Kim's circle of friends, and no remorseful killer had walked in to confess.

The pressure was on, especially since the case was on the front pages, and getting a lot of media. It wasn't just bosses looking over Louie's shoulder, and second-guessing everything Tom Shevlin did—it was the bosses' bosses, the press, and the whole city. Neither Louie nor Tom slept for days after Kim was found dead. They were running on gallons of strong coffee and pack after pack of Marlboro cigarettes.

The case did not quite fit into a known pattern that would determine the course of the investigation, like a domestic homicide, revenge, drug-related killing, a mob hit, or a sex slaying. That meant, in detective slang, Louie and Tom had a "mystery" on their hands—the most difficult type of case. Mysteries were all-or-nothing cases. Detectives who solved a murder mystery sometimes became heroes in the press, and were seen by their children on TV. They had the gratitude of a grieving family, the lifelong career satisfaction of a tough case cracked, and justice achieved. Some got promoted. Unfortunately, most detectives were not psychic, and had to work cases with only their wits and experience. Detectives who failed to solve a mystery often had the same sense of an incomplete life experienced by victims' families, who had been deprived of the closure of an arrest and conviction. All detectives had unsolved cases, but some were condemned to carry that one big open homicide case for the rest of their lives, always hoping to solve it.

Louie and Tom had nothing—but it quickly became worse. In routinely checking for other similar cases, two turned up. On Wednesday, March 1st, less than four hours after Kim was last seen, Mary Ann Maroney, an attractive exotic dancer from Philadelphia, was found alive—but on fire—in a Manhattan apartment at 253 West Twentieth Street. She had also been shot in the face. She died a short time later. Mary Ann, 23, had come to New York to audition for a Manhattan nightclub. On her last night of freedom, Kim had been in a Manhattan dance club—was there a connection there?

The morning after Kim's funeral, the night after the service had been covered on the evening TV news, a third, charred female body was discovered in a suitcase by a Brooklyn school custodian. The corpse was still smoldering behind a Brooklyn elementary school in the low-income, high-crime Brownsville section—about two miles 'from Kim's home. She had been dumped behind a grammar school, doused with gasoline, and set on fire. Dental records would also be needed to determine that victim's identity. At first, investigators suspected the body might be that of missing college student Stacy Pennant—also a popular business student who worked part-time, and drove a Honda. One year older than Kim, Stacy was last seen on February 9th. She had been in great spirits, despite a recent break-up with a boyfriend, said a friend.

"She was laughing," the friend said. "She didn't have a worry in the world."

Stacy had been out to a movie with the friend, whom she dropped off in Canarsie—just two blocks from Kim's apartment. Also, Stacy had worked at night at Kennedy Airport— near where Kim's cell phone had been used. The coincidences of time, place, and circumstance could not be ignored. Was there a sicko serial killer on the loose, who liked to destroy pretty young women with fire? Or were all the cases unrelated? If a serial slayer was at work, the investigation would change direction and become much larger, and city-wide. Louie and Tom had no choice but to investigate, but if the torching cases were not connected, time would be wasted chasing down blind alleys.

"Unfortunately, bodies being set afire are rather commonplace," one veteran city investigator told a *Newsday* reporter. "It's done to obscure the identity, or for whatever other perverse reason they might have, including loathing of the victim."

Every year, hundreds of lives were consumed by the gaping maw of murder and manslaughter in the city of New York. During the previous year, 1994, more than 1,581 lives were terminated by violence in the Big Apple. Only in a big, bad city like New York was it possible that three young women had been torched and murdered in a week—yet were not connected. Louie contacted the detectives working on the other torch murders and exchanged information. No names, businesses, schools, or addresses emerged in common from the three cases. Dental records quickly confirmed that the woman in the torched suitcase was not Stacy Pennant. That woman, an autopsy determined, was four inches shorter than Kim, but was about the same weight and age. Stacy's mother Deva reacted with relief that it was not her child, but her waiting was not over—Stacy was still a missing person. She told investigators that Stacy had lived on the island of Jamaica all her life, and came to New York in 1992 to start a new life in the city. Stacy had not lived with her mother since she was a young girl. Both Kim and Stacy were responsible, and had no drug or alcohol problems. Deva never closed the door to Stacy's room. The mother kept it just as Stacy had left it—hoping for her safe return. Stacy's clothes were still hung neatly in the closet, and her favorite tape cassettes were stacked as she had left them on a shelf. The bed was piled with stuffed animals. A Bible on the night table next to the bed was opened to the Psalm Stacey had read the night before she vanished.

"Everything is just the same for her at home," Deva told a reporter from the *Daily News*. She added that she sometimes thought she saw Stacy asleep under the covers amid the stuffed animals.

"I have negative dreams that she is dead, but Stacey has also told me in a dream that she will be with me, regardless," she told the reporter. "I am just clinging to hope."

Once it appeared that the torchings of the other two women were unrelated, it was back to business. Everyone around the victim would be checked for parking tickets, criminal records, and alibis. Phone records would be checked. Once a person in Kim's circle of acquaintances established confirmed whereabouts for the night Kim went missing, and particularly on the night of her murder, they could be eliminated from suspicion. On television, it was simple. The detectives eliminated suspect after suspect, until the killer was left standing alone. But in real life it was more complex. Often, alibis could not be confirmed independently, which meant that that person could not be eliminated, and the list of suspects would grow—not shrink. Guessing did not count.

The only real items to hold on to were Kim's car, the body, and the torch house. The car had provided little in the way of evidence. Kim's body told part of her story—she was grabbed, robbed, tied up, and not fed for three days. Then she was doused with gasoline and set on fire. No latent prints were found, but fingerprints alone rarely solved a case—outside of movies and television, that is. The zipper teeth found under Kim's fingernail were almost useless. Like hairs and fibers, they were considered general circumstantial "class evidence" in court. A brown hair found at a crime scene might belong to the brown-haired suspect, or it might belong to someone else. There was no scientific way to prove it. The zipper teeth were only of value if a jacket missing four identical teeth was found hanging in the closet of a suspect, or on his back—preferably with Kim's blood on it. It was possible, but, again, something that usually happened only on the silver screen. It was a long shot.

The house where Kim had been killed yielded virtually no clues, but it had led to one person who admitted being in the house while Kim was held there. Wayne McCook, the son of Ruth McCook, may have looked to some like a member of a motorcycle gang, but he was a cooperative, law-abiding citizen who knew nothing about Kim's death. Wayne told Louie how he and his brother Gary had been after his mother for years to sell the house. She had been sick, and she was living with Gary at his Levittown Long Island home. Wayne understood that his mom was sentimental about the house where he and his brother had grown up, where she had been happy with her husband. But it was absurd to pay taxes and heat and electrical bills for an empty house. At least the phone had been turned off, a few months before the murder.

Perhaps it was more than nostalgia. Maybe Wayne's mother did not want to admit that, because her health had failed, she would never again be able to live in her house.

Keeping the house ready for her to visit, ready to move back in, kept alive her hope that she would return someday. It looked like another dead end, but, of course, Louie would leave no phone unturned—he got subpoenas for the phone records from the torch house, and Wayne and Gary's homes, just in case. It was vital to establish who was using the house in the owner's absence. Linking a person to the house might be the handle that would break the case.

Without the house connection, without witnesses or much evidence, the only avenue of investigation left open was the elimination of friends, family, and especially former boy-friends—who would be the immediate priority. This kid Jay, the last boyfriend, was very jittery, and he had a record. Did he have a guilty conscience? Jay's buddy Josh, the Chicken Hawk pimp, looked good—especially because of his arrest for rape and unlawful imprisonment. Did he hit on Kim and get rejected? Did he unlawfully imprison her, too? But if so, why didn't he rape her? Tommy's brother Joseph thought Josh had had something to do with it, but just because these two mutts had records did not mean they were the ones. Jay and Josh both seemed to have good alibis for Tuesday night, and they, along with April, and others, were each other's alibi for the night of the killing. The only way it might be nailed down further was to examine the telephone company records. Once the utility responded to the subpoena and dumped stacks of computer printouts of phone-call logs on the detectives, it might be possible to narrow down the time frame on various events. Also, after the numbers were de-ciphered, and it was determined who called whom from which phone, and when, further suspects might emerge. Maybe. In the meantime, there were several boyfriends to be checked out.

Shawn Hayes, a tall, handsome young man with light black skin, arrived at the Squad Room after Louie called him in for a chat. Shawn was wearing expensive clothes and gold jewelry which seemed a bit pricey for a working man.

"I loved her and she loved me," Shawn said in response to Louie's questions.

He said he had met Kim at a Manhattan club in April of 1994, and exchanged telephone numbers with her. About a month later, Kim called him and they began to date. Shawn said he worked as a clerk in a video store on Avenue D. Without a fixed address, he would stay at the homes of relatives or different girlfriends. In July, Shawn moved into Kim's apartment. Kim always saw Shawn in sparkling lights at a trendy club, or at her apartment. She never stayed with him, but knew he lived somewhere in Manhattan. Actually, Shawn spent a lot of his time in Alphabet City, on the Lower East Side.

Alphabet City sounded like an amusement park for children, but it was a fifty-six-square-block area jammed with crumbling tenements and crowded city housing projects, and plagued with a crime for every letter of the alphabet, especially D for drug dealing, and M for murder. Alphabet City ran from Houston Street north to East Fourteenth Street and from Avenue A east to Avenue D—the "Alphabet" from which the name came.

Shawn said he and Kim had broken up the previous September, after they had an argument about fidelity. Kim had asked him to stop seeing other women. Shawn said he could not be faithful and would continue to date others. Kim had told him to leave, but they had remained friends, Shawn claimed. In fact, two or three months earlier, he said he had met Kim, Jay, and April at a nightspot called Country Club, and ended up taking Kim out to breakfast.

Louie asked if Jay was happy to see Kim leave with Shawn.

"No," said Shawn, he wasn't. Kim, said Shawn, was close with April but she did not care too much for Josh. "She believed that April could have gotten better."

Shawn's alibi was not ironclad, but Louie's gut told him the guy did not kill Kim. Maybe the phone records would tell a different story. But Shawn had an arrest record that showed he was no angel. In either case, he had no evidence against Shawn, and was not ready to go at him yet.

"Look, I don't care about anything you do," said Louie. "We just want to find the murderer of Kimberly Antonakos."

"I'm gonna tell you straight up, I deal drugs," said Shawn, looking Louie right in the eye. "I'm a fucking drug dealer, and I move major fucking weight down in Alphabet City. But I loved her and I didn't fucking kill her."

Louie gave Shawn his card and asked him to call if he heard anything about Kim's death.

"I don't really cooperate with the police—we're usually on the opposite ends of the spectrum," said Shawn. "But, if I find out something, I'll call you."

Louie believed him.

Albert DeSoto, the car salesman, also did not have a rock-solid alibi, and had been dumped by Kim—right after she had taken him home for dinner at her father's house. Kim apparently did not think he had made a sufficient fuss over her on Valentine's Day, although they were together that night. Louie did not see Albert as a killer, but his phone records would also be dumped—just in case.

If the murder had been fiction, Michael Dedely was tailor-made for a dark-horse killer suspect. Kim was his first love, and he still had a soft spot in his heart for her. He saw her from time to time, always for friendship—not for sex. But did he hit on her one last time, for old times' sake, and receive a rebuff? No one had said so. Also, he did not act in a guilty manner. Interviews and investigation were supposed to eliminate suspects. But without independently confirmed alibis, the suspect list was getting bigger, not smaller. And there were a lot more names in Kim's book.

Louie and Tom began using up shoe leather, checking pawnshops in the area, looking for Kim's stolen jewelry—especially the most distinctive piece, the large, valuable gold cross with garnets that Kim was wearing around her neck when she was last seen. She might have been killed just for the money the cross would bring at a hock shop—not to mention her $15,000 car. Tom also put out a teletype bulletin describing the cross and Kim's other jewelry, which circulated around NYPD and went to police departments throughout the state. Soon after the alert went out, an Albany police officer called and said he had a snitch named *Annie, who claimed to know who had Kim's jewelry—including a gold cross. Since they had kept the cross a secret from the public, Louie and Tom were very interested. No, the officer said, he had not told her about the cross—she had told him. Tom asked his brother officer if he believed Annie's story.

"She's been reliable in the past," he replied.

Tom got the woman's number and called her up. He introduced himself, and played it cool. He wanted to hear her story, but did not want to give her any information about the cross. Annie told Tom that she had read about Kim's case in the papers, and something clicked.

"This guy showed me jewelry, and a gold cross he got from this girl," said Annie.

Sometimes, with a single phone call, impossible cases cracked open like a ripe nut. Tom tried to hide his eagerness. He got Annie's address and direction to her home. He and Louie got in the car and drove for several hours, until they stopped in front of Annie's house. When they knocked on the door, it eventually swung open on a huge, fat woman on crutches. Her pale skin was dotted with tattoos, including a skull-and-crossbones on her flabby arm. She invited them in with a smile, and told them she liked men in uniform. "I've dated a lot of cops," she confided.

Tom asked about the cross and Annie gave them the name of the man who had stolen the jewelry and a gold cross from the girl. The detectives had never heard of him. She described several pieces of jewelry the bad guy had taken from Kim. None of them were even close to the real items.

"Was it a little cross, or a big cross?" Louie asked.

"It was a big cross," said Annie. She mentioned that she had once dated a cop in the city who had been killed. When they heard the name of the slain officer, they recognized it.

"How big was the cross?" Louie pressed.

"This big," said Annie, holding her thumb and forefinger about an inch apart—maybe one-sixth the size of Kim's large cross. Louie and Tom looked at each other. Annie was already back on the subject of her boyfriends. Unbidden, she began naming her lost, past loves. Annie did not appear to have much luck with men—every New York City cop she had ever dated was later killed in the line of duty. As she prattled on about non-existent love affairs with dead hero cops, Louie and Tom excused themselves and began the long drive back to the city. They were both exhausted, and angry at the waste of time—but they suddenly began to laugh. In a release of tension, they laughed until tears came to their eyes—there was nothing else to do.

The fat lady had sung, but it was not over.

CHAPTER SIXTEEN

JOSHUA

Louie had begun to wade through lab reports and the phone "dumps" that listed in small type all the calls made from various phones, like the one in Kim's apartment. Analyzing phone dumps was a slow, painstaking process, and required concentration. The sheets for a telephone, like Kim's home phone, would list an exact time, duration of call, and number dialed. That had to be correlated with another list. The second list turned the number dialed into a "subscriber" name and address. Phone dumps took time, not just because it took hours to study the dense stacks of numbers, but because it was a branching process. If several dozen phone numbers had been dialed on Kim's phone, those that could not be easily identified from her phone book might have to be dumped also, leading to a possible infinity of phone calls. On Friday, March 10th, two days after the funeral and the discovery of Kim's car. Louie noticed that, on the day Kim disappeared, sixty-five calls were made from her phone, which might jive with Josh's story that he called everyone in Kim's address book, looking for her that day. But right at the top of the list, the first call made on Wednesday, at 12:10 a.m., was a 917 area code number, which meant it was a cell phone or a beeper. It was listed on the subscriber list as a pager belonging to Joshua Torres. But Josh and April had said they were both at Kim's house and in bed by that time. If Josh and April did not go out, and were in bed asleep, why did someone in the apartment beep Josh from there? Flipping back to before midnight, to the dump sheet for February 28th, Louie saw the same 917 number had been called ten minutes earlier, and also ninety minutes earlier, at 10:41 Tuesday night. Someone had picked up the phone in Kim's house on the night she went missing and beeped Josh's pager three times. Josh, the Chicken Hawk with the arrests for rape, unlawful imprisonment, and gun possession, was probably lying about his whereabouts on the night Kim was taken.

"Oh, look what we've got," Louie said, showing the sheet to Tom. "This is Josh's beeper number." It was Josh's first lie, the first piece of evidence to support their vague suspicion that Josh and Jay had something to do with Kim's death. They both felt they were on the right track, but they were only at the beginning of the road.

"Well," said Tom, playing the devil's advocate, "what else could it be? Did he let someone else borrow his beeper? We'll have to ask him 'Did you ever give your beeper out?' "

Tom felt Josh had a lot of wiggle room. They would have to lock Josh into his alibi story before hitting him with the phone records. Josh had said no calls were made out that night but quite a few calls had been made.

That was Josh's second lie.

Louie kept poring over the dumps and realized that none of the friends in Kim's phone book had been called until five o'clock on Wednesday, and then only a few. But Josh had told Tommy Antonakos at least an hour earlier that he had called everyone in the book.

That was Josh's third lie.

Josh told Tommy that the only one who had not checked back in was Psycho. But Psycho's home was not called for the first time until 9:30 that night, when Tommy and Kim's friends were in the apartment and the search was in full tilt.

That was Josh's fourth lie.

None of it alone would convict Josh of anything. It was circumstantial, and he might come up with likely stories when they questioned him. The phone logs also showed that Josh had called several different women when he was babysitting his son in Kim's apartment—and April was at work. Louie was willing to bet money that April did not know about the calls. If he was right, that might provide them with a little leverage.

Louie told Tom what else he had unearthed and they kicked it around. Was Josh out on both the night of Kim's murder, and the night of her disappearance? When she was killed, he and Jay were out, supposedly looking for Kim's car. But they claimed to have returned to Kim's place, and then to April's apartment before the killing. April said Josh was at home the night Kim was taken. Did he slip out while she was asleep, or was she lying for the father of her child? Or, did he give his beeper to someone else—like his partners in crime—and dial it himself?

Deeper into the phone entries, Louie noticed that a call had been made from Kim's house at 2:48 in the morning, after she was killed, to a Brooklyn number identified as belonging to Josh's aunt, who babysat for Timmy. Josh and Jay had said they had returned to Kim's around 1 o'clock—before she was set on fire. They then picked up April and Liz, dropped Liz off at home, and went to April's place for the night.

Louie decided to call Kim's friend Tara, who had seemed to have a good memory. He wanted to nail down the time that Josh and Jay had returned, because Josh's lies made everything suspect. Tara said she was certain that Josh and Jay had returned at almost three in the morning. They were only there a short time, she said, just long enough for Josh to make a call. It was yet another lie from Josh. The dumps, and Tara's sharp recollection, pinned it down—the only alibi that Josh and Jay had for the time of the murder, was each other.

It was the first ray of sunshine. The lab reports on Kim's

car had been disappointing. Only one fingerprint that had
been recovered from a notebook on the rear floor could be
identified. It belonged to Jay, but, since he had often been
in the car, it was useless. The only thing they had to go on
was the story told by the phone records, and their suspicion
that Josh, and maybe his friend Jay, were dirty.

At 2:45 in the afternoon, while Joey was alone, he picked
up a cellular phone and dialed the number of the 102nd Precinct. When a desk officer answered, Joey asked for the detectives. A phone line in the Squad Room rang and Louie
picked it up.

"One-Oh-Two Squad," said Louie.

"Yeah," said Joey. "I wanna talk to the detective who
has the case of the girl burned in Queens."

"You're speaking to the detective," Louie responded.

"Look, the guys you're looking for are right under your
nose."

"Yeah? Who?"

"Joshua and Jay," said Joey. In fact Josh, or rather, his
beeper number, and Jay's phone number, were *literally* right
under Louie's nose at the time. Speak of the Devil. Also in
on it, the caller claimed, was a guy named Jose, who was
about twenty-five years old, and was also called Joey.

"I overheard them talking about it on a street corner in
Queens," Joey explained. As the tipster spoke to Louie, his
voice seemed to fly away into the distance, and return, fading
in and out.

"It was all over money and the shit went bad and they
had to kill her," Joey said.

There was the missing piece, right there, thought Louie.
It was all about money and things went bad. It was a bungled
kidnap, just like Tom felt. As far as Louie was concerned, it
was a call from Heaven.

"What corner was this?"

"I don't remember," Joey said. Again, the voice faded
away and returned.

"You on a cellular phone?" Louie asked.

"Why?" asked Joey, suddenly paranoid about the over-estimated ability of police to trace calls.

"At times, it's difficult to hear you," said Louie. "Don't hang up. Yo, big guy, I need to talk to you. I'll meet you anywhere, anytime. You call the shots, we got to talk about this further. Nobody will know who you are. Listen, let's meet somewhere at a location of your choice, and talk about this," Louie suggested, in a friendly voice.

"I'll think about it," said Joey, now very nervous. "I'll call you later."

Joey hung up. He had been tormented by guilt, especially after he saw the girl's crying family on television. He wasn't going to meet the cop anywhere, but maybe they would lock up Josh and Jay, and get them off the street. He even told the detective his own first name, and his nickname. Maybe the cop would figure it all out and arrest him, too. If they did, Joey was confident he could make a good deal—he had his insurance on tape—and he was the one who had made the call. Of course, he never mentioned Nick. Joey did not tell Nick he was going to make the call. Joey would never give up his best friend.

When the anonymous caller failed to call back that night, Louie "dumped" the squad phone. When he got the phone records, the call was not there. It was not a direct call, and had come in through the precinct switchboard. It was untraceable.

Tom and Louie had not been around for the first three days of the investigation, when Phil was working it as a missing persons case. After the dumps and the anonymous call implicated Josh, it was time to start over, and examine events from the beginning. Tom first expressed his suspicions about Josh to Tommy Antonakos in a confidential phone call two days later, on Sunday night.

"Tommy, I want to ask you something," said Tom Shevlin. "Who first told you that Psycho did this?"

"Well, Josh told me when I first got there that this guy

Psycho has been bothering her and he thinks he's the one that did this.''

''Okay, so it wasn't the police who told you it was Psycho?''

''No.''

Tom asked the father what Josh had been doing, and Tommy told him about them going to Bushwick with Jay to look at chop shops. Tom Shevlin wondered why they had looked in Bushwick. It didn't make a great deal of sense. Tommy told the detective about searching under the Belt Parkway Bridge, how they went to get ashes and pray at church, and Josh would not go inside. Tom had expected that Tommy would name Josh as the source of the Psycho suspicion. Now it was beginning to make sense, the detective thought. If Josh was involved, he would have been eager to pin the blame elsewhere.

''Why are you asking this?'' Tommy asked, after he finished.

''Well I just want to confirm that Josh is the one pushing this guy Psycho,'' said Tom.

''Why?''

''I've got to be honest with you, Tommy. Listen, I've got nothing to prove this yet, but I believe Josh is involved in this.''

''I don't know,'' said Tommy, obviously surprised. ''I think you're wrong. I think you're going up the wrong tree—this guy's been helping me since day one.''

''Well, how much help has he been? I know you think he's helping you, but all he was doing was steering it toward Psycho, it seems. You guys spent a lot of energy and time looking for this guy Psycho. Something changed in her life in the last month or so—and that's this guy Josh, and he's not a nice guy. Some way, somehow, this guy's involved.''

As the investigator spoke, Tommy listened politely, but he made it clear he was sure Tom was wasting his time. How could a friend of Kim's, who had looked for her, and had helped him direct the search, be involved? Tom did not mention phone records or beepers or girlfriends. If Josh got even a whiff of this in advance, their edge would vanish. He would be ready for them. The only way it might work was to hit him with it cold, watch his face, and see how he changed his story.

"Tommy, this is not a revenge thing. More than one guy did this. If this guy Psycho did this, your daughter would have been beaten up, she would have been sexually molested."

Tom then swore Tommy to secrecy.

"Tommy, don't say anything to anybody, especially to Josh. Keep friendly with him."

"All right, Tom, I'll go along with what you say here," said the skeptical father.

When they were ready to go at Josh, they called him and asked for him to drop in at his convenience. There was no rush, Louie explained on the phone. They were asking everybody back in, and they just needed his help with a few things. It was routine, they told him. Josh agreed to drop the baby off at his aunt's place and stop by on Friday, March 17th, at noon—when April was at work at the law office. Josh was welcomed in the Squad Room with smiles and handshakes. The detectives were grateful for his time and his help, and the interview began in a cordial way, with Louie asking where April was, as if he was sorry not to see her.

"My baby's mother's at work," said Josh, radiating confidence. Josh didn't use April's name in conversation, but referred to her as his baby's mother.

Louie and Tom walked Josh through a series of innocuous background questions, to keep up the pretense that it was just routine. He said Kim sometimes came with April to visit him while he was in jail and again expressed his platonic love for Kim. In fact, Josh cast himself in the unlikely role of Kim's fatherly protector. He would make it a point, he said, to speak to the guys she dated, telling them that they had better treat her in the proper manner, or "they'd have to deal with me." They moved easily to the night Kim did not come home. They gave Josh a pad and pencil and asked him to write down everything he did on that day and the day before. Josh wrote for about ten minutes and then handed them the results. Tom read Josh's written alibi:

> I woke up at 9:30 a.m., drove April to work. Kim went to school. Went back to Kim's house. Clean up Kim's house. Walk the dog. Went to my new house to clean. Around 9 p.m. to 10 p.m., April came to the house to help clean. Then we went to Kim's house, 11:30, 12 o'clock a.m., we went to sleep. The phone rings about 1:30 a.m., 2 a.m.
>
> 3/1/95 I woke up at 9:30, drove April to work. Went back to get cleaned up. April called me 12:30 to 1 o'clock. We spoke then around 2 p.m., and 3 p.m., I spoke to Tommy. I beeped Kimberly. Tommy went to [precinct]. I was calling most of the people in the phone book, Kim's phone book. Tommy and Elizabeth came to the house. Me and Tommy listened to the [phone] messages. Elizabeth stayed at the house when Tommy and me went looking for the car.
>
> Went back to the house to check the garage. We found a earring was the one she had on. Tommy went looking for the car and I went looking for the car. I went back to Kim's around 2:30 to 3 o'clock a.m.

After he was done, Louie and Tom noticed that hours and hours were unaccounted for, with some ten hours on the day of her disappearance a complete blank.

"You were home all night?" on Tuesday night, Tom asked.

"Yeah," said Josh, completely cool.

He said he and April watched the Jenny Jones talk show in bed, and went to sleep at 10:30. He said nobody made any calls out, and only one call came in about 1:30 Wednesday morning, but they let Kim's answering machine get it.

"Are you sure you didn't go out for anything? To the store?" asked Tom.

"No."

"Are you sure?" Louie chimed in. "Not even for milk for the baby?"

"Nah," Josh shot back with disgust. "I don't do that shit." He took umbrage that his detective friends would offend his machismo by thinking he might do woman's work like going for milk—this from an unemployed, common-law house-husband who stayed at home all day to babysit his toddler. They moved on to other items, as if they were finished quizzing him on his alibi. He again stated that he called all of Kim's friends in her phone book before Tommy arrived at the door.

They showed Josh pictures of Kim's charred corpse. He did not turn away, and looked at the shots that clearly showed she was not burned below the waist.

Louie and Tom were good detectives, which meant that they were also good actors. They had agreed beforehand to play the part of bumbling cops who had no clue and were asking the hip street guy, in confidence, to help them out. They hoped it would appeal to his vanity and the urge for the type of control that he seemed to have exerted over the case.

"Listen," Tom said affably, "me and my partner are just average detectives. We have this case here, and we're not getting anywhere. Josh, we're stuck. Help us. How do you think it happened?"

"Well," began Josh, "you got the car. Did you get any prints from the car?"

"Yes, we got numerous prints," Tom said, truthfully.

Actually, the only clear print the lab connected to anyone was a latent left on a note pad on the back floor of Kim's car. It belonged to Jay, but, since he had been in Kim's car many times, it was useless. All the other prints belonged to Kim. But they did not share that information with Josh.

"If you have fingerprints, then how come you don't know who it is yet?" Josh asked, with a sneer.

"Sometimes it takes, like, six months for the prints to come back," but as soon as they did, they would get their man, Tom said confidently—another lie.

"One of them has got to be a weak link," Tom grinned.

Tom figured that anyone stupid enough not to know police looked at phone toll records might be dumb enough to think it took months for latent print comparison. Tom could almost hear the gears spinning in Josh's head—he bought it. He believed he had a few months before fingerprints led to whoever had touched anything in that car or the house without gloves on. A few months until it hit the fan.

"I don't think Psycho did this," Tom said, in a confidential tone.

"I think you're right," Josh agreed, as if he were a fellow detective. "Here's what I figure happened—there were three guys."

Tom and Louie glanced at each other and then back at Josh, waiting for him to explain.

"Well, the way I feel, it's more than one guy. It hadda be three guys," Josh expounded.

"Why three guys?" asked Louie, as a student would ask a professor. Josh explained that they would need their own car, and a guy to drive Kim's car.

"That's two guys," said Louie.

Josh did not explain why a third crook was needed, but Louie and Tom let it go, and let Josh talk.

"The father's loaded," he said at one point, supplying a motive. "They came up behind her in the garage, threw her to the floor, and put her in the trunk of the car. They had to have at least two cars. They went out to Long Island, one following the other. They got rid of the car. The other guy drove the other one back to Queens. The house they kept, that was called the sweet house."

"What's a sweet house?" Tom interrupted.

"A house they had been to before," Josh answered. He

was warming to his subject, growing more defiant and cocky, enjoying it. "They had to burn the house because they didn't want to have to kill her, but shit happens, the shit went bad. They had to burn the house because they had to get rid of the fingerprints.

"It was all over money and the shit went bad and they panicked, and had to kill her," Josh said.

Louie flinched. The words were almost verbatim what the anonymous caller had said.

"But you ain't gonna get 'em, because these guys are tight, these guys are gangsters. They aren't gonna talk to the police. They won't give each other up," said Josh, with what seemed like pride.

"Well, I hope you're right, because, in my experience, if there is more than one of them that did the crime, one will give the rest up," Tom said.

"Not in this case," Josh said. "They're too tight."

Josh was far too arrogant to realize that he had crossed over a line and was speaking for the criminals. He tried to send Tom and Louie off on another wild goose chase by saying that Tommy Antonakos had dealings with the Mafia. That was good, thought Tom, he believed the mob stuff that had found its way into the papers. That might be helpful. They did nothing to set Josh straight about Tommy. Josh was becoming more confident, lecturing the detectives. It was time to catch him off balance and ask a few questions that would get his full attention.

"What's your beeper number?" Louie asked. Josh, a bit puzzled, told him. It was the same one listed in phone company records.

"Ever lend anybody your beeper?" Tom asked.

"No," Josh replied. It was the answer they had hoped for.

"You sure?" Tom pressed, "Maybe to April?"

"No. I never lent my beeper to anybody."

They had locked Josh in. It was time to pull out the phone dump printouts. Time to pull the rug out from under him.

"But I have phone records here that show me your beeper was beeped from Kim's house," said Louie, still with the same camaraderie. He asked Josh to help him understand why—if he was home in bed with April on Tuesday night—somebody called his beeper number from there? If he was next to April in bed, he asked, gesturing to the stack of numbers, why was she looking for him?

"Why would she beep you, if you were there?" Louie asked.

It hit Josh like a sucker punch. He never saw it coming, and he was, temporarily, at a loss for words. Obviously, it had never occurred to him that the police would obtain phone records and use them to catch him in lies. Joshua's face tightened, and his left eye began to twitch.

"Uh . . . Oh, you know, you're right," Josh stammered, with a weak smile. "I had to go to the store."

"For what?"

"For milk for Timmy."

Just like Louie had suggested earlier. Tom bore down on Josh, his voice taking on an authoritative, less friendly tone. Did Josh go out more than once, or just to the store? Tom asked. No, just that one time to the store, Josh answered.

"You sure?" Louie smiled, moving in closer.

Josh said he was sure. Well, in that case, said Louie, how come he was beeped three times from Kim's that night? What was that about? Was he beeping himself? Josh seemed totally at a loss for words. The twitch in his left eye got worse. It had become a full facial tic, distorting his face every few seconds. It seemed to have a life of its own, like the imagined beat of a murder victim's heart that incriminated the guilt-ridden killer in Edgar Allan Poe's "The Tell-Tale Heart." Joshua couldn't stop his tell-tale eye.

"You think I did this?" Josh asked Tom, trying to muster as much indignation as possible in his wavering voice, which was quaking in time with his flickering eye—the eye that had seen Kim in flames. "You actually think I was involved in this?"

Tom explained that they were speaking to every family member, acquaintance, and lover—then they would determine who would be eliminated as a suspect.

"Hey," Tom shrugged, "I don't know. I'm asking you—do you know anything about it?"

"Hey, if I was involved in this, I would have fed her, and she would have been released," declared Josh, with a smirk.

"Bingo!" Tom thought triumphantly. He stole a glance at Louie. Josh had just played their vest card, the holdout—the fact that Kim had not been fed for three days. The autopsy results had not been made public. Only detectives, the medical examiner, and the killers knew that Kim's stomach was empty. If Josh knew she had not been fed, he had to be guilty.

When Louie and Tom seemed unconvinced by his protestations of innocence, Josh asked again if they thought he was involved. This time the detectives answered in unison.

"Yeah."

"I appreciate your honesty," Josh recovered, after a moment.

The guy had brass balls, Louie thought.

"Look, the first guy on board's getting a play"—a deal—said Louie, in a conciliatory voice.

Josh, still twitching, did not go for it. He sat there, thinking, for a while. One of the calls, Josh said after the pause, must have been him calling himself—putting some girl's number on his own beeper, so April wouldn't see it. Again, Josh used Louie's idea—he claimed to have beeped himself. Louie wanted to know why a lot of calls had been made from Kim's the night she was last seen—despite Josh's insistence that none had been made. Josh saw page after page of computer printouts that reinforced his growing paranoia about Big Brother.

"What about all the calls made from the apartment?" Louie demanded.

This time, Louie did not suggest an alternative to Josh. There was none.

"I have no fucking idea!" Josh snapped, his eye still blinking.

No more Mister Nice Guy. Actually, Tom and Louie knew all about the calls and to whom they were made. They began reading out the times, phone numbers, and names of five women who had been called from Kim's house. Josh was fuming, and his eye tic got worse. Two of the women were the girlfriends of Joey and Nick.

"Hey, big guy," said Louie, in a just-us-guys tone, gesturing to the toll records. "I don't want to fuck up your life but . . . if you don't talk to me, I gotta go to April with these."

"Go ahead," Josh said defiantly.

He had cracked, but he did not break. Joshua's walls were still standing. He had declined to confess to murder to avoid getting his baby's mother mad at him. Go figure.

Tom left the room and called Ray Pierce, the department shrink, at headquarters.

"Ray, I feel this guy is the ringleader," Tom said. "This guy does have a record, he has nothing to do all day, except sit around thinking things up. He has no job, and no money."

When he told the psychologist what had happened during the interview, especially how Josh had blurted out that he would have fed her, Pierce gave him a go-ahead.

"You're on third base," said Ray, who said he would write a report to that effect.

Tom felt better. He knew the pressure from above to go after Psycho or look for a mob connection would cease now that Ray Pierce was on board. It was no longer just Tom Shevlin's gut feeling. Tom went back into the interview room. It was time to cut Josh loose. Louie and Tom knew in their hearts that Josh was guilty, but they did not have the ammunition, the evidence, to break down the walls—yet. They asked Josh to take a lie detector test at a later date, and he agreed. Knowing in your heart that Josh was a killer was not enough—it was not admissible in court. Neither were polygraph tests, but it was another step. They needed to build a case, piece by piece, from the ground up, and they needed some luck. But, for now, they would have to cut him loose.

"Listen," said Louie, making a vow, as he looked into Josh's eyes at the end of the grilling. "The next time we talk to you, we will have done our homework."

When a shaken Josh left the Squad Room, Tom lit a cigarette and turned to Louie.

"We're letting a murderer walk right out the door," said Tom, shaking his head.

"I agree with you one hundred per cent," said Louie.

CHAPTER SEVENTEEN

SQUEEZE PLAY

Tom Shevlin felt it was time to call in April, Josh's main squeeze. April worked twelve hours a day to pay for her apartment, car, and everything else for Josh and their child. Josh, the ex-con, sat around all day—watching TV, caring for his son, and speaking to his other girlfriends on the side. He still had plenty of time to dream up felonious money-making plans, and Tom and Louie were certain his criminal career was not over. As long as Josh and April got along, and she supported him in the style to which he had become accustomed, Tom reasoned, nothing would change. April would not be motivated to speak against the father of her child, and Josh would not take any sudden steps. Tom wanted to shake something loose.

When it came to solving a murder, detectives had to field whatever leads bounced their way. Like in baseball, Tom felt that the situation called for the old squeeze play. It was time to try and get Josh away from his safe home plate and get him caught between bases. If they could make Josh a runner trapped between third base and home, surrounded, unable to move, he might make a false move. If not, another player might tag him out in the resulting rhubarb. Either way, the game would be over.

"We've got to shake up his world," Tom said to Louie.

"We've got to do something to change his comfortable little world." Louie could not have agreed more.

When April arrived for her interview, Louie asked her to write down what she had done on the days in question, and she complied. Her time was mostly accounted for. She had either been working, sleeping, or caring for Timmy. After they obtained more background information about April, Josh, and other friends and relatives, they hit her with the phone dumps.

"Look, April," said Louie, broaching the delicate subject, "I don't want you to flip out, but . . ." That wasn't quite true. He showed her the printouts, and explained about the five different women Josh had called. He asked for her help, because Josh had refused to tell them who the girls were. Louie read off the names to April. Her reaction to one in particular was quick and violent.

"He's calling that bitch?" she shrieked, unleashing a string of obscenities aimed at Josh and the woman. When she calmed down a bit, April explained that Josh had dated the woman before he started dating her. Apparently Josh had sworn that the affair was over. April was still furious when she left—a woman scorned. The two detectives smiled at each other. Josh was in for a hell of a night.

Two days later, Louie and Tom dropped by April's apartment to see how Josh and April were getting along. The door was opened by Josh, who did not look happy to see them.

Had the squeeze play failed, they wondered? The door to the bedroom was open, and they saw a plump punk lurking inside.

"Who's that?" asked Louie, thinking the guy looked like the Pillsbury Doughboy.

"Oh, that's Redrum," said Josh.

Redrum, thought Louie, what a cute nickname. It was "murder" spelled backwards, like in that horror movie, *The Shining*, with Jack Nicholson. The one where the little boy saw the word "REDRUM" spelled out in blood, as a warning of a coming bloodbath.

Josh stormed over to the living room and dejectedly plopped his skinny form onto the couch. He made himself comfortable by putting his feet up on a fully-packed duffel bag on the floor. Suddenly, things were looking up. Or did the luggage belong to that Redrum character?

"Listen, you guys are fucking up my life, you're fucking up my life, here," Josh whined. "April will kick me out now—I have to leave. I ain't talking to you no more. You're fucking up my life."

He told Louie and Tom that he had to leave shortly to walk to the store. It looked like Josh also no longer had the use of April's wheels. April was giving Josh the boot, and he was having a bad day. It was wonderful news. Josh was a true sociopath. He took absolutely no responsibility for his own actions. Over and over he told Louie and Tom that they were to blame for what was happening to him. Josh actually seemed to expect the detectives to feel bad, or to apologize. He showed not the slightest remorse for cheating on April— let alone the barbaric murder of a lovely young girl—but he was all whiney and sad about how his comfy life had been made difficult. Who was going to support him? Where could he sit around all day watching the boob tube and getting high? He might even have to get a job! The gall of the man was infuriating. He was the kind of person you just wanted to grab by the throat. Josh was no longer home free. Now if they could just keep him off base, off balance, wondering about who was the weak link—about who would rat him out, they might get their innings.

Jay was next up at bat. It was his turn to answer Louie and Tom's questions back at the precinct.

"Tell me everything you did from the time you woke up on February twenty eight, to the time you went to sleep on March first," said Tom Shevlin, handing Jay a pad and pen. The younger man said he had slept until noon on that Tuesday, the last day he saw Kim.

"I awoke in Kimberly's bed, after staying the night," Jay wrote. "I didn't see Kim that morning, she had already left for work. Joshua, April, and their son also slept over in the other bedroom. When I awoke, April was at work and Joshua was in the living room while his son was playing in the same room. At that time, Kimberly's dog Sugar had made on the living room floor and I cleaned it. After taking a shower I went with Joshua and his son to Joshua's new apartment, to paint. Joshua drove April's car. At Joshua's apartment, I painted the cabinets and doors.'' At about 3:30, Jay said, he and Josh returned to Kim's place, and found her sitting on her couch—watching music videos.

''Me and Joshua sat on the couch and watched the videos with her,'' Jay said.

At about 5 o'clock, said Jay, Joshua drove him home to his sister's house, where he stayed the night on the couch, watching TV and falling asleep about 11:30. He didn't call anyone and no one called him. On Ash Wednesday, at about 10:30 in the morning, Jay said that his brother-in-law the cop woke him up and asked him if he would get up and watch Jay's nephew while he drove Jay's sister to work. Jay took a shower and Josh called.

''Joshua said that Kim didn't come home,'' said Jay. ''I answered 'so maybe she met someone.' Joshua said 'She doesn't do that. She is gone. You should come over here.' Joshua said that he would come and get me.''

''When Josh called, he said 'Kim is gone,' you're sure?'' asked Louie, after reading the finished alibi statement.

''Yes.'' Jay said that Josh picked him up at 3:30 and drove him to Kim's apartment.

''At that time, at Kimberly's, was Tara and Steve,'' Jay continued. ''A little later on, Kim's father came and he sent me and Joshua out looking for her. We went to Bushwick checking chop shops around Flushing Avenue and Troutman.'' Jay described Josh stopping to talk to various guys on various corners in their old neighborhood, but he couldn't remember many details. Like Josh, he could not give a location for more than one chop shop.

''On Thursday or Friday, Kimberly's father, who spoke

with Joshua, sent me and him out to Howard Beach to look at motels for her. He also sent us by the airport," said Jay. On the day Kim was found dead, he said, "Joshua drove me and Shawn to where she was found. We never got out of the car. We just looked at the house then drove away."

Jay, like Josh, volunteered again that Tommy Antonakos was "hooked up with the mob."

Louie and Tom said nothing. They let Jay talk about his underprivileged childhood, and about arriving at the scene of his mother's bloody stabbing murder, moments after it had happened—something he said had broken his heart. He felt that if he had arrived earlier, he might have prevented his stepfather from killing her. He seemed genuinely upset. They handed him the grisly crime-scene photos that depicted, in gruesome clarity, what the fire had done to Kim. Jay seemed shaken.

"What do you know about Kim's death?" Louie asked suddenly, putting Jay on the spot.

"Nothing," said Jay.

He told them he loved Kim, as if he really meant it. Louie told Jay they had fingerprints, but it didn't seem to bother Jay. Louie remembered the name given to him by the anonymous caller, and decided to try it on for size:

"Joey was in on it, too, right?" Louie asked.

Jay froze. They know, he thought. Somebody flipped on us. To Louie it was a shot in the dark. Jay struggled to disguise the fact that Louie had hit a bull's eye. He tried to keep his voice calm as he denied knowing anybody named Joey.

"Do you know who the murderer is?" asked Louie.

"No," said Jay.

"Do you know who murdered your mother?" Louie goaded.

"Yeah, I know who the murderer was."

"Yeah," Louie said. "I believe you know who was the murderer of Kimberly Antonakos, too. I know it."

Jay's denials were losing steam. He was seething with inner turmoil. What did they know?

"This is your shot. The first one who comes in to cooperate will get the best deal," Louie said.

Jay seemed to be thinking it over. Louie then went face-
to-face with Jay.

"You loved her," said Louie, appealing to Jay, as if he
were his best friend telling him his own heart. "You didn't
light the match," said Louie, startling Jay. "Everyone you
love is getting murdered. You're dying inside—you've got
to let us know."

Jay wondered what kind of deal he could get. He had been
looking for a way out, to end it. The detective had punched
the right buttons. Jay's walls were cracking apart, about to
tumble down.

"This guy is good," Jay thought to himself. "He's right.
I am dying inside. I should . . ."

Someone burst into the room and interrupted. A detective
said there was a call for Louie, who left to take it. The wave
of sympathy for Kim, the guilt over her death, and the image
of his dying mother covered with blood, washed over Jay
and receded. Jay had time to think it over, time to regain his
composure. The moment passed. By the time Louie had returned from taking the call, Jay's walls were back up. The
detectives did not mention any other details, but it was obvious to Jay that someone was doing some talking. He would
have to tell Josh.

Louie and Tom let Jay go, not knowing how close they
had come to winning the game in the second inning.

Before Josh came in for his polygraph test, he got completely stoned on weed, thinking it would screw up the results, and allow him to lie without being detected. In the
Queens District Attorney's office, Josh was strapped to the
machine. A cord was placed around his chest to measure his
breathing rate. A blood pressure cuff was attached with Vel-
cro to his upper arm, and inflated—to gauge his heart rate
and blood pressure. Sensors on his hand measured the electrical conductivity of the skin, called the galvanic skin response—a scientific name for sweaty palms. Josh was told

to sit still, breathe normally, and look straight ahead. He could not see the machine, and was to give only yes or no answers. The needle-thin pens hooked up to the various sensors traced parallel tracks on a moving paper chart that slowly spewed from the poly like a fax machine without a cutter. The poly was used by detectives to eliminate suspects and to test someone's guilty knowledge. When they lied, normal people experienced measurable physiological changes. The theory was that untruths could be detected by the box because even the best liar could not prevent his body from betraying him. The machine essentially registered stress, nervousness. Some innocent people looked like crooks on the box, because they were nervous wrecks. There also had been reported cases of mentally impaired subjects confessing to bizarre and impossible acts that showed no trace of deception—because they truly believed what they were saying. That was why the results of polygraph tests were not admissible in court.

And there were ways to beat the box. Intelligence agencies like the CIA gave their agents courses in how to use drugs, muscular control, and other strategies to foil the poly. Josh's secret plan was to use marijuana to suppress his physiological reactions. It was a bad plan. Josh's attempt to fool the machine did not take long. It began at midnight and there were only eleven questions. First, the examiner, Detective Al Velardi, asked Josh a series of innocuous questions, like his name, his age, and address—to calibrate the test. Then Al asked Josh to deliberately lie to the same type of questions he had just answered. When he told the truth, the needles wavered normally. When he lied, the needles wiggled, making dark squiggles on the paper, as they should. So far, Josh's plan was not working. Al began reading the carefully prepared questions aloud to Josh.

"Did you set Kimberly on fire, which resulted in her death on March fourth, nineteen ninety-five?"

"No," said Josh.

Some of the long, thin pens instantly wiggled, as if they

were recording an earthquake. According to the machine, he was clearly lying. Al said nothing. He waited for the activity to subside and then asked the next question.

"Did you take part in the plan that resulted in Kimberly's death on March fourth, nineteen ninety-five?"

"No."

Again, the indicators wobbled, making more squiggles on the paper chart.

"Did you take part in the plan that resulted in Kimberly being reported missing on March first, nineteen ninety-five?"

"No."

Again, the needles traced the jagged pattern of a lie.

"Did you take part in the abduction of Kimberly?"

"No."

The needles jumped again, and again Al waited for the needles to calm down before proceeding.

"Between February twenty–eighth, and March fourth, were you in the house that Kimberly was killed in?"

"No."

Another lie.

"Regarding the death of Kimberly on March fourth, at the very time Kimberly was abducted, were you present?"

"No."

The needles did not jump as dramatically as they had with the previous questions, but they traced a smaller pattern that indicated the subject was withholding information.

"Regarding the death of Kimberly on March fourth, did you abduct her?"

"No."

For a second time the indicators swung in lesser arcs indicating that Josh was hiding something.

"Regarding the death of Kimberly on March fourth, do you know for sure who abducted her?"

"No."

Again, deception was indicated in Josh's answer.

"Regarding the death of Kimberly on March fourth, are you deliberately holding back information about that?"

"No."

This time, the machine registered mixed signals. With inconsistent, unresolved responses, Al could make no conclusion.

"Regarding the death of Kimberly on March fourth, did you set her on fire?"

"No."

Again, it was an inconclusive response. Al read the last printed question, which contained a mistake.

"Regarding the death of Kimberly on March fourth, before March fourth, did you definitely know Kimberly was dead?"

Since Kim had been killed on March fourth, and everyone had been notified the same day, the question was an error.

"No."

That also registered as an inconsistent response.

After the test was over, Josh was unhooked and put in another room to wait, while Louie and Tom conferred with Al on the results. This was the moment when the subject was left to stew a bit, wondering whether he was about to be arrested, grilled again, or set free. Al told them that Josh had failed with flying colors. After a while, Tom and Louie went smiling into the room where Josh was nervously waiting, and shook his hand.

"Thanks for coming in, taking care of that, and getting it over," beamed Louie, as if Josh had passed the test, and all was forgiven.

Josh smiled, too. He thought he had them fooled. He was sure he had beaten the box. He could do anything. He walked out of the DA's office a happy man. Louie sat down to type out a "five"—a DD-5 detective report on the poly exam. He was happy to type the words "subject was deceptive in all questions relating to the abduction and subsequent death of Kimberly Antonakos." Louie and Tom did not want Josh to know he had flunked the lie detector test—they wanted him cocky and over-confident. They wanted him to crow about it. The more people Josh bragged to, the more likely it was that one of them might repeat it to the cops when it would do them some good.

The widespread publicity of Kim's murder had not broken the case, but Louie and Tom got a promising call from the "America's Most Wanted" TV show, which had already gotten results in dozens of major crimes, including murders, around the country. The detectives arranged for NYPD approval, and got Tommy Antonakos and others to cooperate. Some cases were spectacularly broken on the night of the show's broadcast by viewers who called a hotline and turned in fugitive killers. Perhaps this would get someone to pick up the phone and rat out Josh and the others.

Tom and Louie stopped by April's apartment one day, to ask Josh and April to participate in the scheduled filming. The detectives, of course, had an ulterior motive—they wanted to get the couple on video discussing the case, but they especially wanted Josh's bony face and Satan goatee all over the tube. Somebody might recognize him, and drop a dime on him. They called in advance, so that Josh, who had been kicked out, would be at April's place on a visit to his son. Tommy Antonakos had also asked Josh to help with the filming, but Josh refused. He told Tommy that Louie and Tom were persecuting him because he was a street guy with a record. He swore to Tommy that he had nothing to do with it, but he would no longer cooperate with the detectives.

"I ain't talking to them no more. They're fucking up my life," he explained. When Louie and Tom arrived to speak to Josh in person, he was adamant.

"I ain't doing it, man," Josh said. "My life's in danger." Josh did not explain, but they assumed he was still seeing Mafiosi under his bed.

"You gotta do it," Louie argued.

"No. Neither is April."

Josh wasn't having any, and April was a legal secretary who knew her rights. Josh wouldn't budge, and they were unable to force him to appear on the show. Next, they decided to pay a visit to Jay. They had to keep the pressure on. Jay was unpleasantly surprised to see the cops at his door. He wasn't interested in becoming a TV star either.

"We'd like you to come in and take a polygraph examination," Tom told him.

"No way," said Jay.

It appeared as though Jay and Josh were singing from the same sheet of music. As the detectives walked out the door, Jay spoke to Louie.

"There's word on the street that you and Tom get a million dollars to solve the case," said Jay.

It was a statement, but it was also a question.

"Oh yeah?" said Louie, who looked at Tom. Both detectives grinned. They did not deny the rumor, and left, giving Jay the distinct impression that it was true. After all, Tommy Antonakos was loaded, wasn't he? In the car, Tom and Louie chuckled over the million-dollar rumor. It was the first time they had heard it, but they had kept their cool. It was a great rumor. They wished they had thought of it themselves. They would do nothing to discourage anyone from believing it. In fact, they might give it a little help. It might be just the thing to squeeze Josh and Jay between the bases, 'til it hurt—until one of them was sitting in the Squad Room chair giving up the other.

"It might shake things up—get the rats biting each other," Tom grinned.

No justice—no peace.

Beautiful college student
Kim Antonakos.
(Associated Press)

House of horror – the empty Woodhaven, Queens home where Kim was imprisoned by her kidnappers and then burned alive.
(New York City Fire Department)

Kim's charred body *(image, lower right)* was discovered in the cluttered basement by firefighters.
(New York City Fire Department)

Nick Libretti.
(NYPD)

"Joey" Negron and Antonette Montalvo.
(Antonette Montalvo)

Josh Torres.
(NYPD)

"Jay" Negron.
(NYPD)

"Smoked" – the body of Joey Negron is shot dead on a
Queens sidewalk, his watch still clutched in his left hand.
(NYPD)

Joey's black magic Santeria beads he carried
in his pocket – which failed to protect him from his killer.
(NYPD)

Raquel "Blondie" Montalvo.
(Raquel Montalvo)

Detective Tom Shevlin *(left)* "walks" Josh Torres to a waiting police car after arrest.
(Tamara Beckwith, *New York Post*)

An emotionless Josh Torres reads his
written statement to the court before
his sentencing.
(Luiz C. Ribeiro, *New York Post*)

A jubilant Tommy Antonakos hugs Detective Louie Pia after
Josh Torres was found guilty.
(Spencer A. Burnett, *New York Post*)

Tommy Antonakos, praying at Kim's grave.
(John Naso, *New York Daily News*)

CHAPTER EIGHTEEN

SPIRITS

Josh, Jay, Joey, and Nick met on a street corner near Nick's house to discuss their problem. In an isolated spot on a Canarsie sidewalk near an empty parking lot, they formed a circle and resumed their angry, fearful cycle of blame and counter-blame. They made a show of ignoring their victim, like boys whistling past the graveyard. Josh was casually drinking a "Malta" soda from a bottle and all four men were smoking, but they were too busy talking or listening to do much puffing. The rippling smoke from their four cigarettes entwined and rose above them in the calm air, until it became a white spectral shape hovering above their heads.

"Why didn't the house burn up?" Nick asked Josh.

"We messed up. Detectives showed me pictures of Kim, and she was burnt only up to here," Josh scolded, gesturing to his stomach, to indicate fire damage from the waist up. "We did a bad job."

At least one of the others wondered to himself at Josh's use of the word "we." After all, Josh was the one who had gotten the gas, poured it, and lit it up. Nick began kidding Jay, because he seemed sad. Kim had been his girlfriend. But, rather than say he was sorry, Nick needled Jay that Kim was fat and had been heavy to carry.

"She was kinda thick," Nick chuckled.

Of course, Kim was not fat at all. She was slender and sexy.

"She was in the trunk, and I was playing Biggie," said Nick. "We also hit that," Nick leered, meaning that he and Joey had had sex with Kim, which was not true.

"I'm only kidding," Nick laughed, when he saw that Jay was not amused.

Josh laughed, and boasted how he had stood up to a police grilling.

"The detectives on the case, Tom and Lou from the One-Oh-Two were investigating, and questioned me. They're suspicious that it's me. They wanted me to take a lie detector test. I smoked a lot of weed, and I think I passed it," Josh smirked.

Josh was a little leery of Nick, but felt that Joey was not standing up right. He didn't like what he saw in Joey's eyes. He thought the guy was a snake. Of course, Josh was angry at everybody because of the cops and because April had kicked him out. He was homeless, and on a hair trigger. A woman friend of April's mother had made the mistake of accidentally bumping into Josh on the sidewalk, and Josh went off. He viciously punched the woman out and knocked her to the pavement, she later told police. To add insult to injury, Josh had stolen her cellular phone and $400 in cash from her pocketbook. The woman identified Josh as her attacker but he was released on a "Desk Appearance Ticket" and never did any jail time for the assault and robbery.

Like the others, Joey was trying to keep up his cool, macho, I-don't-give-a-damn exterior, but inside, he could not snub Kim's ghost. Joey liked to think of himself as a gentleman, and was very deferential to the opposite sex. He would never have intentionally killed a woman. The bottom line for "Negron Incorporated" was that for all his machismo, Joey could not handle the fact that he had been part of killing Kim. He had not fed Kim because he thought the whole thing was going to be over in a day or so. Josh had kept telling him it would be over soon, and Joey did not want to expose himself to any risk by going back any more than he had to. There had been no problem with the drug dealer's kid, but that didn't drag on for three days.

At one point, Josh turned to Jay with a frightening suggestion:

"We gotta hit Tommy before he hits us," Josh said.

No one else seemed to have the stomach for a plan for going after Tommy Antonakos.

"Yo, the detectives know your name, man," Josh suddenly accused Joey. "How do they know your name? You fucked up!"

"I don't know," Joey lied. "It must have been the duct-tape—fingerprints."

He explained that he had tossed the roll of unused duct tape away after he and Nick had left the car on Long Island. At the mention of the word "fingerprints," Josh scowled at Joey.

"Oh, Homicide chased me the other night," Joey said, suddenly claiming that the cops were after him. It was another lie.

Josh's eyes narrowed as he stared at Joey.

"I'm not gonna burn alone!" Joey threatened.

Joey had announced that he would break the code of the street and "flip" on his accomplices if arrested. It was a dumb, reckless thing to say. Joey felt it was all Josh's fault, and he had no intention of going down because Josh had screwed up, and jammed everybody up. Joey had made the secret call to the cops partly because he was tormented by guilt. He had not intended to kill the girl. It had not been part of the plan. Josh was the man with the plan and his scheme had fallen apart because Josh couldn't get the father to pay the ransom money.

The second reason Joey had made the call was that Josh blamed him for letting Kim die while she was at the sweet house. Joey knew that Josh would come after him—which was why he wanted to get Josh off the street. Joey was in a bind. If he couldn't get the cops to bust Josh and Jay, then the only other obvious solution was to whack Josh first—along with his buddy Jay. Joey had a plan, and had already started carrying his gun in the waistband of his pants—loaded and ready—wherever he went. He might kill Josh in a fair fight, but Josh would not fight fair. If he wasted Josh and Jay, and got arrested for the murders, he might still spend a lot of time in jail—but anything was better than being dead. Joey knew he had no choice now. He would figure out a way to set Josh and Jay up. All he needed was a little luck, and the help of his best friend, Nick.

Josh did not mention to Joey that the cops had said they had fingerprints from Kim's car and the house and would match the prints with names in a few months. Josh knew that couldn't hurt him or Jay—unless Joey ratted them out, unless he flipped. Both Joey and Nick had been in Kim's car, and, if they left their fingerprints, it was their fault. They had arrest records, fingerprints on file, and had no reason to ever be in Kim's car. As soon as the cops got those prints, Josh thought, they would pick them up.

Josh, like the others, became a crook because crime does pay. But there was no honor among thieves and less loyalty among murderers. Before parting, Josh warned them all not to panic—to brace up, and keep their mouths shut—or else.

"Hold your own, or you'll get it," he threatened in a tone of promise, looking directly at Joey.

Before they broke up, Josh took out a match, struck it alight with a snap, and tossed the burning match head at Joey in a flaming arc.

"Flame on, stupid," Josh giggled, as Joey stepped out of the path of the tiny flame, which trailed a slender line of smoke down to the sidewalk.

Josh's message was not complicated—anyone who spoke to the cops would end up like Kim: smoked. It was like a fuse had been lit. They were no longer a gang. They were four guys named Josh, Jay, Joey, and Nick—each worried about what the other three might say or do. Because Kim had been killed, the quartet would always be bound by their common secret. They were no longer friends, although they still pretended to be. They were four enemies chained together by death.

Joey wanted an exorcism, and sought out the services of the ring's witch doctor. Soon after the meeting, Joey drove into Manhattan, to the Lower East Side apartment of the Santeria priestess whom true believers called La Madrina—"The Godmother." He told her everything, and she prescribed a bizarre ritual that she said would free Joey of Kim's spirit.

Santeria, the worship of saints, is a Caribbean religion originally practiced by slaves in the New World. It has a veneer of Catholicism but was actually derived from ancient, African folk magic. Adherents of the religion worship a pantheon of colorful gods and goddesses, and, like in the Old Testament of the Bible, practice animal sacrifice. But followers of Santeria not only had to slit the throats of sheep, goats, chicken, birds, and other animals—they also had to drink their warm blood as a vital part of ceremonial spirit possession. Practitioners used incantations and magic spells to hurt their enemies and help themselves. There were spells to gain money, win the love of another, or drive away sickness. There were also spells to block black magic spells aimed at you, and those specifically designed to help you avoid the police, or win a court trial. The bizarre, exotic ingredients needed for such spells and curses might have seemed impossible to obtain in such a temperate Northern latitude. But the hundreds of thousands of "Santeros" in New York could find bats, vultures, Florida Water, seashells, strange plants, herbs, unguents, oils, lotions, and potions at Santeria stores, called *Botanicas*, in every Latino neighborhood. City workers in public parks routinely cleaned up the bizarre leavings of black magic rites—headless chickens, slaughtered animals, and other odd paraphernalia of urban witchcraft.

When he returned from the sorceress, Joey told the other three gang members that she had commanded that they also come to her. Josh, Jay, and Nick went together to La Mad-

rina, whose temple was in her home. Strange incense, and
spooky "Orisha" music—which included weird yells and
beast-like hoots—filled the "Godmother's" parlor. One end
of the room was taken up by a huge altar of colorful statues
of the Santeria gods and goddesses, and offerings of cigars,
fruit, and rum at their feet. The somber Madrina greeted the
three young men, who each gave her fifty dollars. Madrina
looked like a witch. She was a fat, middle-aged woman, with
an olive complexion and deep mahogany eyes. Clad in a
flowing white dress, she also wore white rags on her head
that held back her black-and-silver hair. Around her thick
neck, she wore several strands of colored beads—one for
each of her Orisha protectors. She also wore a full set of
"war beads" crisscrossing her waist and chest, to ward off
evil spells, like a bulletproof vest.

Madrina parted a set of wine-dark velvet curtains with one
long-nailed hand, and led the trio to a white table bearing a
crystal bowl filled with water. After closing the curtains she
sat and gestured magically with her hands over the crystal
bowl. She gazed deep into the rippling water, as her eyes
darted about. The expression on her wrinkled face changed
rapidly, as if she were watching a silent movie.

"I see bad things happening all around you. I see spirits,"
Madrina told them ominously.

She looked up suddenly and stared at the air behind Josh,
then Jay, then Nick.

"I see a woman behind all of you—and she's following
you!"

In unison, their three heads jerked around involuntarily,
and stared at the same air.

"Her spirit is still wandering," Madrina said. "This is a
very bad thing, because you did it to a woman. The woman
will follow you wherever you go."

Jay was stunned. She knew everything. Josh was also
taken aback. Was she all-knowing, or had Joey spilled his
guts? Josh was filled with murderous fury—he was the only
one who was allowed to blab about their crime.

On previous visits, she had told them that they all had different spiritual guides that looked after them. Now there was a problem with their spiritual guides—especially Nick's—the Madrina said in an angry voice. "Everybody's Santo is crashing," she told the trio, explaining that the guardian spirits who protected them had deserted them because of what they had done.

Joey, she said, had been watched over by Geronimo, the American Indian warrior. Nick, the Madrina said, had been under the protection of a different "Orisha," an African god.

"Your guide is no longer with you. He's not protecting you anymore," the Madrina warned Nick. "You're on your own."

Worse, she said, Nick might share the same fate as his protector spirit.

"Your spiritual guide got murdered in prison," the Madrina said. "They set him on fire in his cell!"

Nick was startled, and his eyes widened with fear at the prospect of being burned alive, like Kim. Nick had been cast adrift in the outer darkness, where there was wailing and a gnashing of teeth. He felt like he was going to get into things and not have someone there for him.

"Damn, I'm fucked up," Nick groaned.

But Josh and Jay were much better off, the fortune-teller said. Both men were under the protection of Chango—the bisexual god of fire, thunder, dance, and passion. They wore Chango's red-and-white beads around their necks. The good news, she told them, was that for half of the year Chango was a male, and for the other six months he was the female saint, Santa Barbara. When Chango was in his male incarnation, those under his aegis could do whatever they wanted to—without punishment. You could murder a thousand people, and Chango would stand by your side. Although they, too, would have to make spiritual amends, Josh and Jay had an easier task ahead of them, she said. The Madrina gave them all multicolored strings of beads, each with an open metal shield medallion with a cross on it.

"These are for protection against anyone who wishes to harm you," she said, warning that they must be worn at all times.

Then she issued instructions for a "baño," a "spiritually cleansing" ritual bath, that would wash away the taint and protect them from evil influences. She also prescribed a ritual exorcism that each man would have to perform separately—as soon as possible. It would, she promised, rid them of Kim's angry ghost. The rite would also block magic from the other side. Her orders, she warned, must be followed exactly if they wanted to be free of the unquiet spirit of their victim. The Madrina also warned that Nick and Joey had to stay away from Josh and Jay.

"You should all stay away from each other for a while," she said.

Silently, separating, all the men went home and performed the same strange exorcism.

Naked, at home, Jay opened the baño, the packet of dark mysterious ingredients that reeked of herbs and alcohol. Following Madrina's instructions, he poured the magic contents into the hot bath water and stepped in. The steamy water released a sweet, heady odor that filled his nostrils. After steeping in the strange brew, Jay opened the drain, stood up, and left the tub, but he did not dry himself. He donned a long, pure white robe over his fragrant, wet body. Next, he gathered the clothes he had been wearing the night Kim had been burned, and wrapped them together. He slipped out into the middle of the cool night, and drove to the middle of the Brooklyn Bridge. Stopping the car, Jay stepped out, wearing his flowing robe, carrying his bundle of clothing. As the Madrina had told him, Jay had tied up his secret with his clothes. It was time to throw his guilt into the ocean, and pray that Kim's haunting spirit would follow it. Jay stepped to the edge of the roadway and threw the knotted bundle bearing his secret over the edge. The pale ball fluttered down into the dark, toward the cold river below, and vanished into the seaward tide. Jay tossed a handful of silver coins after it, turned, and left without looking back. Every time he passed over the bridge, the Madrina said, he would have to throw pocket change, fruit, or cigars as an offering to the forgetful waters below—like a spiritual toll bridge.

Whatever the ceremonial bathing and rituals prescribed by the witch accomplished, it soon became clear that it had not rid Jay or Joey of their guilt, or Josh of his evil thoughts about the others. It may have performed supernatural wonders—but it did not cure any of them of their paranoid fears.

Joey was sitting alone on the couch in the darkened living room of his Queens apartment, as tinny voices came from a small microcassette tape recorder in his hand. He was listening to his insurance—the recording of himself, Josh, Jay, and Nick discussing the kidnapping. He listened to Josh brag about how he had the cops pointed the wrong way, how he had them "looking at Psycho," how the cops "didn't know nothing," how everything was "going good." Yeah, right. He heard Jay's voice on the tape, and Nick's—and his own. He rewound the tape and carefully listened again. The parts that had Josh shooting his mouth off were great. But if the cops grabbed Josh and Jay and took them out of circulation, it was almost certain they would rat Joey out. Joey was prepared, but the only problem was that he and Nick were also on the tape, talking about their part in the kidnapping. Joey decided to erase the parts where he and Nick were talking. Over, and over, Joey pressed the PLAY and RECORD buttons at the same time, to record over part of the tape. Again and again, he rewound the tape and listened to the altered version, carefully erasing more incriminating words. By the time he finished, there were about half a dozen snatches of Josh talking—separated by long, blank pieces of tape. Joey figured it was the best way to protect himself and Nick, but, of course, it wasn't. By expurgating the tape, Joey had rendered the only existing record of the kidnappers admitting their guilt—while Kim was alive—useless in court.

Joey had one other plan that might turn everything around. He had told his friend Nick all about how he intended to deal with the problem, and was just waiting for an answer from Josh and Jay.

"What're you doing?" Antonette asked Joey, suddenly appearing in the living room. "What's that?"

"Don't worry about it," Joey ordered, startled. "Don't involve yourself in my business. Go back to sleep."

As Antonette turned toward the bedroom, she heard Joey again push a button, heard barely audible voices on a tape. She knew better than to press Joey about his business. He didn't tell her what he did to make money, and she didn't want to know. She knew he was up to no good, but he was a good provider, always had money, and treated her well. He loved her, and her son *Bobby, whom he was raising as his own. Lately Joey had been acting very strangely. He was sad, and very nervous. Also, Nick was calling three or four times a day, and Joey would take the phone into the bathroom. She could hear Joey arguing with Nick behind the door, but she could not make out what Joey was so upset about.

Antonette had noticed that Joey was not himself. He was usually such a fun-loving guy. He loved barbecues, playing cards, going to parties, and listening to "freestyle" music, like "TKA," and "Little Sister." Nick was Joey's closest friend. They were like family. Antonette was upset because she felt that if Joey and Nick were fighting, something big was up. Antonette was godmother to Nick's daughter, and the little girl and her son Bobby played all the time.

Antonette had been with Joey for four years. She had first met him years earlier, at Franklin K. Lane High School, after she had arrived from Puerto Rico, where she had grown up. Joey came from a troubled home, but was a good-natured person. She felt he had been dealt a bad hand in life. Little Bobby, fathered by another guy, was eighteen months old when they became a couple. Bobby's fourth birthday was coming up, and he was growing up into a polite young man.

Antonette's sister Susan, and their mother Jeanette, both felt it was due in large part to Joey's good influence. They felt he was special, a sweet guy.

Antonette's little sister Tyisia had a big crush on Joey, who had agreed to be the thirteen-year-old's "date" for her junior high school prom on June 24th, just four days after Bobby's fourth birthday party. Her mother treated Joey like a son. At Bobby's party, while the four-year-old and his friends laughed and played, Jeanette noticed that Joey seemed indifferent. She had already noticed how he was always looking over his shoulder.

"What's the matter, Joey?" she asked.

"My birthday's coming up soon and I'm not going to live to my next one," Joey answered, in a matter-of-fact tone that shocked Jeanette.

"Why?" she asked. "What're you talking about?"

"I got that feeling—I'm not going to make it to my twenty-seventh birthday," was all Joey said. "I got that feeling. I'll be lucky if I make it to my next birthday."

Nick was also nervous, and told Jay he felt vulnerable without his spirit guide. It was very unsettling, he said, "that no one in the spirit world was watching out" for him. He was afraid of the cops, and he was afraid of Josh, and the questions he was asking. Nick took the Madrina's advice to put distance between himself and the others to heart, but he decided to go a step further. He bought an airline ticket and got on a plane to California. Nick went as far away as he could get from the others, without leaving the country.

Without Nick around, Josh concentrated on Joey and Jay. Instead of just leaving Joey alone, as the Madrina had ordered, Josh regularly arranged meetings or just dropped by to repeat his message over and over. He kept telling everyone to play it cool, but he wouldn't let them. Josh—still worried about mob vengeance—was obsessed, and would not let it rest. He had become fixated with keeping the genie in the bottle, and threatened death to anyone who opened his mouth—except himself: He told almost anyone who would listen about the murder. He was the only one of the four who was proud of it, who used it to impress others with how bad a guy he was. Again and again, he would throw lighted matches at people, and joke about the torching. He didn't care who knew—except the cops, that is.

"Flame on," Josh would laugh, as he tossed the matches. It had become his trademark.

After almost a month, Nick returned from California, and things heated up again. Josh believed that time was running out. Soon the cops would match up Joey's fingerprints from Kim's car. Joey was already convinced that Josh was coming after him. Everywhere he went, Joey carried a .380 automatic pistol loaded with ten rounds of ammunition. He wouldn't go down without a fight.

"I'm always on point," Joey bragged.

One night, Joey called Josh and told him he had a paid drug killing for him and Jay.

"I got a hit for you, at a Brooklyn motel on a Friday night," Joey said. Josh said he would think about it.

After he thought about it, Josh picked up Jay and Joey's sister Tina, then stopped at Nick's house, uninvited. Josh saw Nick on the curb, waved, and gave a friendly smile.

"Yo, Nick—get in," Josh said.

Nick got in and they all drove to a friend's house to hang out. Josh was acting strangely, and Jay and Nick had noticed. While Nick was talking to Tina, Josh opened his shirt and showed Jay the butt of a .357 Magnum pistol.

"Yo," Josh whispered to Jay, "I'm gonna murder him as soon as she leaves."

Jay was stunned—at both the murder plan, and Josh's carelessness.

"No, man, why?"

Josh reiterated his reasons for not trusting Joey and Nick.

"I'm gonna be the last man standing," Josh concluded.

"But Tina saw us with him," Jay said, trying for a logical argument.

While Josh mulled that over, Jay thought for the first time, "I'm next."

Josh decided to question Nick about Joey's offer of a murder contract at the motor lodge in Brooklyn. Josh was also agitated about Joey's claims that he had been picked up and questioned by detectives. It was not true, but Josh did not know that. Nick correctly perceived that he was undergoing a final exam, of sorts. When Josh expressed skepticism about the hit scheme offered by Joey, Nick quickly betrayed his best friend:

"Yo, if anything, he was going to get you," Nick said.

Nick explained that the offer of a hit was a set-up, and that when Josh and Jay entered the hotel room, they were the ones who were going to be blown away. As he spoke, Nick made it sound as though he had refused Joey's request.

Suddenly, it was three against one. Nick lived through the night, but Joey's fate had been sealed.

Joey came from a dysfunctional home. When Joey was born, his father was a sixteen year-old boy. At age twelve Joey was already getting into trouble, and went to live with his Uncle Luis Negron and his Aunt Emma in Brooklyn. For three years, Joey was off the streets, and had a stable home life. His aunt and uncle were very religious, and Joey went to church every Sunday. Sitting in the house of God, young Joey often heard sermons of God's love—and tales of eternal damnation for sinners. By age fifteen, Joey ignored the pleas of his aunt and uncle to stay. He went back to the street, and had been there ever since. Occasionally, Joey would drop in unannounced on the couple, just to let them know he was alive. Joey was sorry he had left their home, and he was filled with regret for what his life might have been.

On a warm night in June, Joey showed up late at night and was embraced by the couple. Joey's sister Tina was also there, as was another cousin. As they always did, Luis and Emma tried to talk the nephew they loved off the streets and back into church. They would never give up on him.

"You have to go back to church," said Luis in a good-natured tone. It was not the first time he had implored Joey to return to the fold.

"No . . ." said Joey. Something was different in his voice. "I've done something so terrible, God can't forgive me. I'm going to Hell."

Luis was jolted by his nephew's words. He noticed Joey's eyes were downcast and vacant. Luis suddenly had the chilling feeling that the young man whom he had tried to save from the street had become a lost soul—touched by evil. Joey had not said what the crime was, but the way he had said it left little doubt that it was the sin of Cain—the mortal sin of murder.

"God can forgive anything," Luis declared. "You have to go back to church."

"I can't go back to church," Joey said, shaking his head, and beginning to cry. "God can't forgive me for what I've done. It was too horrible."

It was pathetic to see the strong young man sobbing. Luis and Emma also began to cry. They hugged Joey and tried to reason with him. They knew he had become involved with stealing and drugs, and now, it seemed, murder. They tearfully prayed, and tried again and again to get him right with God, but apparently, Joey had not come for that purpose. He wiped away his tears, and reached into his pocket.

"God won't forgive me for this one," Joey said, finally pulling out a tiny tape cassette, and handing it to his sister. "If something happens to me, give this tape to the police."

Joey staunchly refused to tell them what he had done. He did not want them to know anything. Knowledge was dangerous. He did not mention that he was already being tormented by a devil named Josh, or that he feared death—but that he had a greater fear of burning eternally in Hellfire. His insurance was in place. It might save his life. If not, maybe the tape would bring down Josh, and put Joey on the side of the angels. As Joey walked out the door, his uncle made one last attempt to guide him back to the spirit of God.

"God will forgive anything," said Luis.

Joey shook his head with finality. He knew better.

"Not this," Joey replied, looking at his uncle with haunted eyes one last time, before turning away into the night.

CHAPTER NINETEEN

A FATHER'S PLAN

Tommy Antonakos and his family were despondent. The hard reality of living in a world without Kim—without seeing her beautiful face, or hearing her sparkling laugh—was a grinding pain in their hearts every day. Every night, sleep would bring brief respite, or it might bring Kim herself, as if she were still alive. But every morning, with the sun, Kim vanished again. When sleep ended, it was like waking up to a nightmare. Kim was dead. It was true. It was unbearable, even for a strong Brooklyn guy like Tommy. Often, he had to rush to the bathroom and vomit, as he realized over and over that Kim was dead. The light had gone out of his life.

But he had promised Kim that they would make her killers answer for what they had done. That vow, that mission was the only thing that kept Tommy going—that and his responsibility for his mother, who was also suffering greatly. It wasn't just that he had promised Kim, and felt that she could not rest in peace until her killers were caught. Tommy's soul thirsted for justice. He could not rest until they were behind bars. He had not been to work since the day his daughter vanished, and his business was sliding, but he did not really care. He had more important work to do.

Every morning, Tommy went to see Kim. To her grave, he brought flowers, candles, and stuffed animals, like Sylvester the cat, that Kim had loved so much as a kid. Tommy spoke to Kim as if she could hear, which, of course, he believed, because his faith told him that she was in Heaven.

The investigation seemed to be stalled, and Tommy was willing to try anything. Since the psychic that Marlene had consulted seemed to have been eerily close to the truth, except for that part about Kim being tied to a bed, he wanted to give her another try. He told Louie and Tom that he wanted to use the psychic, but they were not interested. Tom Shevlin thought it was all baloney, and said so.

"I know you don't believe in this stuff," Tommy said to Tom, "but this one might be different."

Tommy had said that the woman's specialty was psychometry, the so-called ability to touch objects and psychically sense information about the owner, or someone who had touched the item.

"Tommy, if you want me to go with you, I'll go," the detective responded, making it clear it was as a favor—not out of trust in alleged psychic phenomena.

Louie Pia and Tom Shevlin met Tommy and his brother Joseph at a condominium apartment in the Bay Ridge section of Brooklyn. They were admitted by Claire Day, a dark-haired, pleasant woman in her forties. The four men and the professional clairvoyant sat down at a dinette table. There was no crystal ball on the table, no crystal bowl of water, or any other fortune-telling paraphernalia.

"We're going to show you some pictures," Louie told Claire. "See if anything means anything to you."

Louie took out about ten photographs and spread them out on the surface of the table in front of the woman. One was a picture of Josh, and another was a photo of Jay. The rest were miscellaneous mug shots of bad guys who had nothing to do with the case. Claire smiled, and picked up the photograph of Josh between the fingers of one hand and held it above the table. Suddenly, her eyeballs began to bounce quickly up and down in her head. Louie and Tom had never seen anything like it. As her eyes jumped violently in unison, like two tiny TV screens on the blink, Claire spoke.

"Cold . . . I'm getting nothing . . ." She dropped Josh's image and picked up Jay's mug shot. Presumably, if she felt that one of the guys in a picture was involved, she would have pronounced it hot. Again, Claire's eyes wobbled vertically, and she also dismissed Jay's photograph. The psychic had just passed over the two guys Tom and Louie were sure were involved.

"Cold . . . nothing." She said. Claire proceeded to feel the remaining pictures, while her eyes wiggled upward and downward. She rejected them all.

"Is there anything you can add to this investigation?" Tom Shevlin asked Claire. He couldn't wait to get out of there.

"The only thing I'm getting," Claire replied, "is that the people who did this went for a trip out West, possibly California." The detectives left to return to their real-world inquiry, convinced that the psychic would never be mentioned again. With a smirk, Tom Shevlin thought it was clever to say that the bad guys went West. Killers might be motivated to leave town—and almost all of the country was west of New York.

Finding the men who killed his daughter was Tommy's full-time job now and he tackled it like an executive. Every morning, bright and early, he was waiting in his car when Tom Shevlin and Louie Pia arrived for work at the precinct. At first, they expected and required Tommy's full assistance, but they had never seen such dedication before. Louie and Tom's bosses required weekly progress reports on the homicide investigation, but Tommy wanted daily updates on what they were going to do next, and how he could help. They suggested that he post a reward and NYPD would make up flyers.

"I'm going to do it myself," said Tommy, who swung into action.

Tommy withdrew $10,000 from his bank and deposited it in an escrow account. Then he took a lovely, smiling picture of Kim in a green cable-knit sweater, wearing a gold locket and a big smile, and took it to a printer. Above Kim's picture, the poster read, in large, bold type: "$10,000 REWARD for information leading to the arrest and conviction of person(s) responsible for the murder of KIM ANTONAKOS which occurred on March 4, 1995." Below the photo was an 800 number that Tommy had set up to ring in his Staten Island home, and the words: "Det. Lou Pia or Tom Shevlin, Queen Homicide Squad," along with a phone number. "Reward is being offered by the family and not the N.Y.C Police Department." That last part might reassure shy tipsters that their call was being answered by a private citizen, not a cop. At least one person out there had already picked up the phone with information that sounded solid. Maybe he would call again.

Tommy arrived one day at the precinct with a large box of hundreds of posters. Some would be plastered around Woodhaven and Canarsie, near where events in the case took place. Louie and Tom took their box of reward posters and made a tour of every borough in the city. They placed reward notices inside the Central Booking areas in Queens, Brooklyn, Manhattan, The Bronx, and Staten Island. All prisoners being fingerprinted, photographed, and booked after arrest anywhere in the entire city would be looking at Kim's face on the wall. The posters were also mounted on the walls of arrest processing rooms, and detective squads inside all of NYPD's seventy-six precinct stationhouses all over the city. The plan was simple. Every mutt collared in New York would know he could make ten grand by ratting out Kim's killers. It might not buy a Q-45 Infiniti automobile, but it was a lot of money on the street. Crooks also knew that they might get a deal for their own felonies, if they could give up the guys who torched the girl in Queens. Since many criminals who got arrested on minor charges were often quickly released on bail, the word got around. Josh, Jay, Nick, and Joey suddenly saw the posters adorning telephone poles, walls and stores in their neighborhoods—advertising $10,000 to anyone who could nail them. The word was out.

But Tommy did not stop there. He began hanging out in front of the house where Kim was killed. He went door-to-door telling everyone about the reward and stapling up reward posters. Then he stopped everyone on the street, and asked them for information. If they knew anything, he told them, they could get rich. The middle-aged businessman sought out street corners where drug dealers and criminals congregated. Tommy spoke to hundreds, thousands of men, women, and kids in Canarsie, Kim's neighborhood, and in Woodhaven, where she was found.

When he did not get results, he started going to the worst, most dangerous neighborhoods in the city, like Jamaica, Queens. He stood in front of crack houses, and passed out halves of twenty-dollar bills, telling the street people who took them that they could get the other half if they found out something useful about Kim's death. He also ventured into ghetto crack houses alone. The image of the successful computer corporation president walking through foul-smelling, crumbling crack dens, passing out reward information and twenties ripped down the middle of Andrew Jackson's stern face, was a surreal one. Many junkies could not believe their eyes. Tommy was warned that handing out cash on the most dangerous street corners in America was an almost suicidal undertaking, but he wasn't concerned about his own safety. He would do whatever it took. The denizens of the neighborhood assumed he was either crazy or a cop. Tommy's family wanted to come along with him on his missions, but he wouldn't let them.

Calls started coming into the 800 hotline Tommy had installed in his home. Virtually every day Tommy reported some new tip to Tom and Louie, who dutifully checked it out, and eliminated it. Dozens and dozens of leads popped up and were ruled out. The low point for Tommy was the night he walked into yet another crack house. As he handed out posters to the stoned and suspicious dopers, he noticed a dazed woman sucking on a crackling crack pipe. Beneath the pipe, at the woman's naked breast, her infant daughter suckled. As the image of the crackhead and her doomed child registered in his mind, Tommy sighed.

"I have to stop doing this," he thought.

But he didn't stop. Even in the lower depths, Tommy felt that Kim was with him. Sometimes he drove back to the house where she had been found and just sat there in his car. Alone in his car in the dark, tears came easily. In a way, Tommy felt, the empty house was Kim's grave—the place where her spirit had left the Earth.

Late one night, after weeks and weeks of false tips, Tommy answered the hotline, and began to write down information from yet another tipster, who wanted to meet with him and get cash up front to name the killers.

"We don't want the ten thousand dollars," the caller said. "We just want five hundred dollars cash."

The voice told Tommy to meet him alone on a street corner in a rough neighborhood. Tommy agreed, even though he knew it was almost certainly a trap. Why would anyone settle for five hundred bucks, when they could get the whole reward? Louie Pia was out of town that night, and Tommy could not reach Tom Shevlin. Rather than call another detective, Tommy decided to go alone. Maybe it was a trap, but what if this is the one—the call that would break the case? He had to go.

When Tommy pulled up to the corner, he saw one seedy—looking guy waiting. He also saw another creep crouching behind a car down the block—not doing a very good job of hiding. That settled it. It was a trap. But rather than drive away, Tommy parked the car. It was a very risky thing to do. In that neighborhood, guns were more common than library books. But what if these guys did know something? What if they were involved? He intended to see it through to the end, no matter what. He owed it to Kim.

The mutts who had lured Tommy to that dark block thought they were facing some old guy from the suburbs, a desperate man who could be tricked and robbed. They had no idea what amount of fury had been pent up inside the strong, dark-haired man. Tommy grabbed a large metal flashlight off the car seat and stepped outside. Keeping the flashlight at his side, he walked toward the waiting man. He could see the second man bracing himself, ready to jump out. Tommy kept walking into the ambush, and gripped the club-like flashlight tighter.

"Let's go up here. We'll talk up here," the first man said, gesturing toward where his cohort was waiting.

Tommy was ready when the figure sprang at him from the curb. He swiftly raised the light, and brought it down hard on the rising figure, with a loud curse.

"C'mon, you fucking bastards!"

Tommy easily clubbed his attacker to the pavement, and quickly turned on the accomplice, who collapsed, whimpering, on the sidewalk. Holding the flashlight over the first guy like the Statue of Liberty, Tommy demanded to know if he had anything to tell him about Kim's death. Of course, he didn't.

"We're crackheads," he whined.

That explained it all. Tommy left them moaning and sniveling on the ground. Tommy did not know that the rats were already biting each other, but he was not discouraged. The next day, after visiting Kim's grave, he was back on the street. He had raised the stakes higher, and the word had filtered down to the dregs of society. Josh and the others knew that many people on the street would gladly inform on them for a lot less than Tommy was offering. The pressure was on. The only thing that prevented all rewards from leading to arrests, was, of course, fear.

You could not spend a cash bounty if you were dead.

CHAPTER TWENTY

FOREVER

Shawn Hayes, Kim's former boyfriend, arrived at work on a fair April day behind the wheel of a gleaming maroon Accura Legend. He parked his luxury vehicle at the curb on East tenth Street near Avenue D in Alphabet City. When Shawn stepped out of his car and into the street, he was in his office. Shawn ran a cash-only business and sales were good. He didn't pay sales tax, and his heroin customers could be relied on to come back for more dope every day. Business was booming, his overhead was low, and profits were high. As Shawn exited the expensive car he had purchased with drug money, he did not know that a competitor had decided to offer him early retirement.

Before Shawn could lock his car, a black BMW pulled up and screeched to a halt. Three Latino men sprang from the "Beemer" with automatic weapons, and opened up on Shawn. Three machine guns exploded simultaneously, with ear-splitting noise and flickering muzzle flashes, as the men calmly riddled Shawn's twitching body with hot lead. By the time Shawn heard the first of dozens of loud bangs in quick succession, several bullets had already penetrated his body. Some slugs passed through him and around him and peppered his car with holes. A few seconds later, when Shawn crumpled to the pavement next to his hot ride, he was dying.

His blood spilled into the gutter, mingling with empty plastic crack vials.

The shooters who had "capped" Shawn hopped back into the BMW, which sped away with squealing tires. Several of Shawn's friends, who had hit the pavement during the fusillade of gunfire, picked him up, put him back in his car, and drove him to the hospital. Shawn was Dead On Arrival.

The next day, April 21st, Louie Pia and Tom Shevlin recognized Shawn's name from a homicide report sheet at the precinct. Detectives kept up with murders around the city like everyone else kept up with sports scores. Had their squeeze play worked? Had it started? Were the rats biting each other—were the perps wiping each other out? Or was it possible that someone else had decided that Shawn had killed Kim, and blown him away in revenge? They knew it was unlikely. Shawn was a drug dealer, and violent death was an occupational hazard, the leading cause of murder in the city. They had to drop everything and make certain that Shawn's murder had no connection to Kim's death. Louie remembered the last conversation he had had with Shawn. He had asked the drug dealer if Josh had ever lectured him about behaving like a gentleman with Kim, as Josh claimed.

"No," Shawn replied. "If he did, I would have kicked his ass. He's a punk."

Just after 9 a.m., Louie called the Ninth Precinct in Manhattan, and located Detective Gilbert Rivera, who had caught the Hayes homicide. Louie explained their interest and Rivera agreed to come to Queens with the case folder. Rivera said there was a drug war going on in Alphabet City, which had already claimed the life of Shawn's partner. Shawn's competitors had also suffered casualties. Everything pointed to a drug-related, drive-by revenge shooting. Rivera said one of the witnesses to the Hayes shooting might be able to identify the gunmen. The witness would also have to look at pictures of suspects in Kim's case.

After a few days, it became clear that it was a drug thing. Louie and Tom were disappointed—not because they thought there was any connection, but because it seemed their squeeze play had not produced results. A series of polygraph exams were arranged for other people in Kim's circle of friends, including April—who passed. She was not lying, the machine confirmed when she said that Josh was in bed with her when Kim was grabbed. Either Josh had slipped out while April was asleep, or he had given his beeper to his confederates, as Tom had suggested.

The tape cassette from Kim's answering machine was sent to the audio lab at Police Headquarters in Manhattan. Tests found the tape blank and possibly erased. It was another dead end.

The investigators took the four bloody metal zipper teeth that had been found under Kim's fingernail to a zipper expert named Roy in the Garment Center in Manhattan, who told them that the teeth were from a cheap "Basic, number four" type of zipper and were coated in black paint. They had been manufactured outside the U.S., he said, probably in Asia, most likely in Korea. India was another possibility. Roy said it was most likely used on a lightweight garment, probably a jacket or blouse. He was surprised when told that the murder victim had clawed the teeth from her attacker's clothing with her bare hands.

"She must have had some death grip to remove that," he said.

On May 15th, Louie and Tom had been putting up WANTED posters in Brooklyn and Queens precincts. They had posted the notices at the Seven-Five Precinct in Brooklyn, and were en route to the One-Oh-Nine in Flushing, Queens. As Louie drove the unmarked car north on College Point Boulevard, he went through a green light at the Horace Harding Expressway—the service road of the Long Island Expressway. Another car ran the opposing red light and sped toward them from the left side. Brakes screeched and the car crashed into them. It felt like they had been hit by a torpedo. Tom's head hit the roof, and Louie slammed into him.

The impact staved in the side of the car, pushing them sideways, and bouncing the car up and down.

When the vehicles stopped moving, Tom was in pain, from what he assumed was whiplash. Arriving cops ticketed the driver of the other car, and put the detectives in an ambulance to Booth Memorial Hospital. Louie was released without major damage, but doctors told Tom that he had suffered a serious injury to a spinal bone in his neck. Surgery was required, they told him two days later. He refused to accept their diagnosis. He got out of bed, put on his clothes, and called his wife for a ride. He rested at home for nine days and then went back to work—but not for long. The pain was constant and unbearable. He began to lose the use of his left arm, as spinal bone fragments impinged on his nerves. The NYPD doctor put him on sick leave and Tom spent a miserable month of convalescence at home.

Tom had been injured in a line-of-duty car accident once before. During a car chase, the bad guy had sped into a construction site, into an excavation and into a wall. Tom's car followed and he ended up pinned inside, under the perp's mangled car. In 1975, he was hit in the face with a brick during a riot. Neither incident had given him a fraction of the pain he experienced from the latest accident.

Tom, sporting a neck brace and a sling for his arm, was a detective, so he decided to investigate his medical condition. He sought out a specialist, who examined him, and administered MRI tests. The specialist told him that he did, indeed, need an operation. A piece of bone would have to be removed from his hip and used as a replacement for his damaged neck bone.

Tom made arrangements to have the operation at a Long Island hospital, but conversations with several people who had had the procedure caused him to cancel. He feared he would lose mobility, and still have pain, as several patients had told him. He was worried that such an operation would render him unfit for duty, and end his NYPD career. He did not even want to consider that possibility. He had a major

case to solve and was not ready to retire. But when he tried
to go back to work, he was ordered to report for a medical
exam. A department physician examined Tom, and told him
he could not return to the job. He needed surgery, and a
further on-the-job injury could result in paralysis. He was
out.

The doctor placed Tom on Restricted Duty, and told him
he'd never be on full duty again. Tom was told to put in for
retirement, but he did not want to leave until he and Louie
had solved the Antonakos homicide. It was the low point on
the roller coaster for Tom. How could he leave the job now?
He had unfinished business. He pleaded with his boss, who
told him that if the guys he liked in the case turned out to
be the ones, he would be allowed to come back for the finish.

At the beginning of June, a few weeks after the car crash,
Lisa Shevlin gave birth to a healthy baby sister for five-year-
old Ashley. They named her Carissa.

Louie was promoted to the Homicide Squad, and Homicide Detective Rich Tirelli was assigned to work with him
in Tom's absence. Rich, a tall, affable redhead, was eager
for a crack at the case. Rich had also grown up with police
work. His father was a Nassau County detective. Louie's
dedication to the case was contagious, and Rich began to
catch the obsession. It was tough for Louie to go back to
work without his partner, but Rich was a good detective and
Louie would keep Tom up to date.

Searching for some kind of link to the murder house,
Louie again pored over reams of phone dumps, looking to
do another Sherlock Holmes, like the one that had snared
Josh in lies. Louie had dumped the phone inside the torch
house, but it had been shut off a few months before the
killing. He also got phone records for Wayne McCook, the
son of the woman who owned the house, and his brother's
place on Long Island. It took time to find out that there was
nothing of interest on Wayne's phone. But going through the
endless lists, Louie found that a single call had been made
from the McCook home in Levittown to an address in Can-

,arsie before the murder. Louie sat up in his chair.

"Whoa—we made a connection to the house!" Louie exulted to Rich one day in June.

It was the first connection between Canarsie and the family who owned the house where Kim was burned. Ruth
McCook, the woman who owned the Woodhaven home,
lived on the island with her son and a grandson—who was
about Kim's age, Louie remembered. Was he the one who
had called the Canarsie number? Of course, it was probably
a simple coincidence, the kind of thing detectives ran across
all the time. The number called was registered to *Nancy
Costello. Louie dialed the number and a woman answered.
He introduced himself and said that he wanted to stop by
and discuss a case because someone in her house might be
a witness.

"Don't get excited," Louie told her. "It's no big deal."

The woman told Louie that she had a daughter and a
twenty-one-year-old son, and she made an appointment for
Louie and Rich to come over the next night. When they
arrived, the woman and her husband told the detectives that
they had no idea who had made the call, and they did not
know the McCook family. Their daughter was not home, and
their son *Lee, who worked as a handy man, also said he
had no idea who had called from Long Island. But Lee spec-
ulated that it could have been made to his sister, or to one
of his friends, who would hang out on his front stoop, and
often used the phone. The kid did not appear nervous at all.
He seemed genuinely in the dark about the call. It was time
to look for any connection to Kim.

"We're investigating a girl that was burned to death by
the name of Kimberly Antonakos," said Louie. Before he
could continue, Lee interrupted him.

"You know, the weird thing about that was she was, like,
my girlfriend when we were twelve years old," said Lee.

Louie and Rich were listening with both ears. It suddenly
looked like more than coincidence was involved.

"That was a terrible thing," Lee said, shaking his head.

"I hope you get the people responsible for this."

Rich asked Lee if he had seen Kim since grammar school, and he said he had seen her around the neighborhood once in a while.

"Ever try to date her again?" Rich asked.

"No. To tell you the truth, she was a very pretty girl and when she got older, she never gave me the time of day. I saw her from time to time," he said.

Lee said his relationship with Kim was kid stuff—innocent puppy love. Rich asked him about his whereabouts on the night Kim vanished and the night she was killed. Lee said he had been right there on his front porch, hanging out with his friends. His parents backed him up. He had never heard of Josh or Jay. The youth did not react like someone with something to hide, and his sympathy for Kim seemed genuine. He seemed to have a good alibi, but families had been known to lie to protect one of their own. Louie felt there were only three ironclad alibis—prison, hospital, or the morgue. Since Lee was not in any one of those places when Kim was killed, he was still in play—still a suspect—but both Louie and Rich felt the kid was clean. That, however, did not relieve them of the burden of fully investigating Lee, and all his friends—and, maybe, their friends, too. It would be a lot of work. Again, a whole host of suspects had cropped up that would be difficult to eliminate.

Back at Queens Homicide, Louie called up Tom, who was laid up at home, and told him where the call had led. Tom agreed it was a hell of a coincidence.

"It's too good to be true," Tom said.

Louie and Rich began what they knew could be weeks or months of investigation to check out Lee and all his buddies. Jeff McCook, the twenty-one-year-old grandson of the woman who owned the Woodhaven house, would also be examined, and his life probed for connections to Kim or the others. They just knew that he, like Lee, would also have a large group of friends who would have to be looked at. The case was turning into a career, but they had no choice. They had to find the other guys. With every name that surfaced, came the names of several friends, and the clubs where they all hung out. There was usually one nickname per person, and occasionally, several aliases—all of which had to be checked out on the department computer, as well as with various witnesses. On some days, it seemed like all the young men in Brooklyn claimed to be rap stars with monikers like "Pretty Boy," or catchy initials in place of a name.

On Long Island, Jeff McCook, an equipment rental firm worker, said he did not know Kim or any of her friends, including Josh and Jay. He also denied knowing Lee, or making the call to Canarsie.

"I've never been to Canarsie in my life," said Jeff.

In answer to Louie's questions, he said he did not have a set of keys to his grandmother's house, never went to dance clubs, didn't know anyone in Malverne where Kim's car had been found, and had never heard of the gang called Together Forever. Fortunately for Jeff, but unfortunately for Louie and Rich, the detectives felt he was telling the truth. As the suspect list grew, even Tom developed doubts. He confessed his fears to his wife Lisa. Josh and Jay must be involved somehow, with Josh as the boss, he said.

"These guys had to do it, but nothing is happening," Tom lamented. He called up Louie.

"Louie, maybe I'm wrong," Tom said.

"Nah," replied Louie. "You're not wrong."

As Josh had said, April also backed out of appearing on "America's Most Wanted." April had said she feared that whoever was responsible for Kim's death would come after her, despite the fact that she claimed to have no information about the murder.

Louie got a tip that Michael Dedely had split with his wife, and arranged to talk to him again. The handsome young man came in to the precinct and admitted that he had argued with Kim before her murder—because he did not approve of the guys she was dating. He admitted going to Kim's school several times. Once, he said, he drove by and saw Kim en-

tering the campus, and twice he had parked across the street
from the College of Staten Island entrance and spoken briefly
to Kim when she arrived. He denied ever going onto the
campus or stalking Kim. When she disappeared, he said he
searched for her in the Mill Basin area. He had also met Josh
and Jay.

"I believe they had something to do with it," Michael
said.

Again, a lie detector test confirmed the detective's reading
of the suspect—Michael was telling the truth when he said
he had no involvement in Kim's murder.

Another tip again raised the specter of mob involvement.
Two brothers, who were the sons of a reputed Mafia member,
were said to have argued with Kim. The brothers, who knew
Lee Costello, hung out near Liz Pace's house. April said the
brothers would shout obscenities at her and Kim when they
were dressed up to go clubbing—criticizing their sexy style
of dress, and their dating of black and Hispanic guys. They
directed the invective at April, she said, not at Kim "because
they would always try to get in her pants but she would
refuse." But Liz Pace said that they did not see the boys on
the night Kim vanished. She also said that many boys in the
area would complain about their taste in clothes and men.
She said the yelling incident had happened months earlier.
When Tommy Antonakos was told of the development, he
asked around the neighborhood, and was told that the brothers had nothing to do with it. Further investigation by the
detectives proved that the word on the street was correct.
Another promising lead had bitten the dust. There was more
work to be done, but Louie did not think it was going anywhere.

"America's Most Wanted" cancelled filming after Josh
and April refused to cooperate. Another opportunity to crack
the case had gone down the drain.

It was a good time for some luck. Murder is forever.
There was no statute of limitations for homicide. The laws
of New York State required that Kim's death be investigated.

The case could never be closed until arrests were made. In a way, it was strange that two men who had never met Kim Antonakos had put every part of her life under a microscope after she was dead. Louie and Tom felt as if they knew Kim. In their own way, just like her father, they had promised her justice, and would not rest until it was done. It didn't matter that they had hit a brick wall, or that Tom Shevlin was incapacitated. Tom and Louie, Rich, and the detectives who succeeded them, would try to lock up Kim's killers for as long as she was dead. The sole bit of good news was that the detectives only had to be lucky once.

To avoid justice, the bad guys had to be lucky forever.

CHAPTER TWENTY-ONE

WHO FRAMED ROGER RABBIT?

Louie was awakened by the phone in the middle of a peaceful June night. For a change, he was not out working overtime, but home in bed catching up on some sleep. On the phone was a lieutenant from the Queens Homicide Squad, who had gotten a call saying that a guy named Sean Rideout, who had been arrested in Brooklyn for a robbery in Staten Island, had a whole scrapbook of newspaper clippings about the murder of Kim Antonakos. The name did not ring any bells with Louie. Sean, the lieutenant said, was facing life in prison because he was a career criminal on probation. He would have to finish his complete sentence, as well as whatever years he got for the fresh robbery. He was in a mood to deal, so Sean began giving up other stickup artists on Staten Island. When Detective Paul Kwiecinski asked Sean why he saved clippings about Kim's killing, Sean said that he knew who had killed her. Louie did not want to get dressed and go into the Brooklyn precinct for yet another wild goose chase.

"Do me a favor," Louie said. "Find out if this is bullshit."

The lieutenant said he would. Louie went back to sleep. The phone rang three hours later. It was the same boss calling. He said it was bullshit, and Louie rolled over again. Soon after, the phone rang for a third time. It was the detective who had collared Sean Rideout.

"You better get down here," the detective said. "This guy's sitting in a cell, he's giving it up." Maybe all those WANTED posters had paid off, Louie thought. The investigator said his partner was interviewing the guy. He told Louie that the mutt was naming five guys—two of them his own brothers. One of the brothers, he claimed, was the driver. He said the guys he was naming were all members of a gang called Together Forever.

Suddenly, Louie was awake—he asked for the names, but Psycho was not one of them. Louie was still skeptical, but he had to check it out. What if these guys had done it as a favor to their buddy Psycho? He showered, dressed, and drove into Brooklyn. When he arrived at the Brooklyn stationhouse, Sean was in an interview room, talking his head off. Louie, who was joined by Rich Tirelli, introduced himself to Sean.

"I'm telling you, my brother was the driver," said Sean. He said that he had nothing to do with the murder, but that he had overheard Together Forever gang members bragging about the torching. It was a deadly serious business, but the story he told took on a surreal quality because of the silly nicknames of some of the gang members Sean said had discussed the slaying, like "Zance," "Elite," "Basher," and "Roger Rabbit."

In April, Sean said, he was at the Brooklyn apartment shared by Together Forever gang members "Roger Rabbit," "Basher," "Elite," and Sean's half-brother Louis. Roger Rabbit's real name was Michael Garrett.

Roger Rabbit had been named after the main character of the 1988 movie *Who Framed Roger Rabbit*. The film was a combination cartoon and live-action film noir detective story that featured a large white cartoon rabbit and actor Bob Hoskins. Produced in a collaboration between Disney and Steven Spielberg, it had eye-popping special effects. The plot turned on the hyper-kinetic, long-eared protagonist, who was framed for a murder in a bizarre 1947 Los Angeles, where the detective and other human beings co-exist in the same city alongside another community of "Toon" characters.

The young man called Roger Rabbit was the author of the "Beauty and the Beast" pamphlet about Together Forever that threatened the death penalty for informing on or showing disrespect to the gang. The others who had allegedly bragged of the murder were TF leader Paul Rivera, known as Zance, Saul Kaleel, who liked to be called Elite, and Sean's two half-brothers, Dave Watts and Louis Rideout. Sean said that his girlfriend *Dolly Tyler was also a witness. Sean told Louie Pia that Zance and Roger Rabbit were sitting on a couch, watching a karate movie, when Zance made a karate punch in the air and said, "That's how I hit the bitch."

"Chill," said Roger Rabbit. "Don't even talk about it. We already burnt the bitch—the shit is dead and over with."

Sean said that Zance's girlfriend, a short white girl with sandy blonde hair, about twenty or twenty-two, came in from another room and scolded the gang leader.

"Why you talking about that?" she asked. "That was my friend, but she's gone now."

A few days later, Sean said, he had witnessed another argument about the slaying in the same apartment.

"They had me drive them to Queens, and the cops could have gotten my plate number," Dave told Sean "That's fucked up. That's foul. I ain't fucking with this shit no more. I ain't going to jail for killing this girl." Dave then stormed out of the apartment, Sean claimed.

"That shook one," said his half-brother Louis.

Roger Rabbit turned to Sean and gave him a warning:

"Don't be talking about this to nobody," Roger Rabbit cautioned. "This is T-F business. You're not a T-F member and shouldn't be talking about shit that doesn't concern you."

Sean said he then went downstairs and spoke to his brother Dave outside.

"They set me up and got me involved in some heavy bullshit," said Dave. "Don't fuck with them—they'll get you in some heavy trouble."

Dave was out on probation and $1000 bail for shoplifting on Staten Island. Louis was already in jail in the Brooklyn House of Detention, charged with the attempted murder of a cop. Sean dictated and signed a statement describing everything he had said.

Louie Pia still didn't see any connection to Josh or Jay, or even to Psycho, but he had to proceed. Over the next few days he worked non-stop. He got pedigrees on the entire cast of characters, and brought in Sean's girlfriend, Dolly. She backed up Sean's story, and also gave a statement to detectives in which she claimed that Roger Rabbit and two guys called Eli and "Forty Cents," joked and laughed about burning a girl alive. Dolly described an entire alleged conversation between three men, complete with facial expressions:

> "Fuck that now—the bitch is dead, we done burnt the bitch," smirked Roger Rabbit.
> "Stop talking about that shit," said Eli.
> "Fuck that, the bitch is dead already," Roger Rabbit laughed.
> "She must have deserved it," chuckled Forty Cents.
> "Fuck her. Word up."
> ("Word up" was street slang for "shut up.")

Louie now had two people giving "directs," saying Together Forever gangsters had joked about killing Kim. In the early hours of June 6th, he went to a phone and woke up Julian Wise from the Queens DA's office at his Manhattan apartment. Julian was wide awake immediately—revved by the developments. He needed closure on the case and was eager to get started, but he was concerned that there was no Josh connection.

"Is this guy just trying to get out-from-under?" Julian asked Louie. "Do you have anything else?"

Louie told him about the girlfriend's corroborating statement. He said the guy was ratting out his own brothers. It

was beginning to look good, but there was a lot of work to
do.

"You gotta come down to the Crown Heights precinct,"
Louie urged.

"You gotta be out of your mind. All right, I'll come but
you gotta get me an escort from the bridge," joked Julian.
"I'm a small Jew in a white car."

The precinct where Julian was bound had four years earlier been the epicenter of riots, in which black street toughs
attacked Jews, after a car in a Rabbi's motorcade had accidentally killed a black child. One young Orthodox Jew, Yan-
kel Rosenbaum, was stabbed to death simply because he was
Jewish.

Louie and Rich tracked down Dave Watts and brought
him into the precinct.

"We know what you did," Louie told Dave, once he was
sitting in the interrogation room chair.

"I had nothing to do with that," Dave protested.

Dave was told he was facing life behind bars—but could
still get a good deal if he told what he knew. But even after
he found out that his brother Sean was giving him up as the
driver, Dave maintained his innocence. He agreed to take a
lie detector test to prove his innocence. It looked like it was
starting to fall apart—bad guys rarely offer to take polygraph
tests. Dave was put on the box and asked only four simple
questions by Queens DA's Office Detective Al Velardi:

"Did you drive anyone to a house in Queens that the
person you now know to be Kimberly was killed in?"

"No."

Dave's vital signs jumped in a characteristic swing. He
was attempting deception, Al decided. He was lying.

"Do you know for sure who burned the person you know
to be Kimberly in the house in Queens on March fourth?"

"No."

Again, the machine registered deception by indicating
strong, inconsistent, and unresolved responses to the question.

"Did you take part in a plan that resulted in the death of the person you know to be Kimberly Antonakos on March fourth?"

"No."

The telltale signs of deception again surfaced.

"Before last week, did you definitely know about the girl being burned in a house in Queens?"

"No."

More deception was recorded.

Two witnesses said that Dave was the driver, and he had just flunked his lie detector test. Either the box was wrong, or Dave was in on it. Louie confronted Dave in a marathon six-hour session, along with Rich Tirelli and Julian Wise from the DA's office. Over and over they asked Dave about the torch house, about Kim's car, about her cellular phone, her beeper, her jewelry, the large gold cross around her neck, and other details of the case.

"All right, all right, I drove there," Dave said, at last.

He told them he was an unwitting accomplice, and that Zance was the ringleader who told him where to drive on the night of the murder. After dictating a statement about how the gang members smelled of gas after returning to the car, Louie and Rich took Dave for a ride. They asked him to direct them to the Woodhaven house, but he said Zance had told him to turn here, turn there, and he did not remember the way. When they pulled onto Eighty-sixth Avenue, Louie asked Dave to identify the house. He looked around and pointed to the house where Kim died. It was the only home on the block that was charred, and had plywood over the windows.

The investigators put Dave on video with his confession, but Julian felt that getting details was like pulling teeth. Dave said he couldn't be sure, but he thought he had seen Zance wearing Kim's large gold cross around his neck after the murder. After the video was complete, a worried Julian paced up and down in the hallway.

"I don't know, I don't know," said Julian to Rob Ferino.

It troubled Julian and Louie that there was no clear-cut motive for the murder. The dots did not yet seem to connect. Louie alerted Tommy Antonakos that arrests might be made in his daughter's case, but withheld details.

Together Forever chieftain Zance was arrested on a charge of murder. Louie asked Zance if he knew anything about the death of Kim Antonakos.

"Yeah, I heard about that," said Zance. "I even questioned Psycho about it."

He said he had heard that Psycho was a suspect, but that when asked, Psycho denied having anything to do with the murder. Apparently, Zance, who had arrests for the theft, robbery, drugs, and gun possession, did not approve of the burning of the beautiful girl. He seemed surprised when Louie told him that he had been named as the head killer. He remained cool and denied it again and again. Zance agreed to go on the lie detector and he passed with flying colors—bad news for authorities.

The detectives picked up Elite, who also vehemently denied involvement. He consented to go on the box, too, and passed. More bad news.

Roger Rabbit's records showed that he was due to show up in court for a hearing on an old charge, so Louie waited in the courtroom and picked him up. They now held five suspects—two of whom were ratting the others out. When Louie brought Roger Rabbit into the precinct, Rich was startled by the suspect's appearance. It was easy to see where he got his nickname, Rich chuckled to himself—Roger Rabbit *looked* like a rabbit. He had a goofy, bifurcated Afro hairdo that flopped off the top of his head and stuck out sideways, like two big bunny ears. He also had large buck teeth, many of which had been covered with shiny gold caps.

They went hard at Roger Rabbit. They told him that he was under arrest for murder, and his eyes popped open in shock. Unlike his cool leader Zance, Roger Rabbit wigged out. When he was told that police had confessions and that he was a main bad guy, he burst out crying, and fell out of his chair like his legs were made of rubber.

"I didn't do it. I didn't do it," Roger Rabbit sobbed, crawling around on the floor on his hands and knees. "I swear to God I have no involvement!" he moaned.

It was quite a performance, his dramatic protestations almost cartoon-like. Louie and Rich had never seen anything like it. Suddenly, in mid-wail, Roger Rabbit's tears shut off like a faucet.

"Wait a minute," he said, calmly looking up from the floor. "What day was this?"

"March fourth," said Louie.

"Fuckin' Zance was in jail in Union City, New Jersey, that day," said Roger Rabbit. "For taking a gun on a plane at Newark Airport."

Louie called the Union City cops, and Zance had taken a collar and was in a cell on that date. But was it really Zance, or was it a set-up for just such an occasion—insurance? Another detective was dispatched to Union City with Zance's picture to compare with the mug shot there. Roger Rabbit was administered a lie detector test and also passed.

A few hours later, the detective called from New Jersey with the news—they were the same guy. Zance had been arrested in January, and served ninety-seven days of a 180-day sentence. He was released until May third. If Zance had been in jail in Jersey, he could not have torched Kim—jail was an ironclad alibi. It was the only occasion on which incarceration was a blessing to a crook. The whole thing seemed to be collapsing like a house of cards. Louie was convinced it had all been bullshit. He felt that Sean was simply trying to avoid spending the rest of his young life behind bars. But why had his brother Dave flunked the poly? They decided to give a second polygraph exam to Dave and he flunked it again. The whole thing was turning into a nightmare—a defense lawyer's dream. There seemed to be only four possibilities. Machine failure seemed unlikely, as did operator error. That meant that either Dave was a very, very nervous guy whose aberrant physiological responses skewed the results, or he was telling the truth. But since the same machine had already cleared Zance, Elite, and Roger Rabbit, how could Dave be telling the truth? The only thing that came to Louie's mind was that Dave might have had guilty knowledge of a different murder—not Kim's. Maybe that was making the box go wild? Louie confronted Sean who stubbornly stuck to his story—his brothers Louis and Dave were in on it, and so were Zance, Elite, and Roger Rabbit. Louie had had enough. He was angry, and had to resolve the conflict.

"You're gonna tell your brother to his face," Louie shouted, grabbing Sean and leading him toward the room where Dave was sitting.

Sean protested, but Louie insisted. As they walked to the room, Sean still swore he was telling the truth. But when Louie brought Sean into the room and put the brothers face-to-face, Sean broke down, wailing and sobbing. He fell on his hands and knees—like Roger Rabbit—at his brother's feet.

"I love you, man," he cried, apologizing for what he had done. "I don't want to go to jail for life. I only made you the driver."

It was over. The whole thing had burst like a cartoon balloon. Roger Rabbit and the rest of the gang had been framed by Sean so he could get out from under the three-time-loser sentence that he faced. Louie, Rich, and Julian did not see any humor in the situation. Julian was crushed. Discussing what had gone wrong, they realized that Sean and Dave had used the questions they asked to supply them with details about the crime. They had fed it right back to them. Louie voided the arrests of Zance and Roger Rabbit, and cut everyone—except Sean—loose. Sean would now go down for his crimes. Louie gritted his teeth and picked up the phone. He was exhausted, but had to tell Tommy Antonakos that the whole thing—a week of work—had been a false alarm.

Kim's killers were still free.

CHAPTER TWENTY-TWO

SMOKED

Joey, glancing around cautiously, pulled his Nissan inside the garage that he rented for $100 a month. He parked and took his gold Pulsar wristwatch with the brown leather band away from Bobby, who had fallen asleep playing with it on their way home from a visit to Antonette's girlfriend. Earlier in the day it had been partially sunny and hot, with a high of 80 degrees. After dark, the air had chilled to almost 65 degrees, with a light breeze. By the time they arrived at the garage, Joey, clad from head to toe in a Fila designer sports outfit, was a bit cold. He was wearing a Yankee pin-stripe short-sleeve shirt, and knee-length denim shorts held up by a brown leather web belt. On his feet were black Fila sports sandals without socks. Joey checked the time. It was 1 a.m., June 23rd. Holding the watch in his left hand, Joey picked Bobby up and put the sleeping child over his shoulder. Joey and Antonette began walking toward Jamaica Avenue, in the direction of their apartment on 107th Street in Richmond Hill, Queens, two blocks away. The clattering of a train on the elevated subway line could be heard receding into the distance. After they had walked half a dozen steps, a thin shadow sneaked swiftly from the shadows and up behind Joey on his right. The man leveled a pistol at the back of Joey's head, pressed the gun barrel against his skull and fired.

BANG!

The explosive muzzle flash of the weapon lit up the sidewalk like a camera's flashbulb and scorched Joey's hair and scalp. A single brass shell casing was ejected from the gun, flew through the air, and landed on the sidewalk with a hollow musical tinkle. Joey never knew what hit him. For an execution, it was swift and merciful—far more humane than the way Kim had died. In a split second, the slug perforated his cervical spinal cord and brain before it passed out of the left side of his face and sped only inches above the head of the dozing tot in his arms. Joey's life functions shut off like a switch. He crumpled to the pavement on top of Bobby, dead before he hit the ground. Incredibly, Bobby was still asleep underneath Joey's body from which streams of dark blood gushed onto the sidewalk in a spreading puddle. Still clutched in Joey's left fist was his watch, which Bobby had been playing with. For Joey, time had run out. Antonette had jumped at the shot, which sounded like an M-80 firecracker going off. She fell to her knees, and saw a man running away toward what looked like a blue Honda with its lights off. He jumped in the passenger seat of the car, which sped away. Antonette, in a frenzy of panic, saw Joey and Bobby both lying still on the pavement in a pool of blood.

"My baby! My baby!" she screamed, as she tugged at her son, who was pinned under the dead weight of her lover.

She probed for a pulse at Joey's wrist, but felt none. She then clawed Bobby from under Joey and picked him up. Bobby had a red bump on his forehead, but did not seem to be wounded.

"Please, somebody, help me!" Antonette shrieked. "Somebody shot my husband! Somebody shot my husband! They shot him! They shot him!"

As she screamed the words over and over, running around desperately, lights went on in apartments and windows opened. She ran toward the corner, cradling her son, fearing that the killer might return. Bobby woke up, unaware of what had happened, and began crying. Antonette shouted to some guys in a passing Bronco. She asked them to follow the gunman's car, and they sped off. Residents began dialing 911. The men in the Bronco returned, and said they had lost the speeding car. Soon, Antonette heard a distant siren coming closer. Tucked in Joey's pants, police found his unfired .380 automatic pistol. Even if he had seen the gunman lurking in the dark, Joey would not have been able to defend himself because he was holding Bobby. He also was carrying a folding knife, a matchbook, five dollars and forty cents in cash—and a brown envelope containing some beads and medallions. They were Joey's Santeria beads, which should have been worn around his neck for protection.

Antonette told police every detail of the shooting. But when they asked what Joey did for a living, she began giving vague answers. She said she did not work, either, but they were able to pay their rent, operate a car, and pay for the luxury of a garage. One of the detectives who responded to the murder scene was Johnny Wilde, a detective who did not work in the One-Oh-Two Precinct, but lived in the area. He liked to keep up on all the crime in his neighborhood, where he worked, and around the city.

"I'm a nosey guy," Johnny would joke when asked what he was doing at a crime scene he was not assigned to. "I'm always sticking my nose in."

To Johnny, it seemed like just another drug hit. The guy was unemployed, well-dressed, drove a car, and carried a gun. He wasn't a cop, he was a mutt on parole. The computer showed that Joey had a history of arrests for assault, weapons possession, selling guns, reckless endangerment, resisting arrest, and attempted murder. The chances were good-to-excellent that he was just another victim of a business dispute in the drug trade. Of course, no one other than the guy's common-law wife had seen or heard anything. After the crime-scene photos had been shot, a van from the Medical Examiner's Office arrived. Joey's body was placed into a body bag, and loaded into the van. The body was taken to the ME's office, where Dr. Kari Reiber, the pathologist who had done the autopsy on Kim Antonakos, was waiting to do a post-mortem exam on Joey's remains.

"Do you know why anyone would want to shoot your husband?" one detective asked the red-eyed Antonette some time later.

"No," Antonette replied. "But I heard from my downstairs neighbor that he had had an argument with someone in the park earlier in the day."

She did not mention Joey's mysterious tape.

Early on the morning of June 23rd, Antonette called Nick to tell him that his best friend had been killed. Nick called Josh to ask if he had heard that somebody had shot Joey.

"That's what happens to snakes," Josh replied. It was both a statement and a warning.

Jay got a call from Joey's mother that her son had been gunned down in the street while holding his kid and walking with Antonette. Jay gave his condolences. Then he picked up the phone and called Josh.

"What's up, Josh?"

"What's up?"

"Guess what happened?"

"What happened?"

"Somebody smoked Joey."

"Oh, really?" Josh asked in a sarcastic voice.

"Yes. Come and check."

"No, I'm not going out there. Come out here," said Josh, obviously unwilling to discuss it on the phone.

Josh had learned to be careful about telephones. Jay jumped in a cab and went to see Josh. He was at April's, babysitting his baby.

"Hey, yo—I wonder what happened? Pretty fucked up what happened to Joey," said Jay, as he walked into the apartment.

"Yo—he deserved it," said Josh.

"Just tell me the truth—I know you did it."

"I smoked his ass," Josh confessed proudly, as his little son played nearby. "He was gonna flip. I knew where he parked his car and I waited on the block for him to come home. When Joey pulled into the garage, he got out with his baby, and was walking up the block. I creeped up behind him. When he was about to turn the corner, I hit him—I shot him in the back of the head—Boom! Joey had the baby in his hands at the time, and he fell on top of the baby. She turned around, and I walked away. I looked back once. I heard Antonette scream. I know the bitch saw me, but I'm not worried. I ran back to the car, jumped in the passenger seat, and the guy took off.''

Jay did not take Josh to task for the murder. In fact, he didn't care for Joey at all—especially after Joey had tried to set them up.

''I got rid of the gun, I took it apart. They ain't never gonna find it. I had to kill Joey because of the fingerprint,'' Josh continued. ''Keep it to yourself. If you say anything. I'll kill you next. If I can't get you, I'll get what's closest to you.''

Jay remembered when he and Josh were kids. When Josh fled his troubled home, Jay's mom took Josh in—just like Kim did later. They had grown up like brothers, but Jay knew that meant nothing to Josh. Jay's sister had kicked Jay out of her apartment that spring. Jay had then moved into a first-floor apartment with an old girlfriend. One night, shortly after Joey's murder, Jay got out of bed at two 2 o'clock in the morning to get a glass of water. As Jay walked into the kitchen, he jumped. Someone was at the kitchen window, peering in at him. It was Josh. He had been peeping into Jay's apartment. Metal security gates prevented him from getting in. Jay was a street guy and he knew the code of the street required that he show Josh he wasn't scared of him—especially since he was. Josh had to go away chilled out. He had to think that everything was cool. It was the street version of a lie detector test. Jay's gut instinct told him that he was not welcoming his boyhood friend Josh—he was dealing with a dangerous, cornered street animal that could smell fear.

"If Josh thinks I'm scared, he'll kill me," Jay thought to himself, as he opened the window.

"What's up? What're you doing?" Josh asked casually.

"Nothin'," Jay said, shrugging his shoulders. He told Josh he had been in bed.

"I was just checking. I just wanted to see how you were doing," Josh smiled coldly.

Josh asked Jay to come for a ride alone with him, as if it was normal for him to drop by, uninvited, in the middle of the night. Jay declined.

"C'mon out. Let's go for a ride," Josh insisted.

"No, man, I'm chillin'," said Jay.

They talked about nothing for a while, tensely shooting the breeze, until Josh returned to the real subject at hand—his adversaries, the detectives Louie and Tom.

"You sure you didn't talk to them?" Josh demanded, staring into Jay's eyes.

"No, man" said Jay, telling the truth with a yawn.

Jay made all the right noises to calm Josh, but was convinced Josh wanted a bloodbath, wanted to be the last man standing. After Josh left, Jay decided that Nick wasn't so dumb to go to California for a while. Between the detectives who wanted him to take lie detector tests, and the million-dollar reward over their heads, Jay felt he might end up in jail. Worse, with the imagined fear of mob vengeance, and Josh running around whacking people, there were just too many ways to die. The next day, Jay began making plans. In a few days, he was on a jet to sunny Puerto Rico with his girlfriend. Jay felt it was time for a nice, long vacation. As Joey's funeral was being planned, his maroon Nissan pulled up in front of Nick's house. Joey's sister Tina and a friend were inside.

"How's your family?" Nick asked Tina sympathetically.

"My brother left a tape, and wanted it given to the police in the event of his death," Tina replied.

Joey's relatives were frightened by the situation he had put them in. They had listened to the twenty-minute tape, but it made no sense to them. It seemed to be some guys talking about a girl and about the cops. It was difficult to understand what was being said, and there were a lot of blank spots. Joey's voice was not on the tape, and neither was Nick's. Nick listened to Tina with growing fear about what Joey had told his family—how he was going to Hell for a terrible sin, and wanted the cops to get the tape because it was about the horrible thing he had done. Tina had no idea that Nick was involved in the crime. Even when Joey had implicated himself in his call to Louie Pia, he had protected his close friend Nick, and kept him out of it. He had even expunged Nick's voice from the tape so it couldn't be used against his buddy in court. But when it came to a choice between the safety of his best friend's widow, and his own security, Nick did not hesitate. He was eager to stay on Josh's good side, keen to prove he was not a snake. As soon as he was alone, Nick drove directly to the place where Josh was staying and told his new best friend about the tape.

The news hit Josh like a shot to the head. Reeling, he unleashed a string of useless obscenities against Joey and his *post mortem* revenge. After his fury subsided, Josh ordered Nick—since he was one of the family—to question Antonette about the tape. Nick did not want to end up like Joey, or in jail, so he became a spy. When Nick asked Antonette what Joey had on tape, she reassured her friend that Joey had made sure he would not be involved.

"You have nothing to worry about," she said.

Nick reported back to Josh, who, of course, was not comforted that Nick was in the clear. He told him to go back. Nick had not quite figured out that Josh was only worried about Josh. He went back to Antonette, who was becoming suspicious about his persistent questions. He asked her if the tape "was about the girl who got burnt."

"No," Antonette replied. "The tape is about something different. It was nothing about that."

Again, Nick dutifully reported to Josh, who did not believe Antonette. What else could the tape be about?

Josh was sick of evasions and decided that if you wanted a job done, you had better do it yourself. When Nick showed up on Antonette's doorstep a third time, this time with Josh at his side, her worst fears had been confirmed. Nick was with Josh. She was terrified.

"I been hearing around Canarsie something about a tape," said Josh in a threatening voice. "Where's the tape at?"

"It was destroyed," Antonette told them.

Josh eyed her with suspicion. He did not believe her. She was lying. He and Nick left, but Josh made it clear they would be back. Josh had to get that tape. If the cops had gotten it, Josh knew he wouldn't still be on the street. If he could get the tape or intimidate those who had it, he might protect himself. But if anybody else got killed, maybe the tape would go to the police. It was a Mexican standoff, but Josh was never one to leave well enough alone. Nick asked Josh if he was going to Joey's wake and funeral with him.

"No," said Josh, "because the detectives, Lou and Tom from the One-Oh-Two, might see me and put it together."

Josh didn't want Nick to go either, but Nick felt that he had to. At the funeral, Nick was spooked—virtually speechless and wide-eyed with fear. Antonette thought that he looked whiter-than-white. It was like he had seen a ghost. She overheard Nick's girlfriend scolding him that he was not supposed to be at the funeral. Nick sobbed as he looked at Joey's casket, surrounded by a garden of sweet-smelling flowers, but he was not crying only for Joey. Nick felt very alone. The Madrina had been right—Nick's spirit guide, his spiritual protector, had left him when he needed him the most.

Tyisia, whom Joey had promised to escort to her prom, and take out to dinner for her junior high school graduation, arrived at the service in her cap and gown. Before the casket was closed, she tearfully placed her prom corsage next to him in the coffin. The minister read from the 123rd Psalm, which looked for mercy from the Lord "as the eyes of a maiden looked on the hands of her mistress."

"Our soul is exceedingly filled with the scorning of those that are at ease and with the contempt of the proud." Joey's Uncle Luis hoped that the Lord would forgive Joey, right then and there.

"I hope that he is with the Lord," Luis prayed.

A few days later, Josh and Nick called Antonette and showed up at her door again. This time, they claimed to be interested in her Aunt Susan's car, which was for sale. But rather than simply look the car over, Josh insisted that Antonette and her aunt drive the car to some place in Queens.

"Where's the tape?" Josh suddenly asked Susan.

"I don't know anything about it," Susan replied.

Susan and Antonette were very suspicious and put Josh and Nick off. Then Antonette heard a terrifying rumor on the street:

"You're going to be kidnapped and killed, and—like an example—put in front of Antonakos' grave," was the word she got from someone who claimed it had come from the killers.

Antonette left her apartment with her son and went into hiding with relatives. She was convinced that she, maybe even her son, would be the next victims—but neither she nor anyone else went to the police. More and more people knew about the tape, and the connection between the murders of Joey and Kim Antonakos, but no one did anything about it. The code of the streets dictated that anyone who squealed was asking for it. The only person who had been willing to talk to the cops about Kim's death had been silenced with a bullet through his brain. No one else was volunteering. While Antonette and her son were in hiding, little Bobby was watching television with a friend when a shooting scene came on the screen.

"That's like what happened to me and Poppa Joey," Bobby told his friend. "I got shot in the head and they killed Poppa Joey. My mother cried for two days."

Bobby then took his pretty, multicolored bouquet of

helium-filled birthday balloons and brought them outside onto the littered Queens sidewalk. Framed by the rusty Jamaica Avenue elevated subway line and the surrounding dingy buildings, Bobby craned his neck and looked up to a visible patch of blue sky above his head. He released his grip on the balloon ribbons, and they flew silently upward. He watched them with a smile as they floated up and away from the dirty street, grinning until they shrank from sight and vanished.

"What are you doing, Bobby?" his Aunt Susan asked.

"I'm sending the balloons to Poppa Joey," Bobby answered. "Poppa Joey is with the angels."

CHAPTER TWENTY-THREE

BLONDIE

Josh loved to discuss his crimes near police precincts—it gave him a real charge. In mid-July, Josh was standing at a pay phone in front of the Seven-Five stationhouse in East New York, Brooklyn, with his friend Mike Castillo. Looking at them from a REWARD poster on a lamppost next to the telephone box was the smiling face of Kim Antonakos. Her eyes were looking directly at them. Josh stared at Kim's image and smirked.

"Do you know who killed Joey?" Josh asked Mike, looking around quickly.

"No," replied Mike.

"I did," said Josh, with a smile.

"What?"

"In the middle of the night, I was watching Joey," Josh explained. "On that night, I saw Joey walking by his house . . . he was walking with his wife and carrying his baby. I went up behind him and shot him in the back of the head."

Josh told Mike about the kidnapping, and how it had gone sour. He said that Joey had to be killed because he had "left fingerprints on Kimberly's car." And was talking to the cops.

"I wasn't going to stand alone," said Josh. "If the cops grabbed Joey, he would have given me up. I had to kill him."

He spoke about the reason for the kidnapping and how he had been the instigator.

"I knew that her father had a lot of money," he said.

Josh explained how they took her to "the hideout" in Queens by Franklin K. Lane High School. This was Joey's sweet house. Joey had used the house in the past for other things. But when they returned to the cold basement after three days, "Kimberly was frozen to death," said Josh.

"It was very cold down in the basement, and he wouldn't give her a blanket or food for two or three days."

In Josh's version of events, Josh was almost an avenging angel, and Joey the rat was the bad guy completely responsible for Kim's death. He described buying the gas can and the gas in detail.

"When we got back to the house, Joey wouldn't go downstairs. I told him he was a pussy. So only Nick and me went downstairs. Before I burned Kimberly, I talked to her. I kissed her on the forehead and said, 'Shit happens. Sorry it had to happen this way.' I put the gas on Kimberly, lit her, stayed there for a few minutes, then left the house," Josh said.

"I had to kill Joey because Joey made a tape about the murder and I was worried about that."

Of course, Josh had no idea that Joey had made a tape until after Joey was dead, but it made a better story that way. Josh spoke as if everything was all over, as if it was history. It had been almost five months since Kim's murder, and Joey was in the ground a month. The cops had nothing. Josh felt he was smarter than the cops. He had gotten away with murder—twice—and was bragging about it in front of a stationhouse. Josh was bad and wanted everyone to know it. Josh's tale was a complete story. There was a brave hero—himself; there was a villain—Joey; and the yarn had a moral: Anyone who tries to talk to the cops gets killed. Mike, who also had an arrest record, had been Josh's friend for about six years. He could have safely walked the few steps into the precinct and reported to the cops inside that Josh had just admitted two murders. But Mike's sister had had a child with Josh's buddy Jay. Mike considered Jay his brother-in-law, and did not want to get him in trouble. Besides, although Mike did not have a college degree, he was smart enough to have no interest in following in Joey's footsteps. He kept his mouth shut.

Josh was glad that he had gotten away with it, but he was still unhappy. He still didn't have his own set of wheels, but was able to occasionally use April's car—the baby-blue Nissan hatchback. It was a far cry from Josh's dream car. He was still a man without a home, and had been forced to stay with various friends and relatives after April ejected him from his comfortable life at her apartment. What Josh wanted was another woman to support him, give him sex, money, a set of wheels, and bed and board. Things were so bad that Josh had actually been reduced to getting a job. He had been hired on a commission basis by a Health Maintenance Organization to try to get people to switch medical insurance carriers.

One of the first people that Josh tried out his salesmanship on, at the end of July, was a twenty-five-year-old mother of four named Raquel Montalvo, whom everyone called Blondie. Blondie—who was not related to Antonette or her mother Jeanette—lived in an apartment on Bradford Street in the East New York section of Brooklyn, and was a widow with long, strawberry blonde hair, and big blue eyes. She was stacked, and very friendly. She had been Jay's girlfriend for a time, but was dating a guy named *Rocky. Josh stopped by Raquel's apartment one day, to ask Rocky to fix the timing chain on April's car. Rocky was not there, and Josh began to chat Blondie up. Also in the apartment were Blondie's children: two boys, aged five and three, and two girls, aged six and eight months.

"I been having problems with my baby's mother," said Josh, who turned on the charm.

He did not mention that April had chucked him out for cheating on her. He lent a sympathetic ear to Blondie's troubles, especially the death of her ex-husband. Blondie's first husband had become a junkie, an intravenous drug abuser, but he was not murdered. He had committed suicide after contracting a fatal disease.

"I know what it's like to have someone die," Josh said, looking earnestly into Blondie's eyes.

"He seems so kind," Blondie thought. "He has kind eyes."

To Josh, Blondie seemed almost perfect. She had a nice apartment, money in the bank, a car, and a hot blue motorcycle. Besides, Josh had heard that Blondie was about to get a big chunk of cash from an insurance settlement. He swept Blondie off her feet with his sensitive act, promising always to be there for her and her kids. Josh asked her if he could move in. It might have seemed unlikely that a scrawny, lazy, shifty-eyed ex-con like Josh would be able to find more than one young woman in Brooklyn willing to keep him—but Josh moved into Blondie's apartment on August 1st. Some young women could not resist falling for the bad boys their mothers had warned them about. When she invited Josh into her bed, Blondie—who herself had never been in trouble with the law—became a two-time loser.

After he moved in, Josh's only visitor was his heavy-set, dark-skinned friend called Redrum.

Josh's beeper went off on a regular basis, and most of the beeps were from Redrum or April. When April beeped him, he would call her back, and often drive to her apartment. He spent a lot of time there, and claimed to be babysitting his son, but Blondie was not happy about it.

Near the end of August, Blondie was in bed with Josh when his beeper went off.

"It's my baby's mother," said Josh, who obviously intended to call the other woman.

Blondie was angry. She was sick of it. The guy was in her bed and he was living off her, but he kept going to see his old girlfriend.

"She keeps beeping you, and you keep running out to

call her," snapped Blondie. "You probably are still seeing her, and, if that's the case, I don't want to be involved with you anymore—I can't trust you."

Blondie did not know she was playing with fire by threatening to kick Josh out.

"The only reason I go over there is because the police are investigating me for something," said Josh. "The police told my baby's mother that they had a witness that saw me cleaning off a car, and also about a partial print on file."

Josh pretended that it had been him, not Joey, who had wiped off Kim's car. When Blondie asked what he was talking about, he said it was better if he did not give her an answer.

"I can tell you what's going on, but you probably wouldn't like it," Josh said.

"If I can't trust you, and you can't tell me why the police are looking for you, then I can't be with you," said Blondie, in an ultimatum that set Josh off.

"They're looking for me because I killed somebody!" Josh screamed in sudden fury, startling Blondie. "Then I had to kill somebody else, because he was trying to put the blame on me, because he made a tape, and was probably talking to the police! I figured I had to take him out before I got caught."

Blondie was sorry she had asked, but Josh could not take back his words. Josh told her the whole story. She had never met Kim, but she knew Jay, Joey, and Nick. Blondie was having trouble believing that Josh had really done what he claimed.

"We had done this before, but it never got this out of hand," said Josh. "We left this girl tied up for a few days, and we were arguing about who was going to feed her."

As usual, Josh embellished his account. He claimed to have kicked Kim in the ribs and hit her in the head, in an effort to revive her. He also claimed to have stripped her of her clothing before he put the match to her.

"Before I lit her up, I kissed her on the forehead and said,

'I'm sorry it has to end this way, but life sucks.' I wasn't sure if she was dead before, but she was dead after that,'' Josh said with a smile.

When Blondie gave Josh a look of disbelief, he got up, rummaged through his things, and pulled out a charred patch of some kind of material. When Blondie asked what it was, Josh replied, "It's a souvenir."

When she saw the burned scrap, a chill went up her spine. Blondie no longer doubted Josh's story.

"Why did you kill the girl like that?" Blondie demanded in an angry voice. "You have no remorse for this girl?"

"No," Josh said. "Why should I? Would you? I have no feeling for nobody," he replied with a sneer that frightened Blondie. "The bitch deserved it, she deserved what she got. She shouldn't've died like that, but the shit went wrong. It was over money. We did it before, but the shit got fucked up."

Josh blamed Kim for dying.

"The father was some kind of big shot," Josh continued. "I believe somebody snitched on me because the father believes I was involved." Josh paused, and spoke again.

"Well, that's not all I did." He told her that he blamed Joey for screwing up the ransom calls, and not feeding Kim or keeping her warm. Joey had to die, he said, because he had been stupid enough to leave a fingerprint on Kim's car. Josh described the hit on Joey.

"Redrum was with me," said Josh, who then boasted about passing a police polygraph.

"I passed it because I was trummed-up on pot," Josh explained with a self-satisfied smile.

"Are you crazy?" Blondie asked. "Are you sick?"

Josh's smile vanished. He glowered at his bedmate and spoke in a calm, icy voice:

"No, I'm not crazy—you're the one who's crazy. Are you going to tell somebody? If you do, you die—I'll kill you," Josh warned.

His eyes, which had seemed so kind, were filled with menace. Blondie said nothing, but knew the threat was not an idle one. Josh settled back in bed. He did not yet have his dream car, but he had Blondie's bike, and another comfortable base of operations. He was still home free. Soon, he was sleeping like a baby. Blondie was not able to go to sleep as quickly. She had learned a great deal more about two murders than she had ever wanted to know. After she heard what Josh was capable of, and saw the look in his eyes when he got angry, Blondie was afraid to throw him out. She suddenly felt like a prisoner in her own home.

Maybe it's all a joke, she told herself, finally. Maybe Josh is just joking.

Soon, she dozed off.

CHAPTER TWENTY-FOUR

DEVIL ON A BLUE BIKE

Blondie was upset that Josh kept getting and answering beeps from April, and leaving her to go to April's place. Josh was also getting beeped on a regular basis by his friend Redrum. On September 3rd, two days after the new death-penalty law went into effect, Josh left the apartment at one in the morning, leaving Blondie alone on a Saturday night. Blondie was very jealous, and very angry. After Josh had told her about the murders, she wanted him out of her house, but she was afraid of what he might do if expelled. She fumed about the situation for hours before taking action. At 4 a.m., Blondie drove over to April's and rang the doorbell. She told April she wanted her to come back with her and take Josh's clothes.

"Come and get his things," she said.

April agreed, but scoffed at Blondie's fear of Josh.

"He's just a wanna-be gangster," she explained.

April accompanied Blondie to her house, and took some of Josh's belongings. Blondie left her motorcycle at Mike Castillo's house to hide it. Josh had begun riding Blondie's motorcycle, tooling around Canarsie on the blue Yamaha 350 with red stripes and telling everyone that the $2,500 'Dirt Bike' belonged to him. Blondie was afraid he might try to steal it. When her eldest son *Luke asked her what was going on, Blondie told him that she was having trouble with Josh and some "bad people."

Sunday morning was a beautiful day. The sky was clear and blue, and the sun began to heat things up to a summery 80 degrees. People on their way to and from church or the nearby park lingered on the street and enjoyed the balmy weather. The sounds of music from different stereos in homes, cars, and on the street filled the air. Blondie was up early. She dressed in shorts and a halter top, fed the baby, and made breakfast for the older children.

At 7:30, Blondie's apartment door exploded off the hinges—kicked in by Josh, who stormed into the apartment spewing obscenities. The noise startled Blondie's eight-month-old daughter, who woke up and began crying. Josh had a wild look in his eye. He punched Blondie in the head, and demanded to know where her motorcycle was.

"What did you do with the bike?" Josh screamed.

"I trashed it," Blondie lied, blood streaming from her nose.

After threatening to torch her home, Josh left. Blondie was badly shaken. She had decided to stand up to Josh, but she had never seen him go off before.

"Get dressed," Blondie told Luke. "These are the bad people, and we have to go to the police."

Blondie called several people, including her friend Mike Castillo, and told him that she wanted to go to the cops because Josh was threatening her and her family. Mike agreed only to come over to watch the kids. But by the time Blondie got behind the wheel of her car to drive to the precinct, Josh pulled up with Redrum. Obviously, someone had alerted them that Blondie was going to the cops. As Josh ran toward Blondie, his eyes were wide with a savage look, and his face was twisted with rage.

"He looks like the Devil," Blondie thought as Josh reached into the car window and grabbed her by the hair on the back of her head.

"You better keep your mouth shut, or I'll kill you!" Josh screamed, shaking her head painfully.

Josh reached down with his other hand, and popped the hood and the trunk open to prevent Blondie from driving away.

"You can be tied up in the garage and burned, too!" Josh threatened.

After demanding the motorcycle again, Josh did something under the hood of the car. Luke, trying to protect his mother, yelled at Josh:

"You're gonna kill my mother, and I'll grow up and kill you!"

Several neighbors on the block had stopped what they were doing and were staring at Josh, who got back into the car and went away. Blondie tried to start the car but it wouldn't turn over. After a few minutes, Mike fixed whatever Josh had done to the engine, and Blondie started the car.

"You can't go alone, I'm involved now," Mike told her. "I know everything that Josh did."

He insisted that he was going to the police.

"Don't you know, Blondie, he was going to tie you up, and burn you in the garage?"

Mike told Blondie that Josh knew about money she had, and money from insurance settlements that she had coming, and wanted to get his hands on it. A short time later, Nick Libretti and another man showed up. With a mean look on his face, Nick warned Blondie not to squeal. After all, if Blondie ratted Josh out, it would be the same thing as squealing on Nick.

"Why would you want to do this to me?" Nick asked.

He asked Blondie to get in his van and take a ride with him, but Blondie was not stupid enough to go. Only the presence of her two brothers protected her from Nick and his friend, Blondie believed.

"I know what you did," Luke defiantly told Nick. "I know everything."

Nick glared at the child with cold eyes.

"I wouldn't want to tie someone up, and burn them up in the garage," Nick told Blondie. "I wouldn't hesitate to tie someone else up. I'm coming back tonight, and I better not find out something happened. I'm going to find Josh, and I'm coming back tonight and take care of this. If they arrested Josh, you're dead. If I have to take your children with me, that's what I'll do. I'll be back." Nick added as he left.

Blondie had no idea that Nick had once put a gun to another child's head and threatened to blow his brains out, but she believed his threat was sincere, anyway. She was convinced that she had to go to the police. But when she got in her car a second time, a vehicle with four men inside pulled into the block and screeched to a halt behind Blondie's car—preventing her from backing out into the street. As Josh, Redrum, and the other men emerged from the car, Blondie became hysterical. She backed the car into her garage, got out and handed the keys to Luke. Josh came running up.

"If you're going to the police, I'm gonna kill you!" Josh yelled, punching Blondie hard in the face.

Blondie staggered back into the garage, and grabbed the first thing she saw—a shovel. She raised it to defend herself, but Josh easily took it away from her. Josh slammed Blondie's face with it and she screamed in pain.

"Stop!" she cried.

But Josh did not stop. He banged her on the head, and in the stomach, knocking her to the concrete garage floor. Again and again, Josh whacked Blondie's flailing knees and legs. Each time, Blondie screamed in pain, and cried "Stop!" before he clubbed her again. Mike, outnumbered four-to-one, did nothing.

"Leave her alone! Let my mommy alone!" Blondie's children screamed at Josh.

He ignored the wailing children and continued to beat their mother, intent on his task, as if he intended to beat her to death. Josh seemed to be enjoying inflicting pain. Also, for a man worried about police attention, he was doing something very stupid. He was attacking a woman in broad daylight in front of her family, a friend, and the entire neighborhood, all of whom could see his face. But Josh could not stop.

"Stop!" shouted a neighbor from her window. "I'm calling the police!"

That broke Josh's concentration. Reluctantly, he stopped, and dropped the shovel. The whole point, he suddenly seemed to remember, was to stay away from the police. Blondie sobbed in pain on the garage floor.

"I'll be back," Josh warned her. "Don't worry, I'll be back to finish this."

Josh and his friends left. Blondie or Mike should have dialed 911, but they didn't. Blondie was intent on preventing Josh from stealing her bike, and Mike wanted to go home. He said he wanted to make sure that his family was safe. A bruised and bloody Blondie had not been at Mike's mother's house long when Josh pulled up in April's van. Josh emerged from the van with a tire iron and smashed the front and rear windshields of Blondie's car, and all the windows on one side.

"I'm going to kill you," he yelled at Blondie again, advancing on her with the tire iron. "I'm going to destroy your life. You won't be walking around, you'll be dead!"

"Leave her alone!" screamed Mike's sister, who came running out of the house brandishing a big knife.

Blondie got on her motorcycle and started it up. She wanted to escape on the bike, but Josh stood in her path. As she revved the engine and advanced toward Josh, he reached into his pants, and pulled out a silver automatic pistol. Blondie was terrified, and stopped moving. Josh put the gun away, and pulled Blondie off the bike. Blondie ran to her car and drove away, convinced that Josh was going to kill her. As she sped down the block Blondie heard the vicious growl of a motorcycle coming closer. She looked in her rearview mirror, through her shattered rear windshield, and saw

Josh advancing quickly toward her. She floored the accelerator, but her car was no match for a bike. To Blondie, it was like Satan was chasing her on a blue motorcycle. As Josh pulled alongside, his face was a mask of fury. He pulled out the gun and waved it. She believed he would fire at her any second. Desperately, she made a hard turn—the wrong way down a one-way street. She sped down one small street and up another, and then another for what seemed like a long time, before she realized that Josh was no longer behind her. Blondie pulled over to the curb next to a pay phone. She believed that her only choices were the police or death. She got out of her damaged car and limped to the phone. Finally, she lifted the receiver, and dialed 911. She told the emergency operator that someone had stolen her motorcycle. He had a gun and had threatened to kill her. Since Blondie mentioned a gun, in addition to the motorcycle theft, the job—a "gun run"—was assigned a high priority and a police car was dispatched.

Minutes later, Officer Jason Houlihan and his partner James Blaha from the One-Oh-Four Precinct arrived to investigate Blondie's complaint. Blondie breathlessly told them how she had been beaten and threatened, and how her boyfriend, a man named Joshua Torres, had stolen her motorcycle at gunpoint. She showed them her registration for the bike, and gave them all the particulars. Blondie urged them to get her motorcycle back from Josh. As a matter of routine, the officers would have simply filled out a "G.L.A"—grand larceny, auto—report, and put out an alarm on the stolen cycle. But before they could do that, Blondie stopped them with an afterthought:

"This motherfucker said he burned somebody, also," said Blondie. "Do you know about where they burned a girl in the basement?"

The question was out of left field, as far as the rookie cops were concerned. They had no idea what she was talking about.

"No," they told her.

CHAPTER TWENTY-FIVE

BLONDIE TALKS

Johnny Wilde was at work in the One-Oh-Four Detective Squad in Woodside, Queens, on Sunday afternoon, September 3rd when Patrolman Jason Houlihan walked in.

"Oh, good—you're working," Houlihan said, by way of greeting. Johnny was a twenty three-year veteran but he never brushed off a rookie. Houlihan told him about the motorcycle robbery complaint that he and his partner had handled. The perp, Joshua Torres, who was also the woman's boyfriend, smashed the windows in the victim's car and beat her with a shovel. The problem was, the victim was telling this big, wild story about the bike thief—that he had also burned some girl to death. Houlihan didn't want to look silly, but he also didn't want to dismiss the woman's claims without the opinion of a more experienced investigator.

"Do you know anything about a girl being burned up?"

"Sure," said Johnny, who had also stuck his nose into the Antonakos torch job in his home precinct. "Where is she? Bring her up and I'll talk to her."

Houlihan brought Blondie upstairs. She was angry, and nervous, but mostly she wanted her bike back. Johnny asked her what the story was.

"He grabbed this girl off the street," Blondie said. "They kidnapped her, tried to get money from the father, and burned her up."

She expected the police to take it from there, and said she was anxious to leave, because a friend named Mike was downstairs with her kids. Blondie said that Josh had told Mike the same thing. After Nick had threatened her kids, Blondie didn't want them out of her sight.

"Let me go take care of my kids," Blondie said, standing to go.

She said she was worried Josh would torch her apartment. Johnny didn't want Blondie out of his sight. He was afraid she might shut down. He was afraid that once she got out, he would never find her again or she might get hurt. Blondie was tough, but Johnny figured she was no match for this animal Josh. He asked her to sit down and wait a minute. He walked downstairs, but there was no guy at the front desk or in the lobby. He walked out into the sunshine and strolled with forced casualness down the block, until he saw a guy sitting with several kids in a smashed-up car that had not been there when Johnny had arrived at work. Most of the windows had been shattered, and were glittering spider-webs of cracked glass. You didn't have to be Dick Tracy to figure out that it was Blondie's car. Johnny walked over slowly. He didn't want to scare the guy away.

"You with Blondie?" Johnny asked in a friendly voice.

"Yeah," said Mike.

"She wants to see her kids," said Johnny.

As the detective walked with Mike and the kids back into the stationhouse, Johnny tried a little bluff. He started talking as if Blondie had told him everything but, of course, there hadn't yet been time.

"That's some story with this guy—a real psycho," Johnny said, shaking his head.

"Wow," echoed Mike. "Can you imagine they did that and this guy made a tape so they were afraid he was gonna give them up?"

Tape? This was too good to be true.

"Right," agreed Johnny, as if he knew it all.

"Yeah, did she tell you about the guy that was walking

down the street and they shot him in the head?''

"Yeah, I know about that, too," Johnny lied. That made it two murders, Johnny thought: the Antonakos torching, and a shooting.

"They're crazy, they do things that are nuts," Mike said.

Once he had Mike and the kids safely ensconced in the precinct, under police guard, Johnny went back upstairs. He told Blondie that her kids were safe, and asked her to start at the beginning. She told him the whole story. Johnny now had a witness who claimed that Josh directly confessed the burning death to her. Johnny reacted with anger to the part about how Josh had kissed Kim and said ''Shit happens'' before lighting the match, but the detective kept it to himself. When Blondie was finished, she asked again when she was going to get her motorcycle back.

"By the way, I just saw your friend, Mike—that's something, the way they did the other guy," Johnny said in an off-the-cuff way.

"Yeah, ain't that something?" Blondie said

She then spilled everything that Josh had told her about that murder. She knew Joey's name and where he lived, and when the hit went down. As soon as Blondie said that Joey was carrying his baby when Josh snuck up on him and shot him, Johnny knew exactly what she was talking about: the guy with the kid. Johnny had been at the scene, and saw the body. It looked like it was not just another drug dealer who had gotten shot after all.

Johnny then interviewed Mike, who told him that Josh had admitted both murders to him on a different occasion. Johnny now had two ''directs'' from people who weren't involved in the crimes. He felt like choking Blondie. She'd known for a month that this guy Josh had burned a girl alive, and killed another guy holding a child in his arms, but she did nothing—until her motorcycle had been stolen, she had been assaulted, and death threats had been made. He felt the same way about her friend Mike, who had known even longer.

Johnny picked up the phone and called the One-Oh-Two Squad. Coincidentally, Louie Pia and Rich Tirelli were working that day. Louie picked up the phone.

"One-Oh-Two Squad—Tirelli," said Rich.

"Hi, it's Johnny Wilde in the One-Oh-Four. Listen, man you got that fuckin' Antonakis case?"

"Yeah," said Rich.

"I got a girl here, a girl and a guy, who both say another guy confessed to the Antonakos homicide, and another killing," said Johnny.

The Antonakos thing, Johnny told Rich, was a kidnapping for money that went bad. Also one of the perps had made a tape about the kidnapping and was himself killed by another bad guy.

Rich asked to speak to Blondie and Johnny put her on the phone.

"I have information about that girl Kimberly Antonakos," Blondie told Rich.

"What do you have?" Rich asked.

"The guy who stole my motorcycle did it."

Rich handed the phone to Louie.

"What's his name?" Louie asked Blondie.

"Joshua Torres," she said.

Louie jumped like he had been hit with a jolt of electricity. He told Blondie to put Johnny back on the line.

"We'll be right over," he told Johnny, and hung up.

"We got to get over there," Louie said, pulling on his jacket.

He and Rich rushed out to the car and Rich drove quickly to the One-Oh-Four. Rich looked at the expression on Louie's face. He felt it looked exactly like one of his kids at Christmas, unwrapping a new toy. But Louie was also apprehensive. They had worked so hard on the case. This woman Blondie was Josh's new girlfriend and she was giving him up—it looked like the squeeze play had worked, after six months. But after the long, frustrating roller-coaster ride, it seemed almost too easy. Louie had not forgotten the Roger Rabbit fiasco, and neither had the DA's office.

"I hope this girl has good information," Louie said nervously, as they pulled up to the precinct.

CHAPTER TWENTY-SIX

ROUNDUP

Louie got a written statement from Blondie, while Rich did the same with Mike in another room. Johnny sat in, to make sure the stories were the same he had heard earlier. Prosecutor Gene Reibstein arrived and met Blondie, and then Mike.

"That's some shit she's saying in there," Mike said to Gene.

"Yes it is," Gene agreed.

Louie was energized. Blondie was tall, robust, and unkempt after her ordeal, but she was a good speaker, and Louie believed her. He listened as she told how Josh had described killing off one of his co-conspirators, the guy's name was Jose but everyone called him Joey—just like the anonymous caller said back in March. It was beginning to make sense. It certainly fit in with Tom and Louie's feeling that it had been a kidnap that went bad. Louie could not wait to get his hands on the tape made by Joey Negron, that he'd supposedly given to his wife. Louie also couldn't wait to get Josh back in the chair, but there was homework to do first, work that had to be done discreetly so as not to alert Josh, Jay, and this new guy, Nick—*and* Louie had three quick calls to make.

Tom Shevlin was still laid up on sick leave at his Long Island home. Tom was wearing a neck brace, his arm was in a sling, and he was under heavy medication to kill the pain from the car crash almost four months earlier. It was tough even to pick up the phone and put it to his ear without moving his neck.

"It finally happened," said Louie.

Tom knew immediately what "it" Louie was talking about.

"It worked—we got this girl . . ." Louie said, describing Blondie and her story.

A big smile spread across Tom's face as he listened. The squeeze play had worked at last. Josh had been caught off base by his own big mouth. It looked like Josh had finally talked himself into jail—but they had no proof yet.

"Make sure you keep them under wraps," Tom said.

Louie agreed with Tom, and went back to work. Next, Louie touched base with Greg Lasak, the head of the Homicide Bureau of the Queens DA's office.

"Louie, have you got the right fucking guy here?" asked Lasak, who did not want to see a re-run of the Roger Rabbit episode.

"Yes," Louie told him. "It's Joshua Torres."

Lasak took Louie's word that they were on the right track, and gave his blessing. Lastly, Louie dialed Tommy Antonakos' home on Staten Island.

"Hello?"

"Tommy, did I wake you?"

"Yeah."

"Sorry."

"Yeah, no problem."

"Listen, Tommy—we got it, man," Louie told him. "I can't tell you much now, but maybe in a day or two . . ."

Louie explained that they had witnesses who were giving Josh and Jay and others up for killing Kim. He did not give details, and swore a jubilant Tommy to secrecy. He told him it could be days before they were ready to make an arrest, and to sit tight.

The first order of business, Louie felt, was to find Joey's

widow. She was supposed to have the tape he had made, and she probably knew something. She was also a witness to her husband's murder. They could not waste any time. If Josh got any inkling that they were on to him, he might start wiping people out. Or they would discover that he was "in the wind"—on the lam.

On Labor Day, Monday, September 4th, 1995, Louie and Rich went out to look for Joey's widow Antonette Montalvo. She was not at home. Motor vehicle records told the detectives that Antonette had a blue Buick Century four-door registered in her name. They found her car parked down the block. The last thing they wanted to do was alert anyone that detectives were suddenly hot on the Antonakos case. Louie stopped a passing cop on a scooter and asked him to help out. The uniformed officer went door-to-door, asking if anyone knew who owned the Buick. At one apartment, they were told that it belonged to their friend Antonette, who was visiting. Antonette told the officer she was sorry the car was parked illegally, and that she was leaving soon, and would move the car. The cop thanked her and reported back to Louie and Rich. At 7:30 that evening, Antonette emerged from the apartment building, along with her son Bobby, and a man. They got into the car and drove away. Louie and Rich followed and waited until they were out of the neighborhood before they pulled them over to the curb on Jamaica Avenue, near Highland Park. Louie flashed his detective badge.

"We'd like to speak to you about your husband's death," Louie said.

Antonette was surprised at the sudden interest, but agreed. She asked that she be allowed to drop her son off at her mother's house first. Rich and Louie followed Antonette down Jamaica Avenue, into Woodhaven, Queens. Antonette made a left turn on Seventy-ninth Street, and parked in front of her mother's house. Jeanette Montalvo opened her front door, welcomed her daughter and everyone else inside, and ushered them into the living room in the rear of the first floor apartment Baby, the family dog, ran in between the arriving legs, with her tail wagging. When Louie looked out of the living room window into the rear yard, it was still light outside. He saw a fence, and, behind it, the rear and side of a house that looked familiar.

Suddenly, Louie felt a chill on his spine, and goose bumps going up the back of his neck. Everyone else looked at him as he stood staring out the window. The detective seemed to have zoned out.

"We're here," Louie thought to himself, in a rush of emotion. "This is it. We're on the right track."

Louie spoke to Rich, Antonette, and Jeanette, and then asked to use the phone. Jeanette handed him her portable. He quickly dialed Tom Shevlin's home number.

"Tom, I'm standing in this woman's living room, and I'm looking at Kimberly's crime scene!" Louie said triumphantly. "The mother-in-law's home faces the crime scene!"

"Bingo!" yelled Tom. "I'm coming in!"

At last, they had their connection to the house and to Josh. Tom called his boss, who had said he would allow Tom to come off sick leave temporarily. He told the lieutenant about the new development, and asked to be allowed to come back to wrap up the case.

"If it's the people you say it is, by all means, you can come in," the lieutenant said.

Tom hung up the phone. He had waited for six months, and he knew he was going to have to wait a few hours or a few days more. It didn't matter—as long as he could be part of locking up that smug, evil Josh, he could retire a happy man. Tom struggled to his feet from the couch. His wife Lisa shook her head, but knew better than to try to talk Tom out of going back to work—it wouldn't have done any good.

Antonette accompanied Louie and Rich back to the precinct and Louie asked about the rumored recording:

"Do you have that tape?" Louie asked.

"No," said Antonette. "If he gave it to anyone, he'd give it to his father."

She said that Joey's father lived in Florida, and gave them the number. Antonette stuck to her story that she had not seen the face of her husband's killer, but she was cooperative, and gave them permission to look through Joey's stuff. At her apartment, they found Joey's address book with Nick's name and phone number. They looked everywhere for a jacket with missing zipper teeth but found none. Antonette said she could not remember if Joey had thrown out any jackets. They found a set of handcuffs, and the microcassette tape recorder Antonette said that Joey had used to play the tape. There was a tape inside—apparently blank— that may have been erased. It was sent to the police lab for possible audio enhancement.

When the detectives told Antonette that Nick may also have been involved in Joey's death, she told them where to find him: at his girlfriend's house. Louie went back to the phone dumps, and found that Nick's girlfriend's number had been dialed from Kim's apartment on the night Kim vanished. Antonette's number had also been dialed, and both numbers were called the next morning. Louie realized that the calls were not to two of Josh's girlfriends, but to Nick and Joey, his co-conspirators. Because the phones were registered in the women's names, and the investigators did not know who Nick and Joey were, Louie and Tom believed they were calls to Josh's girlfriends—and he did not correct them. It was frustrating to see that there was an indirect connection there all the time, but—unlike Claire Day—they were not paid to be psychic.

Rich checked out the gas station where the bad guys had bought the gas to torch Kim. It was a dead end—nobody remembered anything. The station did not have a video security system, so there was no chance that the arson killers had been caught on camera.

By the afternoon of September 6th, it was time to round up the bad guys. Louie and Rich went to Blondie's house, and found her standing in the middle of her ransacked apartment. While Blondie was with the cops, someone had broken in and stolen her TV, VCR, stereo, and almost everything else of value, including her pocketbook and credit cards. Many things were smashed, including a plaster statue of Jesus. Blondie was furious, and said she had been getting beeped by Josh. She told the detectives that she believed Josh was responsible for the theft and vandalism. Blondie believed it was another warning. Louie asked her to lure Josh out with a promise to give him the registration to her motorcycle. As they stood next to her, Blondie called Josh at his aunt's house.

"I don't know why you're beeping me," she told Josh. "I'm sick of this—meet me in the open."

She told him she would let him keep the bike if he left her alone, and offered to meet him right away. Blondie listened as Josh responded.

"No, someplace public," Blondie said. "The McDonald's on Hendrix Street and Atlantic Avenue? Five o'clock? Okay."

Josh warned her not to try anything funny, or he would "take somebody with me."

The day had been clear and hot, but, as the sun sank lower in the west, it became muggy, and the temperature dropped to 70 degrees. Two teams of four detectives staked out the meeting spot, and Louie waited in a car around the corner. Louie knew that if Josh saw him, it would blow the arrest—he would either run or fight. Rich and another detective were concealed around the corner, and the other detectives waited inside the fast-food joint, posing as dinnertime customers. Blondie was waiting alone on the corner opposite the McDonald's at five sharp, but there was no Joshua in sight. After a long ten minutes, the detectives began to get nervous. After fifteen minutes, Rich figured that Josh was not coming, and he discussed it with Louie by radio. Blondie had grown impatient, also, and had picked up the pay phone and dialed home. But just when they were about to fold up the surveillance, Josh drove down the street at the wheel of April's baby-blue hatchback. Of course, they could not tell if Josh had come loaded for bear, and would have to proceed as if he were armed and dangerous. Blondie hung up the phone as Josh turned the corner and stopped the car. Blondie approached the vehicle and the detectives got ready.

"I hope we can end this," Josh said to Blondie with a smile. "And . . ." Josh stopped talking suddenly. He turned his head to the left and right, and saw four detectives rushing toward him—converging on him with guns in their hands.

"Police!" Rich yelled. "Put your hands up!"

Josh did not put his hands up. He turned to Blondie with a look of murderous hate in his eyes.

"If you set me up, I'll kill you," Josh snarled.

"Back up!" yelled one detective, ordering Blondie to move out of the line of fire.

But Blondie could not move—she was frozen with fear, convinced that Josh was going to start shooting. The detectives rushed past her, grabbed Josh, who did not have a gun, and pulled him out of the car.

"Put your hands on the car!" Louie ordered, pointing to the hood.

Josh ignored him.

"Put your hands on the car!"

Still, Josh ignored Louie. He was busy giving Blondie a death stare.

"What're you looking at?" Louie asked Blondie, pretending not to know her—for her protection. "Get the fuck out of here!"

Louie yoked Josh around the neck above his red-and-white-stripped shirt—pulling his hands behind his back at the waist of his Guess designer jeans as Rich handcuffed him.

"What the fuck are you doing?" Josh screamed, struggling to break free.

They handcuffed his wrists behind his back and walked him around the corner, to the unmarked car. Josh was put in the back seat. Louie Pia sat in the front. The detective turned to Josh, smiled, and then uttered a dozen words that he had waited six months to say:

"You're under arrest for the murder of Kimberly Anto-nakos—we got you."

It had been a long six months, and at several points, Louie didn't think he would ever get to say it to anybody. It felt so good to finally collar Josh.

"What are you talking about?" Joshua said, making a sucking noise with his tongue and his teeth. "You ain't got shit!"

Josh was playing the hard-ass. He would be a tough nut to crack, but Louie now felt like the Energizer Bunny—he was ready to stay up for days interrogating Josh and Nick, if he had to. They drove Josh and his son—who had been in the back seat—to the nearby One-Oh-Six Precinct, and put Josh in a room. Josh's son was upset at his daddy's arrest and began crying. A female cop took Bobby to play and have snacks in another part of the stationhouse. Louie and Tom walked into the room with Rich and beamed at Josh. Tom had just taken off his neck brace and arm sling because he did not want Josh to see them. Rich read Josh his rights.

"I told you the next time we talked, I'm gonna do my homework," Louie told Josh. "I told you the next time we bring you in, you ain't leaving. You ain't going nowhere but to jail—we got you for Kimberly's murder."

Josh his goateed chin held high, glared back with his best tough-guy look, the most confident young man in the world.

"Get the fuck outta here, you ain't got shit," Josh said. "Fuck you! I'm tired of this shit!" Josh stood up to leave.

"You ain't going nowhere!" said an angry Tom Shevlin, who grasped Josh's shoulder with his left hand and pushed the shorter man back into the chair. As Tom shoved Josh back down in the seat, he felt a searing pain burn up his arm all the way to his shoulder and neck.

"Oh, shit!" Tom cried, grabbing his shoulder with his other hand and grimacing in pain.

Rich stood over Josh to make it clear that he was not

leaving. The detectives decided to let Josh stew a while, while they went out to look for Nick Libretti. Again, they wanted to get the bad guy out in the open—not inside an apartment, where he might barricade himself, shoot it out, or take hostages. Louie and Rich went back to Antonette's apartment.

"We gotta get Nicholas," said Rich.

"I'll do it," she said.

Antonette beeped Nick, who quickly called back. Antonette had Caller ID on her telephone, and when Nick called back, the name Helen Libretti—Nick's mother, who had done so much to keep her son out of jail—along with her address, was displayed on the tiny Caller ID screen.

"Nick? Listen, there's a guy that owes Joey money, and I want to go collect from him, but I don't want him to bullshit me . . ."

Antonette had used Nick's magic word—money.

"OK, I'll meet you outside in fifteen minutes," she said.

Louie called the detective squad in the precinct where Nick's mother lived, and and asked them to rush over there and grab Nick. After she had set Nick up for the police, Antonette began to cry. Joey was dead, and Nick—his best friend—probably had something to do with it. She felt very alone, and scared.

A surprised Nick was picked up on the corner of Pitkin Avenue and Eighty-Fifth Street, after he emerged from the safety of his mom's house, wearing button-fly cargo pants and a long-sleeved shirt over a white t-shirt.

"We're detectives," Joe Miles told Nick. "What's your name?"

"Nicholas Libretti."

"Put your hands on the wall," Miles ordered Nick.

He complied, and went meekly with the detectives.

"Where are we going?" Nick asked from the back seat of the unmarked car.

"To the One-Oh-Six Precinct," Miles replied.

"Why?"

"When you get there, you'll find out."

Meanwhile, Tom continued to question Josh, who was still doing his tough-guy act, in a large room normally used for lineups. On one wall was a big one-way mirror. Behind the mirror was a small dark room, from which witnesses and victims viewed lineups of bad guys without being seen. Tom did not admit it, but Josh was right—they didn't have shit. They had enough for an arrest, but not for a reliable conviction. They still had to find the switches to flip that would make Josh and Nick talk. Tom did not want to see Josh walking out of a precinct scot-free for a second time.

First, they would have a go at Nick. They fortified themselves with more detective fuel, drinking the first cups—that would add up to gallons—of strong coffee, always on the brew in Squad Room. Louie and Tom had already smoked five packs of Marlboros. They sent out a detective for seven more packs of butts. It was going to be a long night.

Louie, Tom, and Rich went into another room with Nick Libretti. At first, after he was read his rights, Nick denied everything and played dumb. But when he was told that they knew everything, and began describing the torching of Kim in detail, he stopped protesting and started listening. The detectives acted like they didn't care whether Nick spoke to them or not. They told him they didn't really need anything from him because they knew it all already. They were just a couple of good guys offering him a break. Louie took out a picture of Kim and looked at it.

"She was a good-looking girl, a beautiful girl," said Louie, showing Nick the smiling photo of Kim.

The picture had no effect on Nick. Trying to get sympathy for Kim or her family out of Nick was a waste of time. He didn't speak the language. The three detectives looked at each other. Rich left and went back into the room where Josh was waiting, and began to needle him.

"Hey, Josh, your man Nick is in the other room, and he's giving you up," said Rich. "He told us you started this— you're the guy that did it all, you're the guy that made everything happen here. You're the guy that killed Kimberly Antonakos—that's the bottom line.''

"Yeah," said an arrogant Josh, who would not believe that Nick would talk. "You don't have shit. Nick ain't here."

Rich wanted to keep Josh talking, but he didn't want to get him angry or make him try to leave. That would not look so good from behind the one-way mirror. Rich kept telling Josh how much they had against him, but Josh calmly denied it again and again. Josh was just biding his time. He knew that eventually, April would miss him and the baby, and start looking for him. Next door, Louie and Tom began telling Nick the same thing that Rich was telling Josh: Your partner is ratting you out, and putting it all on you.

It was the oldest trick in the book.

"Listen, man, you're going to jail—there's no fuckin' doubt about it," Louie told Nick. "Your fuckin' guy next door is giving you up . . . He's making you the heavy, he's making you the ringleader, the guy with the match."

Nick was rattled, but he shook his head and kept his mouth shut. His expression showed he doubted that big, bad Josh was spilling his guts.

"You don't think he's fuckin' talking?" asked Louie, getting to his feet. "C'mon, I'll show you."

Louie and Tom took Nick down the hall and into the viewing room. Nick looked through the one-way glass and saw Josh talking his head off to some detective. Nick couldn't hear what was being said, but Josh and the cop looked real friendly, and Josh seemed to be telling the detective some story, and the detective was shaking his head up and down, and smiling. Then Nick saw the detective stand up and say something to Josh, as he warmly shook Josh's hand. Rich closed the door on Josh and joined Nick, Louie, and Tom in the hallway.

"Hey, Nick, you see that?" Rich beamed. "He's even shaking my hand."

Nick's body sagged and they led him back to the interview room. If Nick had been able to hear what was being said between Josh and Rich, he would not have been so crestfallen. Far from cooperating, Josh had simply mouthed more cool denials:

"I had nothing to do with her murder," Josh told Rich. "I was her friend. I tried to help her family out. I can't believe these guys did that, whoever did this," Josh said, sucking his teeth for emphasis.

When Rich had stood up to leave, he reached out to shake Josh's hand, and Josh took it, as most people did in that situation. But Rich had not been thanking Josh for his cooperation. What Rich said, as he smiled and pumped Josh's hand for the benefit of an audience of one behind the glass, was quite different from what Nick had feared:

"I'll see you in jail, asshole," a smiling Rich told Josh.

Back in the interview room, Nick sat with his hands folded on the table in front of him. He was wearing a green, long-sleeved denim shirt over a t-shirt. He had close-cropped hair, a mustache, and a scraggly beard along his chin line. His brown eyes shifted back and forth from under dark eyebrows. He looked like a cornered animal, searching for some way to escape. Louie and Tom gave it to him.

"I don't believe you lit that match," Tom told Nick in a sympathetic voice. "I don't think you actually did the murder." If he was not the one who had set Kim on fire, then he could cut a deal, Tom said. "If you didn't light that match . . ."

"OK, I'll tell you what happened," Nick said. "We wanted to let her go in the park. Joshua gave us the suggestion that if we took Kimberly, we'd be able to get money for her from her father."

Nick said they did not think Kim was burned alive.

"We thought she died in there, so we just freaked. Joshua threw gas on her and . . . just lit her up. I never knew her."

Nick said that Josh was the mastermind who had laid it all out about two days before he and Joey took Kimberly. Nick could not even remember the last name of the girl he had kidnapped and helped burn alive.

"Josh told us how she would come home, and how Joshua wanted us to go about obtaining her," said Nick. "It was late at night. We were just going to wait for her to pull in from the bar and we're just gonna grab her. We walked in behind her. She got out of her car. It was chilly. Joey grabbed her mouth."

Nick described binding the struggling Kim with duct tape, throwing her in her own trunk, and driving to the Woodhaven home. He said that his dead pal Joey did almost everything by himself—grabbing and taping Kim, lifting her into the trunk. Nick shifted blame to the point where he claimed that Joey had lifted the squirming, 115-pound Kim out of the trunk himself, taken his keys out of his pocket with one hand, unlocked the front door with the key, and carried her into the house "like a bride."

"I didn't go totally down in the basement," Nick claimed, although he did not explain how he could have held a flashlight on Kim, and seen Joey tie Kim up, unless he had gone downstairs.

"He sat her down in a chair and taped her . . . to the pole. I was just waiting for him," Nick lied, eager to remove himself from the action as much as possible.

"Joshua had the idea," said Nick, happy to have someone else to blame. "Her family would give money for her . . . because her family had money. We didn't really know how long, we thought it was gonna be a one-day thing."

Josh insisted that he could not participate in the kidnapping "because he didn't want to be implicated," said Nick. He couldn't remember the name of the town where he and Joey left Kim's car.

"It was just random. We left her car parked on a side street," Nick said. He told them about driving back to Queens, and returning so Joey could wipe the car clean of prints.

"He cleaned it, he wiped it down . . . I guess for fingerprints."

Nick detailed stealing Kim's jewelry, and said he was the

one who tried to use Kim's cell phone. At a meeting after Kim was taken, said Nick, he learned "that Joshua tried to contact her father and nothing happened. He played a tape demanding money and the father didn't say nothing." Josh said he would try again. But after the psychic incident, "We decided that we hadda get her out. We went down and we saw her, and she appeared to be dead. It was cold. We freaked out. We panicked and we just looked at her. Joshua kicked her in the shin pretty hard. We didn't know what to do. We were gonna take her body out . . . She was stuck to the pole."

After a discussion, Nick said that the three men decided "that we should just burn the whole house down. We went to the gas station. Joshua bought gas. Joshua went down, poured the gas all over her, and just lit it up. He put it on her head."

Nick described the sound, as the gasoline ignited:

"*Wooosh!*"

"We all felt like this shouldn't have happened in the first place but we felt we had no alternative," Nick said. Josh, he said, later told him that he was a suspect.

"I heard he used to get picked up by the cops . . . on a regular basis," said Nick. Josh told him "that they are suspicious that it was him and they wanted him to take a lie detector test. He said he smoked a lot of weed before and he thinks he passed it. We were all scared about each other talking about it."

When asked about his friend Joey, Nick responded without emotion.

"He got killed. He was shot in the back of the head," Nick said. Josh, he said, told him, " 'That's what happens to snitches.' He felt like Joey deserved it."

Nick mentioned that he split to California after the case hit the press. Louie asked Nick whether Kim had pulled any teeth from a zipper on Joey's clothes—or his. Nick said he knew nothing about it. Not once in his modest confession did Nick mention Jay. He only talked about Joey—who was dead—and Josh, whom he had seen was already in custody, and seemed to be ratting him out. Louie then asked Nick to make a written statement of what he had just said, and he agreed.

"Do you want to write it out?" Louie asked him.

"My handwriting's bad—you should write it out," Nick said.

They went through Nick's story again. Louie wrote it down on a legal pad, and then read it aloud to Nick. On the last page, Louie drew a diagonal line from the end of the statement to the end of the page, so that nothing further could be added to the statement. Nick then signed it. They were then joined by Julian Wise from the DA's office, who had cut short a California vacation to be in on the arrests. Julian introduced himself to Nick, and asked him if he was willing to make a video of what he had told the detectives. Nick also agreed to that. The camera was set up, and Louie sat on one side of the room while Julian asked Nick questions. Halfway through the tape, Julian could not help feeling anger.

"Sitting across from me is a guy who was involved in burning a girl alive," Julian thought. He wanted to reach out and smack Nick in the head, but he restrained himself and did his job. Rich went back to have a go at Josh again, using what Nick had just said. When Josh again told Rich that Nick was not there, Rich was glad to prove it.

"You don't believe me. You don't think Nick is here? C'mon, I'll show you. He's giving you up."

This time Josh watched Nick talking through the one-way mirror—but this time it was really happening. Back in the room, Josh was less cocky, but still would not talk.

"You're going to jail," Rich told Josh. "Now I really got you, because we got your boy giving it up in the other room. He told us you started this—you're the guy that did it all. You're the guy that made everything happen here. You're the guy that killed Kimberly Antonakos—that's the bottom line, Josh."

Tom entered the room and listened, as Rich gave Josh details of the crime.

"I even know the gas station you went to," said Rich. "We know where you bought the gas can."

"I don't even know what you're talking about," Josh sniggered, then he made that sucking sound with his teeth again.

"You don't even know what I'm talking about?" Rich said sarcastically. "It's a twenty-four-hour station. You know what they've got? Video cameras! Joshua, I got you on tape, I got you on camera! We see you going in and buying the gas!"

Rich then laughed triumphantly. It was a marvelous performance.

Josh sat bolt upright, and the color drained from his face. The haughty smirk fell from his white face and his jaw hung open in shock.

"All right, I . . . I didn't want to tell you," Josh blurted, as one of his eyes began to twitch. "I didn't buy the gas . . . I only bought the can!"

Rich, with a twinkle in his eye, looked at Tom—who could hardly believe that Rich's bluff had worked. When Tom saw Josh's eye fluttering, it seemed like Morse code for victory. Of course, there was no video. Rich had just faked Josh out of his socks and into prison. Suddenly, Josh's tough-guy, screw-you act was gone—just like a switch had been flipped. He was friendly and smarmy, looking for a play, a deal—eager to be the rat. It looked like the elusive Josh would also soon be starring in his own video—the one kind of confession that could never be explained away in front of a jury.

"Can you help me out . . . can you help me?" Josh implored, his eye continuing to blink involuntarily. "Listen, man, I gotta be honest with you, those guys did it—Jay organized the kidnapping."

Josh said the whole thing was Jay's idea—it was all Jay, Joey, and Nick, Josh told them, as he began to weave a tale.

He put Jay in his role of mastermind, and himself in Jay's shoes as the reluctant, frightened, after-the-fact cohort. Josh also seemed to be maneuvering, trying to find out how much the detectives knew.

"Listen, they didn't even let me know where they took her, where she was being held," Josh claimed. "After three days, they finally took me to the house where they were keeping Kim. I never went into the house."

"Josh—you weren't in the house?" Rich asked. "I got your fingerprints in the house. How are your fingerprints in the house?"

Josh did not answer. He just sat there, thinking and blinking. Rich could not believe Josh was finally talking to him. Both he and Nick had fallen for the simplest trick detectives had. Josh was blaming it all on Jay, Nick was blaming it all on Josh, and they both blamed it on the dead guy. Rich asked Josh about Joey's tape and Josh admitted that he had asked Antonette where it was. As Josh began to talk himself deeper into the kidnap plot, there was a knock on the door. It was two in the morning, and Rich had just asked Josh about Joey's tape. Josh admitted that he had questioned Antonette about the tape. Another detective was at the door and asked Rich to step outside. Rich had no intention of interrupting Josh. He told the detective that he was busy. Very busy.

"Please," the detective insisted. "I gotta talk to you—outside."

Once the door was closed, Rich made his impatience clear.

"What's up?"

"Cut it off—he lawyered up," the detective said.

"You're fucking kidding me," said Rich.

April had found out that Josh was in police custody and she called a lawyer. The lawyer had just called the precinct and ordered the cops to stop questioning his client Joshua Torres. The lawyer also directed that Josh could not sign anything. Rich cursed. He had been so close.

After Nick finished his videotaped confession—during

which he never expressed the slightest remorse—Johnny
Wilde stuck his head into the room, and saw Nick sitting
alone.

"Hey, how's everything going?" Johnny asked.

"Fine. I should be out of here in a little while," Nick
smiled.

Johnny ducked back into the hallway, where he saw Rich.

"We got another idiot in there," Johnny told Rich, who
nodded his head. Then Louie, Tom, and Julian went in to
the room to wrap things up.

"You feel good you got that off your chest?" Louie asked
Nick.

"No, not really," Nick replied. "Am I gonna get the reward money?"

Louie fought to keep a straight face at the cold-blooded,
greedy gall, the sheer stupidity of Nick Libretti.

"I'll check into it," was all Louie could say, as he fought
to keep a straight face.

"Can I go home now?" Nick asked Tom.

He was serious. Tom, with a smirk, thought Nick was as
sharp as a doughnut. Nick turned to Julian.

"Do you think I'll get a long time?"

"You know," said Julian, on his way out the door,
"you're an asshole."

It was time for paperwork, and one other thing.

"Louie," said Tom, "give Tommy Antonakos a call."

Louie picked up the phone.

"We arrested Joshua Torres, and a guy named Nick Libretti, for Kim's murder," Louie told Kim's father.

"Who?" Tommy asked.

He had never heard of Nick.

"Where are you?" Tommy asked. "I'll be right over."

Nick's sister, who was a corrections officer, showed up
and was allowed to speak to her brother, who admitted his
guilt to her. When told that her brother had confessed to a
murder, she cried, and asked if Nick could get a deal from
the DA's office. Rich told her that they had no control over

the DA's office. She asked if her mother could visit with Nick before he went to jail, but by the time Helen Libretti arrived, she was not able to see her son alone.

A jubilant Tommy arrived a short time later with his brother Joseph. Louie and Tom came down to see them and there were hugs and handshakes, as the detectives told them what had happened. Tommy was elated. Six months of frustration lifted from his shoulders, now that the men who had burned his little girl alive were no longer walking around. To Tommy, Josh was the Evil One, the Devil incarnate. Tommy had kept his promise to Kim. Remembering how he had refused to believe it was Joshua, he turned to Tom Shevlin:

"You son-of-a-bitch, you were right all along," said Tommy.

"You bringing him out the front? I'm gonna wait for him outside the precinct."

The press was alerted by the department. Reporters, photographers, and TV crews began to gather outside the precinct to catch "the Walk"—the ritual promenade of the suspects past the front desk of the stationhouse and the waiting press outside, for the trip to Central Booking. Some time later, an exhausted Julian left the precinct clutching the only copy of the Nick Libretti videotape. "What happens if I get into an accident?" Julian wondered to himself, as he walked out of sight of the precinct on the dark city street.

"Now I can leave my job," Julian thought to himself. "I've had enough. We got those guys."

No sooner had the thought appeared in his mind, than Julian was grabbed from behind. Strong arms pinned his arms to his sides. Julian wheeled around, ready to defend himself, thinking it was a mugger.

It was a beaming Tommy Antonakos.

"We got 'em, didn't we?" Tommy said.

"Yes, we did," said a relieved Julian, who was overcome with emotion.

He hugged Tommy back. Julian wanted to tell Tommy the unvarnished truth, but his voice choked up as he spoke.

"Tommy, let me explain," Julian said. "The case against Josh is not good."

He explained about the lawyer, and how Josh had refused to sign any statement or make any videotape. Julian wanted Tommy to understand that it was not going to be a walk in court.

"It makes no sense," Tommy said.

"Not everything makes sense in the criminal law in New York State," said Julian.

Upstairs, as Louie Pia and Tom Shevlin typed up their arrest reports, sipped more strong coffee, and puffed on more cigarettes, they were both aglow with their accomplishment. They would not end up bitter and disappointed because they had failed to solve the biggest case of their careers. They had done it. With Kim's murder, Louie and Tom had solved twenty-one homicides as partners. Their work had made a difference. They didn't get mushy about it, but they both knew it was over. At least their partnership had ended on a high note of justice. Deep down in their hearts, both men felt good. They had locked up Kim's killers. No one could ever take away what they had done.

Suddenly, Louie looked up from his typewriter.

"Tom, you remember we went to that psychic with Tommy?"

"Yeah, I remember that we went to the psychic—why?"

"Well, she said they went to California. Nick went to California," Louie said.

"Yeah," said Tommy. "She did."

The two detectives just looked at each other. Tom shrugged. Go figure.

When they were ready, Louie and Tom brought Josh out and put him in an unmarked car. He was morose, and filled with self-pity. He had been to jail before and knew it was not fun. None of the killers could be charged under the new death-penalty law that had taken effect a few days earlier, but Josh and Nick were facing twenty-five-years-to-life in prison. To a young man, it seemed like forever. Josh would be an old man when he emerged from a penitentiary. Once they were in the car and on their way to Central Booking, Louie had something to say to the silent Josh before he disappeared into the system.

"It's all over, pal," Louie said. "It took six months, but we finally got you. You're going to jail for the rest of your life—you set Kimberly Antonakos on fire."

"If I get more than fifteen years, I'll kill myself," Josh moaned.

Louie refused to get his hopes up—he knew that Josh had never kept his word.

Later that morning, Louie, Tom, Rich, Julian, and others joined Queens DA Richard A. Brown for a packed press conference.

Brown called Kim's murder "one of the most savage and brutal homicides we had seen in Queens County. Kimberly was a twenty-year-old college student in the prime of her life. It was a horrendous crime. This is one case that I will not forget because it was so horrific, because of the manner in which this young woman was killed."

The DA praised Tommy Antonakos for his dedication to helping to find his daughter's killers. Brown felt that Tommy never wavered in his commitment. Brown and everyone else in his office marveled at Tommy's strength in the face of tragedy. For Brown, it was a sad but moving experience. That day, for the first time since Kim had been killed, Tommy met a newspaper reporter to express his feelings. Al Baker from the *Daily News* met Tommy and his brother at the Arco Diner in Bay Ridge, Brooklyn—where Tommy and Kim had met for dinner at least once a week. They sat at the same table every time. This time, Joseph sat in the corner chair, Kim's chair. Tears came to Tommy's eyes as he spoke of the arrests.

"You sort of daydream to yourself that when you find these people, your daughter is going to come back. Let me tell you, I just came from the cemetery—she is not coming back. If she were here right now, I would say to her, 'I'll miss you for the rest of my life, and you're never going to be away from me,' " Tommy said through his tears.

"She never is," Joseph comforted his brother. "She never is, Tommy. She's never away."

Tommy buried his face in his hands.

"Maybe I shouldn't have bought her the new car. I should have made her come back to live in Staten Island. I think about it all the time. Where did I go wrong? Where did I go wrong?"

Tommy talked about Kim's job, school, her childhood, and her first communion party at the Tavern on the Green.

"She was just like gold, this kid. She never realized how pretty she was. Even though she had more than the next kid, she never made you feel she was better than you. It was her goodness—that was her weakness," Tommy lamented.

He said that he never suspected Josh Torres for a second, because he was his daughter's friend.

"The first words from him were, 'I called around. I called all her friends . . .' To Kimberly, I know that I was her hero," Tommy told the reporter. "I have no doubt that when they had her tied up, she had in her mind, 'Where's my Daddy? When is my Daddy going to come and get me?' My daughter caught the worst break you can catch," Tommy said, his face flushing red with fury. "She caught the worst break anybody could catch in their life."

Once his anger had subsided, Tommy's tears returned, as he spoke again of the arrests of Josh and Nick.

"I know it sounds crazy . . . It makes so little difference as far as getting my daughter back, but at least I know my daughter is saying right now, 'It's good, Daddy—it's good that you got them off the street.' "

CHAPTER TWENTY-SEVEN

THE CASE GOES SOUTH

Blondie felt better after Josh and Nick had been arrested and held without bail, but she still did not feel safe. Josh's threat that he would kill her still rang in her ears. Because Josh had arrived with several men when he attacked her with the shovel a few days earlier, she was afraid one of them might come after her. Her fears seemed to be realized just a few hours after she saw Josh taken away in handcuffs. At 8:30 that Wednesday night, Blondie was standing outside her apartment when she was accosted by a portly figure with a crooked baseball cap over a crewcut. She later told police that she recognized the dark-skinned face of one of Josh's friends, whom Josh had told her was at the wheel of the getaway car the night that Josh killed Joey: Redrum. He was four inches shorter than Blondie, and was dressed in blue jeans and a green t-shirt.

"I'm going to smoke you, if you talk," Redrum threatened Blondie. "Nothing better happen to Josh. You better not have gone to the police—Josh is going to know."

Before he left, Redrum lifted up his shirt and exposed the butt of a black gun tucked into his pants for Blondie to see. Blondie reported the threat to the cops and made a criminal complaint for menacing against Redrum, whose real name was Peter Rodriguez. Redrum had been arrested upstate three years earlier for possession of two ounces of crack cocaine. He was on parole until 1999.

Blondie asked for police protection and was given it. After discussing it with the detectives and the DA's office, Blondie decided to enter the Queens District Attorney's Office Witness Relocation Program with her kids. Mike Castillo and Blondie's brother also decided to enter the program. They packed their things, and were driven to an isolated hotel on Long Island. Blondie and the others were warned to sever all contact with their friends and family, except in controlled situations, because their lives were in danger.

Joey's widow Antonette was surprised to hear Nick's voice on the phone. Nick protested his innocence, and told her he was not involved in Joey's murder. That was, of course, literally true, but completely false. Nick had betrayed Joey to Josh, and Antonette believed she was going to be next. Nick was charged with Kim's murder, but because Kim had been killed before Nick was sentenced to probation for his previous robbery, he was not guilty of a violation of his probation. After she overcame her shock at hearing Nick on the phone from the Rikers Island lockup, Antonette asked him about Kim's murder.

"What got into you guys with this girl?" she asked.

"I can't talk now, they're calling me for chow," Nick said, and hurriedly hung up.

Antonette did not think anyone was calling him to dinner—she felt that he just didn't want to answer the question. In a second call, Nick continued to be evasive. On the evening of September 28th, Antonette returned home to discover that Nick had called a third time from jail—and left a message on her answering machine. Incredibly, Nick was asking her to visit him.

"I would like to see you and kick some shit around," Nick said.

Was Nick interested in protesting his innocence in person—or was there some message he had for Antonette that he did not want to say over the phone, or record on an answering machine? Antonette was alarmed, and reported the contact to Louie, who asked her if she would visit Nick in jail while wearing a "wire"—an electronic bug. Antonette said she would have to talk to her family first, but that she was trying to disentangle herself from the mess Joey had gotten her into—not get deeper into it. She would not wear a wire on Nick, or anyone else.

Louie Pia and Rich Tirelli searched for Jay, starting with his family and friends, but he had split to Puerto Rico and had not returned. Josh had named Jay in his interrupted confession, but Nick had not. There was no real evidence against Jay, but the cops still wanted him. Next, they contacted Joey's father in Florida, who said that he had heard of the tape but did not have it himself. He named several family members who might have it, including Joey's uncle Luis Negron.

"Listen, I don't have the tape at home. It's in my locker at work," Luis told Louie when reached by phone.

A week later, Luis turned over the tape, and Louie, Tom, Rich, and Julian were able to hear a very rare piece of evidence—a clandestine recording of kidnappers during a kidnapping. The problem was that the tape had been tampered with. It was marred by erasures, which left large holes in the recording—holes large enough for a defense lawyer to drive a truck through. Also, it was difficult to understand what was being said at various points. Since the tape would probably be thrown out of court, it was decided not to introduce it into evidence.

After Josh's arrest, the car he had been driving was impounded by police, and searched for evidence from the two murders. Josh had told Blondie and Mike and others that he had used April's baby-blue Nissan Sentra hatchback the night he shot Joey—a somewhat conspicuous and unlikely getaway car. April called Louie repeatedly, demanding to know when she was going to get her car back. Louie thought Kim's good friend since childhood might want to help put her killers away, but she said she could not help—she just wanted her car back.

"I can't tell you if he was involved, but even if I knew . . . he's the father of my baby," April told Louie.

Blondie also wanted her set of wheels back—she called Johnny Wilde virtually on a daily basis, wanting to know when she was going to get her motorcycle back. She and her four kids were crammed into a hotel room on Long Island. Also under wraps in the same spot were Blondie's brother and Mike Castillo. Blondie kept asking Louie if he had arrested Redrum, but Louie had no witnesses or evidence that would have allowed him to charge Redrum with complicity in Joey's murder, or with anything else. Neither Blondie nor Mike had heard Redrum admit involvement in the hit. What they said they had heard from Josh was hearsay evidence, and not admissible in court.

The arrests were front-page news, and led the evening television news broadcasts. The horrific story of a beautiful college girl burned alive struck a primitive chord of shock and outrage in readers and viewers. How could such an act of barbarism take place in the middle of modern civilization?

Blondie called Louie and told him she was stunned to see "Blondie" mentioned in a *Daily News* story—as the woman who had informed on the killers. She felt it endangered her life, but, of course, the men who wanted her dead already knew her real name and what she looked like. Blondie complained that in the rush to safety, she didn't have milk or food, or diapers for her children. She threatened to leave the hotel.

"I need somebody to come and take me shopping," Blondie said.

"Stay there. We'll be out—we'll get some food for your kids," Louie promised her.

Louie and Tom drove out and helped Blondie adjust. It was difficult to care for a baby and three other kids in a small hotel room. Blondie was supposed to be hiding out. Her life depended on keeping a low profile, and preventing the bad guys from learning her whereabouts. On the weekend after the roundup of Josh and Nick, Blondie picked up the phone and called the *Daily News*. She was angry, and wanted to speak to somebody. On Monday, September 11th, the *Daily News* ran an exclusive interview with "Blondie" by columnist Mike McAlary. The article, under a headline "KISSED, THEN SET AFLAME," included a smiling picture of Kim and an account of Josh kissing Kim on the forehead, telling her, "I'm sorry it has to end this way, but life sucks," before setting her on fire. Needless to say, Louie, Tom, Rich, and the prosecutors were very unpleasantly surprised to see that the star witness whom they had secreted in their Witness Relocation Program was calling people—much less blabbing to the press. Blondie had not yet appeared before the grand jury that was expected to indict Nick for second-degree murder, and Josh for the murders of Kim and Joey Negron.

Louie and Tom drove out to see Blondie to find out what was going on. Blondie got in their car and they drove to a pizzeria to get a pizza for her kids. She denied speaking to the press, despite a story that was filled with her quotes. She accused Louie of leaking her name to the press. Louie told her he had not. As Blondie denied leaking to the media, her beeper went off. Tom and Louie looked at each other in amazement.

"Are you beeping people?" Louie asked. "Are you making calls from the hotel? You're not answering your beeps, are you?"

Blondie was evasive, so Louie asked to see the beeper. The pager contained a phone number with a 212 area code—Manhattan.

"Whose number is that?" Louie demanded.

"I don't even know what number this is," Blondie claimed.

Louie picked up the car's cell phone and dialed the number. A *Daily News* columnist answered.

"Are you talking to this guy from the *Daily News*?" Louie asked in an angry voice.

"Since the article was written with my name in it, I wanted to talk to a reporter to, basically, straighten out whatever was being said in the newspaper," Blondie admitted.

Louie was furious. He felt that Blondie was not only accusing him of leaking to the press in an attempt to cover up her leaks, but was also endangering the case against the killers, and might be endangering her own life.

"You're on my ass, and you're calling the *Daily News*?" Louie asked, incredulously.

He lectured her sternly about talking to the media, and told her not to answer beeps—unless she wanted to get herself killed. Blondie stopped talking to the press, but she was not happy living in a hotel room. As the weeks went by, she became more and more unhappy. She began fighting with her brother and with Mike Castillo. The idea of spending a year in hiding until Josh and Nick came to trial seemed like forever. Blondie began to realize that becoming the state's star witness against the killers might mean a life sentence of fear for herself and her family. Blondie begged to be moved to a real apartment and eventually she was relocated to one above a bar on Montrose Street in Brooklyn. Louie and Tom and the NYPD were no longer responsible for Blondie's safety—that had been taken over by detectives in the Queens DA's office—but it was still their case.

Nick was not enjoying his stay at Rikers Island. Shortly after the front-page newspaper stories about Kim's murder, and Nick's past use of a .45 automatic against the heads of a woman and child, Nick was attacked by a gang of five inmates, who tried to slash his throat. It's a curious fact that drug dealers, thieves, rapists, and killers in jail are always glad to see someone accused of more heinous crimes—like child molestation—so they can feel superior to them. In Nick's case, the jailbirds were filled with righteous indignation at his dirty deeds. When the C-95 Cellblock inmates surrounded and grabbed him, Nick at first feared that it was a Mafia hit—until one snarling inmate spoke:

"So you like killing girls, and pulling guns out on kids?"

Nick jerked away, just as the home-made "shank" blade lashed for his throat. It caught him on the cheek—gashing open the skin beneath his beard, but missing the vital arteries in the throat. There was a lot of blood, and Nick was rushed to King's County Hospital in Brooklyn. His wound was stitched, and Nick was able to have visitors—like Jay, just back from Puerto Rico and still tan.

Jay thanked Nick for not mentioning him in his first statement to the cops. He was grateful, and wanted Nick to stay loyal to him. No problem, Nick told Jay, but he and Josh needed a favor from someone on the outside. They wanted Blondie and Mike Castillo "out of the way" and they expected him to handle it, with assistance from Redrum.

Soon.

Jay felt that he could not say no. If he refused, Nick could rat him out, and he would also be in jail. Or, worse, he might just be added to their hit list. Jay decided to play along with the game. He didn't want to kill anyone. Maybe he could stall them.

Although Blondie, her brother, and Mike had been warned by the detectives from the DA's office to cut off all contact with their old associates, the good advice was ignored. Blondie was still responding to numbers on her old beeper—and calling them back from her new unlisted phone. One night in November, two months after the arrests, Blondie's unlisted phone rang.

"Hello?"

"Hello. Do you know who this is?"

Blondie recognized the voice—it was her old boyfriend Jay.

"Yeah, I know who it is. How did you get my number?" Blondie asked.

"Where you living, baby?" Jay asked Blondie.

"How do I know I can trust you?" Blondie asked.

"I want to meet with you," Jay told her, assuring her he meant her no harm, that he simply missed her.

"I don't want to meet with you because I've got a bunch

of maniacs out to kill me," said Blondie. "I don't trust you. How do I know you're not trying to hunt me down?"

"No, I'm just confused," Jay said, protesting that he had not kidnapped or burned Kim.

"And you didn't do anything to protect her," Blondie countered.

She knew that Jay had been involved with Josh and Nick and Joey in the killing, and she didn't trust him. Jay repeatedly asked Blondie to give him her address, or meet him somewhere. When she hung up the phone, Blondie was convinced that Jay was trying to set her up for Redrum to kill her. She knew that Redrum had talked to Josh in jail, and Blondie believed Josh was pulling the strings from behind bars. If Redrum really had been with Josh the night Joey was killed, then he was motivated by more than just loyalty to Josh. That made four convicted felons who might get off—if Blondie disappeared.

Blondie called Louie and told him what had happened, and begged him to arrest Redrum. Again, she was told there was no evidence against Redrum. Louie again scolded her for contacting people when she was supposed to be in hiding. Someone she had contacted had obviously given Jay her unlisted number.

One night, Blondie got a call from a woman who knew Jay. The call confirmed her worst fear—Jay, the woman said, was supposed to kill her for Josh and Nick. The woman said she was calling to warn her, and offered to let Blondie listen in on a conference call with Jay—without his knowing it. Blondie quickly agreed. The woman warned Blondie not to speak, and punched a few buttons. Blondie then heard a phone ring.

"Hello?"

It was Jay. The woman on the other end chatted with Jay about a few things, and then asked him why he was going to get rid of Blondie.

"I don't know if I can do it," Jay told the woman.

Jay said that Josh and Nick wanted it done, but he seemed reluctant to do the job.

"Why are you asking me all these questions?" Jay asked, suddenly suspicious.

The phone call shook Blondie. She felt as though she couldn't take it anymore. She feared she might have a nervous breakdown. She had to do something.

A week later, Blondie called Louie again. She claimed that her brother had slapped her around during an argument, and she was thinking of having him arrested. She said her brother had threatened to reveal her new address to the guys who were looking for it. Louie and Tom arranged to meet her and drove to her apartment. Blondie got into their car to discuss her plans, but first she asked if they had locked up Redrum yet. When Tom told her they had not, and could not arrest Redrum, Blondie shook her head.

"Jay's back in town," said Blondie. "He got my number."

The detectives were concerned that Jay was trying to find her, but she didn't know where Jay was, and he didn't know where Blondie was. The news was welcome, and both detectives made a mental note that it was time to start looking for Jay again.

"You gotta lay low," Tom told Blondie.

"Well, I'm going away in two days."

"You're going away? Where?" Tom asked.

"The Poconos or Florida."

"You're going away in two days and you don't know where?" Tom asked, incredulously.

"I may be gone for a week."

"Where did you get the money for this?" Tom demanded. "Who's paying for this?"

"Friends, relatives—because of the stress I've been under," Blondie said.

"We need to hear from you," Tom ordered. "Give us a call in a couple of days."

Tom did not think that Blondie was telling them the truth.

He felt she was hiding something. They warned her to be careful and not to talk to her old buddies, and to keep in touch with them—and with the detectives from the DA's Witness Relocation Program, who were responsible for her.

Louie and Tom felt it might be good for her to get away— maybe she would relax, and it couldn't hurt to put some distance between her and the guys who were looking for her. Although she seemed calm, it was obvious that her situation had taken a toll on her—she looked exhausted. Maybe a little vacation was just what their stressed-out witness needed. She promised that she would be careful and keep in touch.

As Tom had suspected, Blondie was lying to them. She did not go to the Poconos, or Florida. She went to Kennedy Airport, and got on a plane to Ecuador in Central America. Two weeks later, Blondie returned to the U.S., stepping off a jet at Miami International Airport. After clearing customs, Blondie was scheduled to board another plane bound for New York.

Florida was a major point of entry for illegal drugs into America, and the U.S. Customs Service carefully examined arriving baggage—and people. Routinely, customs agents searched bags, and questioned arriving foreigners and U.S. citizens about their trips abroad. In addition to smuggling drugs inside bags, canes, souvenirs, food, radios, and hundreds of other objects, drug "mules" swallowed prophylactics filled with dope. But ingesting enough dope to kill an office building full of people was dangerous—a race against the clock. The idea was to swallow the latex balls as close as possible to landing, and then recover them as they emerged from the body, often with the help of laxatives. If there was a long delay, stomach acid might burst the rubbers, releasing a massive overdose inside the body. Sometimes, men and women collapsed at the airport and died a painless death from the fortune in dope released suddenly into their system. Federal agents used detailed profiles of drug smugglers to spot dope couriers. They also used drug-sniffing dogs, and portable x-ray machines to ferret out contraband.

But, usually, the best instrument of criminal detection was the human brain.

A female customs agent at Miami International Airport noticed that the passport of the woman in front of her gave an address in New York, a major market for drugs—and that the woman had come from Ecuador, a major source of drugs. She casually asked Blondie if she had been visiting family in Ecuador.

"No, business" said Blondie.

The agent felt that Blondie seemed very tense. She kept asking questions.

"What do you do?" she asked Blondie with a smile.

"I'm an interior decorator," Blondie replied.

The agent, glancing at Blondie's exterior, did not think Blondie looked like an interior decorator. She didn't look like a business traveler.

"Do you have a business card?"

"No, I work out of my house," Blondie replied.

"Do you have any swatches?" the agent asked, trying out a little interior decorator jargon on Blondie.

"What's that?" Blondie asked.

When a purported interior decorator did not know that swatches are small samples of material, it was time for further investigation. The agent asked Blondie to step into a side room. Once there, she searched Blondie's luggage. When the officer did not find any interior decorator materials, she told Blondie that she was going to be searched. Blondie sighed and told the agent that she was carrying things under her clothing. Blondie opened her clothes and began pulling out objects that looked like bulging, beige sausages from her bra and underwear. The agent quickly recognized them as prophylactics filled with drugs—some kind of white paste. Her suspicions had been confirmed—Blondie was a "mule," a drug courier. Blondie admitted that she had also secreted drugs inside her vagina. Blondie was taken to a local hospital, where an emergency room doctor removed more drugs. When all the bulbous, balloon-like shapes had been deposited on a table and tested, they amounted to more than a kilo of concentrated heroin paste. The dope could be purchased outside the U.S. for about $130,000, but it was worth about a million dollars when ''cut'' with powdered milk sugar, and put into the arms and noses of junkies on the streets of New York.

Blondie did not make her New York connection. She was handcuffed, advised of her rights, and arrested for narcotics trafficking. Blondie, facing heavy time behind bars on her first arrest, began pleading and crying. She spun an incredible tale of shadowy drug figures who were holding her children hostage in New York, but it was to no avail—the people who had arrested her were going to make a federal case out of it.

Julian Wise was sitting at his desk in the Queens DA's office, when he picked up the phone and heard a man identify himself as an assistant U.S. attorney in Miami.

''Hello. What can I do for you?'' asked Julian.

''Do you know Raquel Montalvo?''

''Yes . . .'' said Julian, suddenly apprehensive about his witness.

''She was just before a federal magistrate, and she was yelling out your name.''

Blondie, he said, had been busted at the Miami airport ''for bringing in a kilo of heroin.''

It was a while before Julian could answer. He was stunned. Julian felt like he had been punched in the stomach. What the hell was Blondie doing in Florida smuggling drugs? He told the U.S. attorney that Blondie was a cooperating witness, that she was needed to put away killers in two murders. Her life was in danger. Julian asked the federal attorney to help—he had to salvage Blondie as a witness.

''We'll do what we can,'' the U.S. attorney replied before hanging up.

That did not sound very hopeful. Julian could not believe it. After all they had been through with the Antonakos case, it had finally seemed to be going well. Now, his star witness, who had never been arrested before, had been busted—for international drug smuggling.

"My entire case against Josh Torres is sitting in a Miami jail cell," Julian thought, hopelessly.

The Queens DA's office detective in charge of Blondie's witness relocation called Louie to give him the bad news. .

"Your main witness has been arrested for muling over a kilo of heroin from Ecuador," he told Louie, who could not believe it.

But there was more. Louie called a DEA agent he knew in Miami, who told him something that was even more alarming: Blondie, the agent said, was telling federal officials that gangsters were holding her kids hostage and had threatened to kill them unless she became a drug mule. It was a plan to discredit her as a witness, she claimed.

"They made me do it because I'm a major witness in a murder case in New York," Blondie told the feds. "They've got my kids!"

It was a nightmare for the detectives and the prosecution. An NYPD Emergency Services team was immediately dispatched to Blondie's place on Montrose Street in Brooklyn to rescue her four kids. The cops, clad in black, wore bulletproof "flak vests" that said POLICE in large orange letters. Carrying shotguns and machine guns, the SWAT team bounded up the stairs to the second floor. They stormed the apartment, ready for a firefight or a hostage drama, but found only a terrified babysitter. There were no hostages, no drug gunsels, no kidnappers. The kids had been watching TV when the police commandos burst in. It would have been better for the case if the police had rescued Blondie's kids from a gang dispatched by Josh and his evil minions. Blondie was obviously lying about her children being held hostage at gunpoint. What had made their star witness suddenly go off on a criminal escapade? Julian and Louie would make every effort to keep Blondie out of jail, and rehabilitate her as a witness, even though their star seemed to have fallen to

Earth. Julian beeped his boss, Gene Reibstein, over and over, to tell him about Blondie.

"It's Blondie," a distraught Julian told Gene when he called back.

"Did she get killed?" Gene asked.

Julian detailed the disaster for Gene.

"Jesus!" cried Gene. "Holy shit! This is not a good thing. What are we going to do now? We are in a lot of trouble."

It soon became clear that federal authorities in Miami were not going to let Blondie go. She claimed to be cooperating, but she stuck to the same story that had already been proved to be a lie—that mysterious bad guys had set her up at the behest of Nick and Josh, and were threatening her kids. Blondie claimed that two shady guys whom she knew only as Manuel and Osvaldo were behind it all, and that Nick Libretti had sent them to get her out of town. The feds believed that Blondie had made up the whole story and was refusing to tell them who was really behind the drug importation scheme. Blondie was not going to get a deal, so a trial date was set in Miami. Louie went to Miami and spoke to Blondie, who protested her innocence.

"If you don't believe me, ask my girlfriend in New York," Blondie suggested.

Meanwhile, back in New York, Julian and Gene were trying to prepare Mike Castillo to fill Blondie's shoes at the trial. The problem was that he had a criminal record, and seemed reluctant to testify. During the trial preparation period he got into another scrape in Atlantic City but was not arrested. He would also be vulnerable to a defense lawyer. Gene was afraid to rest the whole case on Mike.

When he got back, Louie went to Washington Heights and looked up Blondie's girlfriend, *Martha, who was supposed to corroborate the tale of Blondie's frame-up. But after interviewing the woman, she folded up and admitted that Blondie had called her and asked her to lie.

"Blondie told me to make the whole thing up," Martha said, shaking her head. "I've got a family."

She told Louie that Blondie had run drugs before—but had never been caught.

"It's all bullshit. She's been doing this for years," Martha claimed.

A year after Josh and Nick were arrested, Julian and Louie flew down to Miami to testify on Blondie's behalf. It was a last-ditch attempt to save her as a witness. If the jury could see the crime-scene photos of what had been done to Kim, perhaps it might make the difference between a conviction and an acquittal. Louie was angry at Blondie, but still felt she was a great witness in the Antonakos case. In his heart, Louie felt that she had done the right thing, and he tried to help her. He would do everything that he could, but he could not be a party to perjury—even if that meant that Blondie might go to jail, and Josh and Nick might go free. He had no choice.

The defense had also arranged for Blondie's friend Martha to fly down to testify for the defense. After the defense lawyer spoke to Martha behind closed doors, he told her that she would not be called to the stand and could go right back to New York. But Louie stopped her in the hallway and handed her a subpoena—from the prosecution, whom Louie had informed about the perjury scheme.

Louie took the stand in Blondie's trial on September 3rd, 1996—one year from the day that he had first met her. Louie told the jury how vital Blondie's testimony was, how the killers might get off if she were not free to testify. Unfortunately, on cross-examination, he was also forced to tell the court that he knew nothing about Blondie's claims, and that she had lied about her kids being held hostage. It was strange to see Blondie—who was to have been the main witness for the prosecution in New York—sitting as the defendant in Miami. Blondie then took the stand in her own defense, and wove her tangled tale of fear that she said had forced her to become a drug mule to save her kids.

After Blondie stepped down, the federal prosecutor put Martha on the stand. She told the jury that Blondie asked her to come to court and lie. It was devastating to Blondie's defense. The jury did not buy Blondie's story, and quickly found her guilty of drug smuggling—and an additional charge of perjury. Blondie was later sentenced to a minimum of 15 years in a federal penitentiary.

"She played both sides of the fence, and she lost," Louie thought after the verdict.

That was bad for Blondie's kids and for Tommy Antonakos—and good for Josh Torres and Nick Libretti.

Back in Queens, Gene Reibstein felt that Blondie was finished as a witness. A defense lawyer would easily be able to discredit her now, by portraying her as a drug dealer looking for a way out of jail, and a convicted perjurer, who could not be believed.

The upstanding citizen and mother of four who was supposed to put Josh and Nick away, was herself going to stay behind bars—maybe for longer than Josh or Nick would ever get for burning Kim alive.

It seemed as if the whole case against Josh and Nick had gone south with Blondie.

CHAPTER TWENTY-EIGHT

GOING ALONG WITH THEIR GAME

Louie was dispirited, but he would not give up. He had been forced to help put his own star witness—Blondie—away, but he had one last plan to put Josh behind bars. The plan was simple: find Jay and get him to testify against Josh. Louie had checked with Jay's relatives, old girlfriends, and friends, but could not lay his hands on the elusive suspect. Josh's statements—before his lawyer called the precinct—had put Jay into the kidnap gang, but there was no real case against Jay. Louie hoped that the threat of a murder rap might get him to cave in, and nudge him into the witness box to fill the void left by Blondie. Jay was the only one who fit the bill—if he could be found. He had to give it a shot. It was Jay or nobody. Louie knew it was a long shot—and his last shot. They had tagged Josh out in a squeeze play, and Louie would be damned if Josh was going to win the game.

"We can't count on this guy Castillo," Gene lamented to Rob Ferino one morning, after Mike Castillo had been arrested on some minor charge. "We gotta figure a way to win this."

It looked like Josh might beat the rap. Just two months after triumphant arrests, the case was in ruins. Gene knew Louie was hunting for Jay but there was no guarantee that he would find him. It certainly seemed unlikely in the extreme that a guy who participated in the murder of his own girlfriend, and then fled the country, would suddenly agree to cooperate, when they had almost nothing on him. Gene was wrestling over what to do. It now seemed like a good idea to put Nick on trial first—because he had made a vid-eotape that Gene felt a jury would have to believe. Gene feared the only way out was to offer Nick a deal—give him fifteen-years-to-life, in exchange for which he would testify against Josh at the trial. It would be a bitter pill to swallow—for the detectives, the prosecutors, and especially the family. It would mean that of the three surviving bad guys, only one would get the heavy twenty-five-years-to-life behind bars, the second would get a lesser sentence, and the third, Jay, would walk away. Unfortunately, the criminal justice system, like politics, was the art of the possible—it just wasn't nec-essarily *justice*.

Nick did not have a court-appointed lawyer. His mother had hired Harold Levy, an experienced criminal attorney.

"My guy's innocent," Levy told Julian by phone. "I'll even let you speak to him."

Nick and Levy came in for a deal conference but they quickly rejected the fifteen-year offer. It was too much time, they said. Nick was used to really good deals.

Gene felt he could not offer Nick a shorter sentence for his testimony. This was not, after all, the "Let's Make a Deal" game show—Nick was up to his neck in the kidnap and murder. Gene and his boss, DA Richard A. Brown, had to face the public and look Tommy Antonakos in the eye. For the second time, the case against Josh Torres had fallen apart. Josh seemed to have the Devil's own luck.

Pete Donohue, a *Daily News* reporter assigned to the Queens courthouse, had been working on the Antonakos story—which had quieted down. Pete was a very persistent reporter, and was always roving the corridors of the court-house looking for a good story. On January 6th, 1997, Pete went to Justice Thomas Demakos' third-floor courtroom and made a routine request of the court clerk—to be allowed to see the Josh Torres court file, to find out if there was any new material inside. Leafing through the thick file of legal papers in the file, Pete saw the familiar criminal complaint, the indictment, and other documents on the case. Then he noticed a copy of the defendant's statement to Detective Richard Tirelli on the night of his arrest. Pete began reading the statement, but stopped when he found something new on page eight:

"In sum and substance, the defendant stated: B-Q organized the kidnapping of Kimberly Antonakos."

Josh's statement fingered "B-Q" as the mastermind behind the bungled Antonakos kidnapping and murder. That meant that a fourth guy involved in burning Kim alive was still at large. Earlier in the same statement, Josh had told Rich that "B-Q" was the nickname of Jay. Pete knew when he had a story, and he filed it for the next day's paper. It ran on page 22, under the headline "FOURTH SUSPECT IN TORCH SLAY?" The story quoted an unnamed law enforcement source:

"We believe there is a number four. He is an un-arrested person who was probably involved in this."

Josh's unsigned statement was in the open court file by mistake. Prosecutors and police were not happy to see the story. For Louie, it looked like another deadly blow—Jay might see the story and go on the lam again, or he might lawyer-up. Either way, Louie figured he was screwed again.

Jay had seen the newspaper story saying that he was the mastermind of the kidnapping, and he already knew Louie was looking for him. But rather than get on another plane, Jay did something much smarter—he played it cool. Jay called Louie and said that he had heard Louie was looking for him, and he wanted to come in and talk. Louie was stunned.

For once, a press leak had helped the case.

After several weeks of delaying, Jay arrived at the Queens Homicide Squad in Forest Hills with his police officer brother-in-law, who brought him in to speak to detectives. Jay looked like a hard street case. He removed a jacket to reveal a white tank shirt. Jay's muscular torso was dotted with tattoos, including one of Jesus and a cross on his right arm. The most striking was a tattoo of a heart broken in half over his own heart—with the word ''MOM.'' He was cordial, and seemed relaxed with Louie and Tom in the interview room. Rich Tirelli, Gene, and Julian were also there. At one point, Gene called Rob Ferino at home and told him to come down.

''We've got Jay, and he's talking to Lou Pia and Tom Shevlin,'' an excited Gene told Rob.

On the way to the One-Twelve Precinct Homicide Squad office, Rob picked up a six-pack of beer—just in case there might be anything to celebrate.

After a few preliminaries, Jay gave a statement in which he claimed to have been kept in the dark about the kidnapping until after Kim had been killed. After that, he said, he kept quiet out of fear of Josh. It was a self-serving statement, one designed to provide the minimum admissions and get Jay off the hook. In return, he expected a slap on the wrist and minimal jail time—or none at all. Louie took a seven-page statement and had Jay sign it.

''This guy's lying to us,'' said Gene at a conference outside the room. ''Now that we know he was there, he's got to do some jail time.''

Jay had admitted criminal behavior, and now they had a grip on him. If Jay and his lawyer agreed, it would be a Devil's bargain—one that would let a lesser player off easy, while, hopefully, convicting the other two killers. Louie and Tom went back inside and confronted Jay, telling him that they believed he was more deeply involved. He had confessed to crimes, and had confessed to hindering prosecution, which carried a maximum sentence of five-to-fifteen-years in prison, they told him. Jay repeated that he did not know anything about Kim's murder until after she was dead.

''What do you know about the tape that Joey made?'' Louie asked.

The question stopped Jay in his tracks. The tape, Louie told him, was made while Kim was alive.

"You're on it," Louie said.

Jay quickly changed his story. His second story was that he had found out earlier—after she was kidnapped, but before her death. Gene was still unhappy. He confronted Jay about the latest version of his story and yelled at him:

"I don't believe a fucking thing you're saying, and I'm not putting you in front of a jury with that bullshit," Gene said angrily.

Even though he expected it, Gene was furious that the guy was still angling to wiggle out of responsibility for his involvement. Kim had been his friend, and lover, and—at the very least—Jay had admitted that he knew who kidnapped her. Rather than dial 911, Jay had helped his buddies cover it up.

"Nobody in the world would believe you," Rob chimed in.

"What you're saying makes no sense at all," said Julian.

"Well, I'm getting out of here," said Jay, rising to his feet.

"You're not going anywhere," Louie yelled. "You're under arrest."

Louie's statement startled the prosecutors, who knew they could not make an arrest.

"You're better off cooperating with us than going to jail," said Julian.

But Jay was angry and wanted to go home. Apparently, he thought everyone would believe his improbable story, and just let him walk out the door. Rob Ferino advised Jay of his rights and took an audio statement from him, in which he admitted going to the Woodhaven house, but said he refused to go inside. Jay began talking about Kim and about his hard life. Jay told Rob about his son Brandon, who had died of a liver disease.

"I was too busy screwing girls to save my son's life," Jay said.

He told Rob about seeing his mother's body just after she was stabbed to death.

"He stabbed her over and over again," Jay said, shaking his head.

Rob thought Jay seemed to express genuine remorse about Kim, and sorrow over the untimely deaths of his mother and son. Rob thought that perhaps Jay, unlike Josh and Nick, had a conscience. Rob knew that Julian felt that Jay was in on the kidnap plot from the start, and that a deal would essentially allow Jay to get away with murder, but Rob wasn't so sure. He felt that Jay seemed to have a spark of decency. Jay's statement might have been unbelievable, and self-serving, but at least they now had an eyewitness to events that could convict Josh. This time, it was agreed, the witness was going to jail—to protect him and the case. The problem was where to hide Jay until the trial. Hiding a criminal in a jail was like hiding a tree in a forest. But if they sent Jay to jail in the city—to Rikers Island—his whereabouts might soon be known. Jay might end up dead, with a sharpened spoon sticking out of his neck. Julian called a friend of his in the correctional system, and they decided to hide Jay on Eastern Long Island—in the Suffolk County Jail in Riverhead. Louie and Tom made the eighty-mile drive with Jay and lodged him in a cell inside the suburban lockup under the name of "Junior Cortez."

Jay did not settle in easily. He got into fights on a daily basis. He was given a court-appointed lawyer named Warren Silverman, but he was not happy. He called Julian, Louie, or Rob Ferino every day. Rob was a rookie and had more time than anyone else to listen to the griping of a witness. Jay was beginning to trust Louie, but Rob was at his desk most of the day, and was more reachable. Rob had a sympathetic ear, so Jay called him three or four times a day. Jay complained about jail conditions, the charges against him, and life in general. Jay also spoke fondly of Kim.

"She treated me like an equal," said Jay. "I think about her all the time."

Jay spoke about visiting the Madrina, and Rob was beginning to believe that he felt real guilt and remorse.

"Everyone in my life who I'm close to dies," Jay grumbled to Rob one day. "I believe every time I try to turn my life around, something happens, and I lose."

"Here's your chance," said Rob.

After some hemming and hawing, Jay said that he wanted Rob's advice, and presented a hypothetical situation to the young prosecutor:

"If three guys robbed a bank, and a fourth guy found out about it," Jay began, and then changed his mind, moving the scene to a grocery store robbery, where the owner was tied up by the robbers, who later return to let him go.

"Suppose that guy just stays in the car," while the others went inside, Jay said.

The bad guys are startled to find their victim no longer alive, and exclaim, "Oh, God, he's dead" before going to a gas station to buy gas to burn the grocery store down, Jay said.

"What does that make this guy guilty of?" Jay asked.

"I'm not sure," Rob replied. "Maybe we should talk." It looked like Jay was about to drop the other shoe. It also looked like Rob the rookie had scored.

When Jay and his lawyer Warren Silverman came in for a conference, Gene offered Jay two-to-six years in jail—instead of the maximum five-to-fifteen. Louie told Jay that at last he had a chance to turn his life around and do the right thing. Jay's lawyer told him to forget it—he was going to walk Jay right out the door. The lawyer stood up. They had suddenly reached the see-you-in-court moment. The case against Josh Torres had all fallen apart for a third—and probably last—time.

Jay was in turmoil. He wanted Josh and Nick to stay behind bars—he believed his health depended on it—and he was looking for a way out.

"I'm not gonna go anywhere in life if I don't stop being a loser," Jay thought. "It's time to do the right thing."

"No. I wanna come clean," Jay said aloud at last, rejecting his lawyer's advice—and making it clear he knew how weak their case against him was:

"I know you guys can't get me for murder."

With a sigh, against his lawyer's advice, Jay finally admitted that Josh had told him about his kidnap scheme weeks before it had been put in motion. But Jay still maintained that he never believed Josh would do it. He said he only found out that Kim had been grabbed the next morning, when Josh called him at his sister's house. Jay accepted the 2-to-6-year deal, and signed a written cooperation agreement. Jay wanted them to believe he was not a monster. He said he had asked Joey and Nick where Kim was being held:

"Tell me where she's at—I'll go feed her," Jay said he had told his cohorts. "Bring her a blanket. Don't let anything happen to her."

He claimed that both Josh and Joey had threatened him, but he did not put a stop to it "because I didn't want to tell on my friends. Even though I was away from Joshua and by myself with my sister and her husband, who was a cop, I didn't tell anybody of what I knew to try to stop this kidnapping. I knew I was misleading Tommy Antonakos, and the police," said Jay, "but I was just going along with their game."

At last, Gene felt, they had a case that could be presented to a jury. Prosecutors quickly went to a judge and argued that they had a witness in two murder cases, whose life would be in danger if he were named before trial. Jay had to be kept a secret from the defense, and everyone else, they argued. One witness—Joey Negron—had already been killed, and others had been threatened, the judge was told. On January 16th 1997, the judge issued a court order allowing the Queens DA's office to keep Jay a secret witness, and directed that all records and files bearing his name be changed to the fictitious name "Junior Cortez."

This time there would be no leaks to the press, no wandering witness extending a two-week vacation into a fifteen-year term at a federal penitentiary.

Louie, Tom, and the prosecution team were back in the ball game.

CHAPTER TWENTY-NINE

TRIAL

Criminals out on bail, sometimes accompanied by their spouses and families, as well as witnesses, prosecutors, cops, defense lawyers, and other citizens entered the Queens Supreme Court building on Queens Boulevard in Kew Gardens by striding up wide marble steps into an open, two-story lobby. In a hurry to meet their various appointments with justice, they walked quickly past a huge, bright, two-story-high mosaic of multicolored tiles that decorated both sides of the lobby. Not one of them glanced up at the large, dramatic figures embroiled in epic struggles of crime and punishment, punctuated by flashes of lightning, that had been created thirty-five years earlier when the building was constructed. On the left wall was a morality tale in marble—the naked female figure of TRUTH towering above the scene, and revealing the figures that personified the Seven Deadly Sins that led to crime:

VANITY, clutching a mirror, sat inside his own castle in the air. His gold crown had been knocked off by the haughty gold mask he wore strapped over his face. ENVY's green face was twisted with jealousy of the others. HATE bared his snarling teeth, like a beast closing in for the kill. Barely clothed in a low-cut crimson gown, LUST was a study in sexual seduction. SLOTH slept snared in a spider web. GLUTTONY, a fat, slobbering pig munching food, wore a dirty gold crown lopsided over one of his pink ears. In the center, Av-ARICE, bedecked with a string of pearls and gold earrings, gloated over her coveted treasure box of gold, pearls, and cash.

Perhaps the intent of the parable in stone had been to force miscreants to recognize themselves among the seven sinners, and mend their evil ways. If so, the work of public art had not been a great success. Most criminals, it seemed, did not respond to moralistic art unless, perhaps, it was a metal sculpture: a steel jail cell door clanging shut behind them. On the adjacent wall, over the entrance to the elevators, visitors walked under another female figure—the lady JUSTICE in her flowing robes, whose eyes were not blindfolded. Her double-edged sword lay at her feet. In her right hand, she dangled the Scales of Justice. With her free hand, Justice pointed to the object on the lower scale, which tipped much lower with its heavy burden: a single human heart. The other, lighter scale, floating high in the air, bore a huge, heavy book of LAW. The message, for those who cared to notice, was that Justice was not blind—and that a heavy heart outweighed the system.

The drama of the murder trials of Joshua Torres and Nicholas Libretti played out two stories above the allegorical art in the lobby, inside the wood-paneled courtroom of New York State Supreme Court Justice Thomas Demakos. A stern, no-nonsense jurist with short, silver hair, and gold-rimmed glasses, Demakos, also of Greek heritage like Tommy Antonakos, had already presided over trials for some of the most violent and disturbing murders in the history of the county. Demakos was the judge for the murder trial of the three men who assassinated Police Officer Edward Byrne on the orders of infamous crack ringleader Howard "Pappy" Mason, to avenge his arrest. Earlier in the year, Demakos had sat on the College Point Massacre trial. He also presided over the shocking slaying of Bonnie Mejia—a witness to a burglary, who was murdered by the burglar in order to prevent her from testifying against him. As in the Antonakos homicide, the body of the young mother had been horribly mutilated, in an attempt to hide her identity and destroy evidence of the crime.

Many of the principals in the Antonakos murder case against Josh had already passed by the mural, and attended a series of evidentiary, pre-trial hearings. Josh's lawyer Andrew Worgan had challenged his client's arrest and tried to get the case thrown out, claiming that Josh had not been properly read his rights. When the trial began, Worgan might tell the jury that police had arrested other men for the crime—when Roger Rabbit and his gang were busted—and that Josh was also the wrong man. On May 20th, 1997, Louie Pia was called to the stand by Gene Reibstein at a hearing. Lanky and soft-spoken, clad in a dark suit and tie, Gene wore a neat salt-and-pepper mustache and beard. He artfully guided Louie through an uneventful direct examination. Few in the courtroom who did not know Gene would have guessed that the dignified prosecutor, in his spare time, was a road warrior who raced through his Long Island neighborhood on a skateboard or roller blades. On cross-examination, Worgan brought up the Roger Rabbit debacle:

WORGAN: Had you ever arrested anybody in this case prior to the arrest of Mr. Libretti and Mr. Torres?

REIBSTEIN: Objection.

THE COURT: Sustained.

WORGAN: What about Mr. Watts?

REIBSTEIN: Objection.

THE COURT: Sustained.

WORGAN: Did you ever take a statement from Dave Watts?

REIBSTEIN: Objection.

THE COURT: I'll allow it.

WORGAN: Did you ever take a statement from Mr. Watts?

PIA: Yes.

WORGAN: Concerning the death of Miss Antonakos?

PIA: Yes.
WORGAN: And in that statement, did he mention Mr.
   Libretti at all?
PIA: No.
WORGAN: Did he mention Mr. Torres?
PIA: No.

After the hearing, Gene decided that the incident indicated
that Josh's new defense lawyer, Martin Chandler, would
probably do the same thing at trial, and perhaps push it further. He might even talk of a police frame-up in his opening
statement, based on the voided arrests. Gene was concerned
about the issue—he was afraid it could prove to be a major
bump in the road. But Louie had no problem with any of it.
Louie felt he had nothing to hide. In fact, he knew a jury
would understand that the voided arrests proved the detectives had checked out every lead and followed them to the
end—and even admitted when they were wrong. That was
the opposite of a cover-up. Gene agreed with Louie, but he
knew that a good defense lawyer could exploit the false step
by investigators. Chandler was a good lawyer and might create doubt in the minds of jurors—possibly enough reasonable
doubt to let Josh walk out of the courtroom a free man. It
would be a safer bet to somehow exclude the whole Roger
Rabbit thing from the trial. The only way to defuse the issue
was to prevent Louie Pia from testifying, Gene felt. Tom
Shevlin was now retired, but he was not there for the mis-
taken arrests. Rich Tirelli was there, but Louie had been the
arresting officer. As the October trial date approached, Gene
decided that he would not call Louie to the stand. Louie was
furious. He believed that Gene was being over-cautious, and
did not want to be denied his chance to take the stand and
help put Josh away. Gene told Louie that he still might decide to put him on the stand, but on the first day of the trial,
Gene gave Louie the bad news: he would not call him for
the entire trial. Louie was angry and felt almost as if he were
being punished for the Roger Rabbit embarrassment, but he

understood Gene's reasons, and knew that he only wanted to make sure Kim's killers were convicted. Louie swallowed his pride and helped Gene with the case.

On Wednesday, October 30th, 1996, Josh sat calmly, confidently at the defense table with his lawyer Martin Chandler, as the trial began. Josh was dressed in a suit, dress shirt, and tie. For many people who walked into the courtroom, it was the first time they had ever seen Josh clad in traditional, semi-formal attire. But Josh's sartorial splendor would not end up on the nightly news. Justice Demakos had denied media applications to videotape the trial, after Josh's lawyer objected, saying that his client feared for his life. Josh sat in the front of the courtroom as if he didn't have a care in the world. He seemed completely confident that he would get off. In fact, Josh's self-centered expression was a mirror image of the visage of Vanity three floors below his feet. Josh, of course, knew what had happened to Blondie, and that Mike Castillo could be easily discredited by his lawyer. He also knew that the case against him for Joey's murder was even weaker than for Kim's murder—they had no bullet, no gun, and no witnesses who saw him do it. Josh's expression of smug amusement during the opening proceedings was good news for the prosecutors. It told them that their secret witness—Jay—was still a secret. For all Josh knew, his buddy was still hiding out in New Jersey somewhere. If Josh had known that his man B-Q, his homeboy from the "hood," had turned state's evidence against him, Josh would have been wearing a different face.

Tommy Antonakos was not allowed to enter the courtroom, nor was anyone else who was scheduled to appear as a witness before the court. Gene rose from his seat next to Julian Wise and Rob Ferino at the prosecution table to give his opening statement to the jury who would decide Josh's fate:

"Thank you, Your Honor. Good afternoon, ladies and gentlemen, Your Honor, Mister Chandler. At approximately four o'clock in the morning of March first, 1995, twenty-year-old Kimberly Antonakos, a kind, generous, pretty young woman with many friends, was kidnapped from her garage on the order and directions of this man,'' Gene said, pointing an accusatory finger straight at Josh. Gene detailed the kidnap plot, and told how Kim was taken. As he spoke, he looked at one juror, and then another, and another.

"They took her to a house, a vacant house. There was no heat in this house—this is wintertime. In that darkness, they sat her on a chair. They then strapped her to a pole in that basement. They then left her in that cold, in that dark—tape around her eyes, hands cuffed behind her back—attached to that pole. They gave her no blankets, they gave her no food, they gave her no water. They left her there in that cold, dark place alone. They left her there for three days,'' Gene said. The jurors were rapt, as Gene described the murder.

Josh "took a can of gasoline and poured the gasoline all over her head, and he poured some around,'' said Gene, his voice rising in volume and outrage. "But he made sure he put it on her head first, and then he took a match and he lit the match and dropped it on her hair, and then he ran out. Kimberly Antonakos burned to death that night. Think about her three last days in that basement—the confusion, the fear that she went through.''

"Objection!'' Chandler shouted.

"Overruled,'' Demakos said immediately.

"The flame came through this man,'' Gene charged, pointing again at Josh. "The flame came from his hand!''

Gene then spoke of Kim's kindness to her friends, particularly April and Josh, whom she had allowed to stay at her place when they had nowhere else to go.

"How many people, ask yourself, would extend themselves this far?'' Gene asked, turning back to the members of the jury. "Kimberly says, 'Well, you and Josh and the baby can come and stay with me until you find a place to stay, and they do. And they stay there for over a week . . . This man decided that the best way he could pay Kimberly, pay back her kindness, is he says, 'I can kidnap her. I can

make money off of her. I can get Nicholas Libretti, and Joey
Negron'—two people that do not know her, but know him—
'I'll get them. We'll kidnap Kimberly because I can see she
has a lot of money. I will kidnap her, and we will hold her,
and we will make a lot of money.'

"This man has a nickname. He gave it to himself, and it
is somewhat revolting," Gene said, sarcasm dripping from
his voice. "He's 'K-Q'—that stands for 'King Quality.'
That's what he thinks of himself—he's a king! K-Q sits right
over there. King Quality!"

Gene then told the jury that Josh killed Joey to silence
him and prevent him from going to the police. The prosecutor described a distraught Tommy Antonakos arriving at
his missing daughter's apartment and being assisted in the
search for Kim by her friend Josh.

"And he is greeted by this man, and he is duped for the
next several days by a concerned friend," said Gene.

He gave an account of how Josh claimed to have called
everyone in Kim's address book, but was actually leading
Tommy and the police astray and after Psycho—whom Josh
had designated as the fall guy.

"The ransom demand was never conveyed for this young
lady. Mister Antonakos would have paid every penny that he
could have found in order to have his daughter returned. He
never received a ransom demand. You will hear why not.
Fearing a kidnapping has gone wrong, and fearing discovery—should anything be left that could be traced back to
him, he decides to destroy all of the evidence, and a big part
of the evidence is Kimberly Antonakos. So he goes to a gas
station. He buys a can of gas, and he comes back. He goes
downstairs, he pours the gasoline all over Kimberly, and
lights a match, and drops it on her head, and then runs. He
comes home, and pretends shock and dismay the next morning—when she's found, and she is identified," Gene said.

Three months later, "in fear that Joey Negron would give
him up," he said, Josh murdered Joey:

"He sees Joey Negron walking down the street with his

common-law wife, holding their young son. He comes out from the shadows, and puts a gun right to the back of Joey Negron's head, and fires one shot while he's holding his young son. The bullet travels right through Mister Negron's head. He falls to the floor. He is dead.

"He drives off in a blue, four-door Japanese car that is seen leaving the scene. That's his family car.

"Ladies and gentlemen, these are the facts—these are the gruesome facts. This is what he did. From the mind and hands of that man, two people died," said Gene, locking eyes with the defiant Josh sitting at the defense table.

"Two people died because this is the way Joshua Torres covered his tracks so that he does not get caught for kidnapping. Kimberly Antonakos dies so he does not get caught for kidnapping, and for the murder of Kimberly Antonakos, his companion dies. Ladies and gentlemen, there is a particular cold-bloodedness that you don't see in most homicides. It comes from this man. It comes from his mind and it comes from his hands."

Gene then outlined the charges and what kind of evidence and witnesses they would see and hear in the coming weeks.

"When I come back to ask you to give a verdict that you know is the truth—that this man committed murder twice over—a kidnapper who repaid kindness with killing. A guilty man, guilty as charged. Guilty as proven. Thank you, ladies and gentlemen."

Gene took a seat and Chandler rose to make his opening remarks for the defense. They were very brief, just over one hundred words:

"Ladies and gentlemen, it's not my burden to make an opening statement," said Chandler. "You understand I don't have to do that. But what I have heard is a mystery. There's no question about the fact that two people are dead. There's no question about the fact that one body was burned. But what I'm talking to you about is the story that you heard—because that is the District Attorney's story. You listen to the evidence, and you decide if he has lived up to proving

to you what he has just said. I'm sure that when you hear
the evidence, your verdict will be Not Guilty,'' said Chandler. "Thank you very much.''

The next day, Gene, assisted by Julian Wise—who had
returned from a leave of absence—and Rob Ferino, began to
unfold the prosecution case against Josh. Gene was the lead
prosecutor, the most experienced, and he began calling witnesses to set the scene and tell the story of what had happened to Kim—all a preparation for the eventual unveiling
of their star witness. Each witness was called and entered
through the swinging door at the rear of the courtroom. They
walked past the spectators, the lawyer, and the jury, and into
the witness box. They then raised their right hands, and
swore to tell the truth, the whole truth, and nothing but the
truth.

The People's first witness was John Cuniffe, who testified
how he had smelled smoke, discovered the fire next door,
and dialed 911.

Fire Lt. Fred Reich then took the stand and described
entering the basement of the burning house and supervising
the firefighters who extinguished the blaze. When he spoke
for the first time about finding Kim's body, ''slumped over
in a chair,'' a hush fell over the courtroom.

''She had been burned severely,'' Reich said. ''I radioed
to the chief that we had found a victim and that I felt it was
a homicide, and he asked me, 'Why do you think that?'
'Well, the person's hands were behind them in the chair.
They were slumped over, and to me that indicates some foul
play,' so we immediately backed off and tried to preserve
the crime-scene area.''

He described removing his air mask and smelling gasoline, which, he said, caused ''an irritating feeling around
your eyes, you start to tear. You get a slight sting in your
throat. You can actually taste it a little bit, gasoline or flammable liquid.''

''Ever seen anyone bound, taped, and deliberately set on
fire before?'' Gene asked Reich.

"No," he replied, shaking his head sadly. "That was the worst I have ever seen. Never seen anything like that before."

"Thank you very much," said Gene. "No further questions."

The jury was then excused from the courtroom, so that the lawyers could have a conference on which photographs of Kim's charred body would be admitted into evidence, and shown to witnesses and the jury. Chandler objected to several photos, but the judge admitted them all.

"They don't appear to be that gruesome that the prejudice far outweighs the relevancy," said Demakos. "I'll permit them."

A police officer followed Reich and gave similar testimony. Next, Rob Ferino called Fire Marshal Stanley Jaremko, as an expert witness on the origin and cause of fires. Jaremko told the jury three basic causes of fire—an act of God, an accidental fire, and arson. He also recalled that cold night in that burned-out basement in Queens almost a year and nine months previously. The victim, he said, was found locked in a frozen position—even though the chair she had been sitting in had crumbled to pieces after being partially consumed by the flames.

"That was another indication in a fire that's set that you can understand. In the old days, with the witches burned at the stake, they would put up a stake, put you in the middle, the body was there, they start the fire," Jaremko told a horrified jury.

"The wood, whatever is burned, starts first, and gets a good-sized fire, and goes up, naturally burns the victim. On this one here, the chair, the bottom of the chair was not burned, indicating that the fire was started over the height of the chair."

It was not an accidental fire, Jaremko said, and it blazed for about twenty or thirty minutes before it was extinguished. Rob showed the fire marshal the black-and-white photographs taken of the fire scene, with Kim's body sprawled on

the cluttered cement floor. He then showed him close-ups of
Kim's burned wrists—with unburned bands where tape had
given protection from the fire. Next Rob showed him a single
grisly picture of the victim's blackened upper body and head.
Rob then asked to show the pictures to the jury.

"Denied," said Demakos.

After lunch, Gene called Wayne McCook, who told the
court about his mother's house, where Kim had been killed.
He described the empty house, the missing front-door key,
and said he had never heard of Josh, Nick, or Joey. During
the routine questioning, as he described picking up mail at
the house on a regular basis, the attention of some of those
in the courtroom began to wander. Gene thanked him and
said he had no further questions—but the court did.

"When was the last time you said you were at the house
to pick up mail prior to being called about the fire?" asked
Demakos.

"The morning of March third," Wayne replied, with a
pained look on his face.

"You were there the morning of March third?" the judge
asked, his voice rising.

"Yes, sir," Wayne said sadly.

A gasp came from the spectators, as they realized that
Wayne had been only yards from Kim while she was still
alive. The missed opportunity for a rescue that never happened cut through several hearts in Kim's family like a knife.
When Wayne had found out that Kim had been alive when
he had been there, it affected the former soldier deeply. He
was stricken with un-earned guilt, and had lain awake at
night, second-guessing his routine actions:

"If only she would have been awake," Wayne thought.
"If only she had been conscious, or made some kind of
noise . . ."

The next morning, November 1st, during a sidebar, Justice
Demakos refused to let the prosecution introduce several
color crime-scene photos into evidence.

"There are three I will not permit to be introduced into

evidence because they're too gruesome—they're unnecessary," said Demakos.

The judge later allowed the jury to see three black-and-white photographs of Kim's body. Two were the least shocking shots of Kim's corpse in the basement and the third was a closeup of Kim's burned hands.

Julian Wise called detectives from the Crime Scene unit and Missing Persons Squad to testify about finding Kim's earrings in the garage and in her trunk, and other details. Gene Reibstein then called Kim's friend Liz Pace. After testifying about her night out with Kim, and how her friend vanished, Liz spoke about how Josh was Tommy Antonakos' right-hand man during the search.

"Did Tommy rely on Josh?" Gene asked.

"Yes," said Liz.

"Objection!" said Chandler.

"Strike the answer," Demakos ordered.

"Josh ever bring Kim back alive?" Gene pressed.

"No," said Liz.

"Thank you very much, Miss Pace. I have no further questions," said Gene, who then sat down.

Chandler questioned Liz about Psycho.

"I know of him, yes. I never met him."

"You know of him through Kim?" Chandler asked.

"Yes, I heard."

"Did she ever express to you any fear of this person?"

"Just that he was obsessed with her. She never really told him where she lived or anything."

Tommy's friend Gina Cuozzo stepped up next, and Gene asked her if, during the search for Kim, they had stopped anywhere.

"Yes, we stopped at church. It was Ash Wednesday, so we stopped for the ashes services at the church in her neighborhood," Gina said. "Tommy turned the car off and he and I went to get out of the car, and he turned and asked Josh if he wanted to come in and say a quick prayer—and Josh said no."

"How far was it from where the car was parked, and stopped, and you guys got out, to the door of that church?"

"Objection, Your Honor," Chandler interrupted. "I'll ask it be stricken."

"No," Demakos responded. "Overruled."

"Thank you, Your Honor," said Gene, turning back to Gina. "You can answer the question."

"It was probably as far as I am sitting from that door," she said, pointing a finger to the rear door of the courtroom.

"And Josh stayed in the car?"

"Yes."

"To what door?" Demakos asked.

"The exit door," Gina said, pointing again.

"It's approximately forty-three feet," Demakos noted for the record.

"You and Tommy go into the church?" Gene continued.

"Yes."

"Say a prayer?"

"Yes."

"Get ashes?"

"Yes."

"Come back out?"

"Yes."

"Josh still in the car?"

"Yes."

Gina said Josh told everyone in Kim's apartment that he was going out to Bushwick to look for Kim's car after he and Tommy had found Kim's earring in her garage.

"When was it he made this announcement?" Gene asked.

"I'm not sure of the time. Right before the detectives got there . . . from the precinct in Canarsie."

"When they arrived, Josh was gone?"

"Yes."

On Monday morning, November 4th, Gene stood up and asked another witness to the stand:

"At this time, The People call Thomas Antonakos."

Tommy answered Gene's questions and told the jury his

address in Staten Island, his age, and his business interests. Tommy described Kim's birth, his estrangement and divorce from Marlene, and the happy times when Kim would visit him on the weekends, and watch Sylvester and Tweety cartoons. Gene brought him through the years and up to the time Kim moved into her own apartment. Tommy detailed his alarm when he had heard that Kim had not come home, and how he left work and drove to Kim's place in Canarsie— where he met Josh for the first time. He described how a helpful Josh had told him that he had used Kim's address book to call all her friends, to see if he could locate her. The only one who had not called back, Josh told Tommy, was a guy named Psycho.

"I'll ask you something," Gene said to Tommy. "You mentioned that was the first time you saw Joshua Torres— do you see him in the courtroom today?"

"Yes."

"Please point him out."

"That's him," said Tommy, pointing to Josh, who was dressed in a beige shirt and tie, and wearing glasses that heightened his new image of a harmless, innocent man.

When Gene tried to have Kim's address book admitted into evidence, the defense lawyer objected—because it also contained a diary with a poem written by Kim. The lawyers argued about it during an off-the-record sidebar.

"It really appears to be a poem written by the deceased," said Chandler. "I don't think it has any bearing." The judge excluded the diary, but Kim's address book was admitted. Tommy described how Josh helped him look for his daughter, how they found her earring in the garage, and how they searched for Kim's car on the street, and under the Belt Parkway bridge—where Josh warned Tommy to watch out for the rats. Back in the car, Tommy said he had told his daughter's friend that he was scared.

"We stopped at a church," Tommy said, his voice choking with emotion. "It was Ash Wednesday, and I felt I wanted to get ashes, and ask God for some help."

Tommy burst into tears, his body trembling.

"Do you need a moment?" Gene asked, quietly.

"I'm okay," Tommy said, after a moment, struggling to regain his composure. "Just . . . he . . . we got to the church, and I got—me and Gina—I thought we were going to go into church just to say a prayer, and Joshua wanted to stay in the car, so me and Gina went into church, and we got our ashes, and I prayed . . . you know, you pray because you're scared, you're scared . . ." Tommy said, tears coursing down his cheeks.

"It's all right," Gene consoled him. "Did you ask Josh if he wanted to go into church with you?"

"Yes."

"Did he go into church with you?"

"What did he say?" Demakos interjected.

"He just didn't want to come in," Tommy replied.

Again, Gene asked how far away the car was from the door of the small white church.

"To, maybe, where the exit signs are—that's as far from the car—to the exit sign," Tommy said.

"Approximately forty-three feet," Demakos added.

"Thank you, Your Honor," said Gene.

"Were you thinking that he was helping you at the time?" Gene asked Tommy.

"Oh, sure."

"You don't know what he was thinking, do you?"

"No. I had no doubt he was trying to help me at that time."

"How much sleep did you get in the next few days?"

"Not much, not much sleep—you don't really think about sleep when your kid is out there."

During the emotional testimony, Josh sat in stony silence, unmoved. Josh also remained impassive later, when Tommy sobbed as he told the jury about learning from Louie and Tom Shevlin that Kim was dead—and had been burned to death.

"I just got an eerie feeling, I got a bad feeling, when

these other detectives came in,'' said Tommy, bursting into tears again. ''And then they all came back out, and they told me that they had found Kim.''

In her seat on the courtroom pew, Tommy's mother Betty also began to weep. Gene asked Tommy if he saw Jay at Kim's funeral.

''Yes . . . We hugged one another, you know. It was sorrow, and stuff like that.''

''Did he cry?'' Gene asked.

''Yes.''

''Jay was crying?''

''Yes.''

''Did you see Josh at the funeral?''

''Yes.''

''Was Josh crying?''

''No.''

Gene questioned Tommy about several matters and then paused before asking his last two questions.

''Have you worked at all since Kim was found?''

''Sustained,'' said Demakos, before the defense lawyer could voice his objection.

''How often do you visit Kim in the cemetery?''

''Objection!'' Chandler shouted.

''Sustained,'' Demakos said.

''I have no further questions,'' said Gene, walking away. ''Thank you, Mister Antonakos.''

Under cross-examination by Chandler, Josh's defense lawyer asked Tommy what the police had told him about how Josh had become a suspect. Tommy responded that Louie and Tom Shevlin had told him about discrepancies in Josh's story.

''Did they tell you what the discrepancies were?'' asked Chandler.

''Yes. Just, you know, discrepancies.''

''Did they tell you they asked him to take a lie detector test?''

''Objection!'' shouted Gene.

"Sustained," Demakos ruled.

"They . . ." Tommy began.

"Don't answer the question," Demakos ordered.

Lie detector tests were not admissible as evidence. The only reason a defense lawyer would ever mention a polygraph exam was if his client had passed one. The prosecutors did not smile at the defense tactic. A judge could stop a witness from answering a question, but a jurist could not unask a question, once the jury had heard it. Even if a judge ordered that the question be stricken from the record, he could not remove it from jurors' minds. Obviously, Josh had told his lawyer that there was a lie detector test that exonerated him—and the lawyer believed his client. Josh still thought that he had fooled the Box. After Tommy was finished with his testimony, Gene asked the judge if Tommy could join his family in the audience for the rest of the trial, but Demakos refused, saying Tommy might be recalled to the stand.

Kim's childhood friend Tara Pappaccio broke down in tears on the stand when Gene asked her if she missed Kim. Tara said that she had adopted Kim's pets. Kim's kitten Spike had died, but Tara still cared for Kim's dog Sugar. Her testimony was low-key, but crucial, because she clearly remembered Josh and Jay arriving back at Kim's apartment "about three a.m."—which meant that their only alibi for the time of Kim's murder was each other. Tara testified that Josh drove her home on the night Kim was killed. As they left April's apartment, Tara said she gave a warning to Josh:

"When we were leaving, as far as I was concerned, the person who did this to Kim could have been any monster on the street. I told Joshua to lock the door because April and the baby were in the house. He said, 'Oh, don't worry about it—if anybody comes to take April, they'll have a big fight on their hands.' "

After lunch, Gene could delay no longer—he had to notify Josh's lawyer that the prosecution had a secret witness, giving the defense just two days to prepare for a cross-examination.

On Wednesday, despite the warning, Josh seemed shocked when Jay's name rang out in court.

"The people call Julio Negron," Gene said.

"Julio Negron," a uniformed court officer said loudly through the open side door of the courtroom, where Jay had been waiting in protective custody. Josh reacted to Jay's name echoing in the courtroom as if he had suffered a series of electric shocks. When Jay entered, the two old friends locked eyes. One look told Josh all he needed to know. He was not going to walk. He was going down. Jay really was going to give him up. The mask of arrogant Vanity instantly fell away from Josh's face, revealing the naked face of Hate underneath for everyone, including the jury, to see.

"Could you please tell the jury your name?" Gene asked Jay, after he had been sworn in.

"My name is Julio Negron," Jay replied, in a weak, hesitant voice. It was the first time he had been in court without being the defendant. All eyes were on him, and he was about to violate the First Commandment of the Street—Thou shalt not rat. Jay could clearly see the punishment for breaking the code of silence—death—burning in Josh's cold eyes.

"You have to speak louder," Demakos told the witness.

Jay raised his voice and told the jury that his nickname was B-Q—and that Josh's nickname was K-Q.

"Do you know what it stands for?" Gene asked.

"King Quality."

"Do you see King Quality in the courtroom today?"

"He is over there—sitting next to the court officer," Jay said, pointing to the glaring defendant.

Gene wasted no time on preliminaries, and brought the jury back to the night of Kim's murder—to the moment of moral choice for the four suspects, while she was still alive. Gene began questioning Jay about sitting in Joey's car outside of the house where Kim had been held hostage:

"We were debating about who was going to go in and let

her go. We decided Josh Torres and Nick Libretti would go down and let her go,'' said Jay.

''Joshua had a feeling that everything was falling apart—the plan to get the money for her—everything was just breaking down, so he talked about it then, and decided to let her go.'' Jay told the jury of the confusion that ensued after Josh and Nick found Kim frozen and apparently dead.

''We were all bugging out. I mean, I couldn't believe she was dead—none of us could believe it. It wasn't supposed to happen. She was supposed to be all right. She was supposed to be released,'' said Jay.

He described how Josh bought the gas, and said that Josh and Nick had gone back into the house, while, he claimed, he and Joey had remained inside the car.

''You were there, too!'' Josh erupted at his former friend, jumping to his feet behind the defense table.

Josh, who had just admitted in open court that he was involved in the murder, turned toward the jury and growled at them in a guttural voice, choked with hatred:

''If he didn't do anything, why is he copping a plea?''

Chandler got his client under control, and back into his seat.

Jay's damaging testimony continued on rails laid down by the prosecution team. He described how Josh kissed Kim, and then burned her, as well as Josh's threats to him to keep quiet. He also described how he and Josh had pretended to help and console Tommy Antonakos and his shattered family. Either Jay was a good actor, or what he had done had made him soul-sick. His voice quavered with emotion when he described attending Kim's funeral. The jury's eyes were riveted on the witness.

''There was a lot of family, a lot of friends,'' Jay said. ''It was really crowded. I didn't want to go to the casket at first, I was still feeling like shit, because I knew what had happened. I was coming to the funeral, and I was going to have to face the family, being a piece of shit.''

The twenty-three-year-old man began to cry.

"Excuse me?" Gene asked, apparently also hearing Jay's thoughts for the first time.

"I was going to have to face the family, being a piece of shit," Jay repeated, reaching for a tissue.

"You mean yourself?"

"Yes."

"Go ahead."

"I walked in and the first person, one of the first people that greeted me was her mother—came up to me, hugged me, and she, like, 'Jay, you know, it's going to be all right,' and I was, like, 'Yeah, I'm sorry, Marlene, you know, I offer my condolences.' I had to be a hypocrite. I mean I was sorry, and I am sorry, but I was acting like I didn't know nothing about what happened to her—and I did."

Jay then told the jury how he cried at Kim's coffin, and how her unsuspecting father hugged him and vowed to get the guys who had killed Kim.

"I told him, 'Yes, we will—and when we do, I want a crack at them' " said Jay.

"You're getting your crack today," Gene consoled him.

"Mister Reibstein!" Demakos scolded.

"I apologize, Your Honor," Gene replied.

Slowly, methodically, Gene walked Jay through events up until the time he decided to cooperate, including Josh confessing that he had murdered Joey. On cross-examination, Chandler grilled Jay on his criminal record, and got Jay to admit that his first story to police—that he had found out about the kidnap plot only after Kim's death—was a lie. The thrust of the defense case was that Jay was one of the full plotters—maybe the mastermind—and hoped to get a share of the ransom loot. The only reason he became a prosecution witness was to get off with a slap on the wrist and get away with murder. Chandler forced Jay to admit that when he found out by phone that Josh had kidnapped his former girlfriend Kim, he had not been threatened by Josh. Still, he had failed to report the heinous crime to his brother-in-law the police officer, who was just a few feet away—not to mention to Kim's terrified dad:

"So when you received that information, you were not under any threat of any kind—is that correct?" Chandler asked.

"Yes, sir," Jay replied.

"And you liked her a good deal—is that correct?"

"I loved her, sir."

"And you didn't say *boo*?"

"Boo?"

"You didn't say anything?"

"I didn't tell anybody."

"To anybody?"

"No, sir."

Chandler interrogated Jay about the first time he met Tommy Antonakos, who had awakened him while he was asleep on Kim's couch:

"He told you to go back to sleep?" Chandler asked.

"Yes."

"And you went back to sleep—correct?"

"Yes."

"With a clear conscience?"

"Objection!" said Gene.

"Withdrawn," said Chandler, after scoring his hit.

"Were you upset that Josh was misleading Mister Antonakos?" Chandler asked later.

"Was I upset?" asked Jay. "I was going through a whole lot of changes. I felt a lot of feelings."

"You were thinking about that money?"

"Objection!" Gene protested.

"Sustained," Demakos agreed.

The questioning became even more heated when Chandler demanded to know why, when Jay heard Josh say that Kim was dead, he did not rush in to see if the woman he loved really was dead. The defense lawyer hammered Jay with his admittedly false first statement to cops, and then loudly confronted the witness, as if he might break down when accused of being the mastermind:

"Did you kidnap Kimberly?" Chandler thundered.

"No, sir," Jay denied.

"Did you ask for a ransom?"

"No, sir."

"Did you burn the house down?"

"No, I did not," said Jay, remaining calm.

"Did you talk to Kimberly or have any connection with Kimberly while she was abducted?"

"No, sir."

"So, what did you do?"

"Objection!" Gene interjected. "He's doing two-to-six!"

"Mister Reibstein, I don't need any comment from you, either," the judge cautioned.

"I apologize, Your Honor," said Gene.

"Why is he going on the top count if he didn't do anything?" Josh shouted to the jury.

"Who said he didn't do anything?" Gene countered.

"Please, Mister Reibstein," Demakos said, trying to regain control of his courtroom. "I think it's time for a ten-minute recess." The judge dismissed the jury, and then cautioned both lawyers.

"Mister Reibstein, no remarks like that again."

"I apologize."

"And, above all, don't go talking to the defendant," said Demakos, turning to Chandler. "And you better advise your client . . ."

"I have," Chandler said.

"Anything he says is being taken down," said Demakos.

The next day, a series of witnesses came to the stand for the prosecution, including Tom Shevlin—who was glad to come into court to testify to against Josh. He and Louie had eaten, slept, lived, and breathed the case, and it was gratifying to finally be able to tell it all to a jury. On cross-examination, Chandler tried to show that the things that Josh had admitted to Tom and Louie a few weeks after Kim's death had all appeared in the newspapers.

"And all of this information that he provided in the statement was all material that was in the papers, is that correct?" Chandler asked.

"Sustained, as to that," Demakos said, anticipating a prosecution objection.

"I'd like him to answer," Gene told the court.

The judge had already ruled, preemptively, that Tom did not have to answer, but Gene surrendered the prosecution's objection.

"You want the answer?" Demakos asked.

"Yes," Gene replied.

"You want the answer, Mister Chandler?" the judge asked, in an uncertain tone.

Demakos may have been trying to warn the defense lawyer that if a prosecutor as sharp as Gene Reibstein wanted to hear the answer, perhaps a defense lawyer should withdraw the question. But Chandler went full speed ahead with his original line of questioning.

"Yes, I want an answer," Chandler insisted.

"All right," said Demakos, turning to Tom in the witness box, whom he began to question: "Let's narrow it down then, please. Okay? He told you, I believe—correct me if I'm wrong—he told you that he believed three guys did it, is that correct?"

"That's correct," Tom answered.

"Was that in the paper?"

"No."

"He told . . ."

"May I inquire along those lines?" Chandler interrupted, trying to take back his cross-examination before it got away from him.

"No," Demakos responded, and continued asking Tom questions: "Let's get it out—he told you they put her in the trunk, is that correct?"

"He told me that," Tom said.

"Was that in the newspaper?"

"No, it was not in the papers."

"He told you that it was a 'sweet house'—was that in the paper?"

"Well, the house itself was, but it wasn't really as a 'sweet house,' " Tom said.

Chandler resumed his cross-examination, but the damage had been done. After probing several matters inconclusively, Chandler said he had no further questions, and then sat down next to Josh, who urgently whispered an important question that he wanted his attorney to ask. Chandler shot back to his feet.

"Any re-direct?" Demakos asked Gene.

"No, Your Honor."

"I'm sorry," Chandler apologized, "a bit more, Your Honor."

Chandler turned back to Tom.

"Detective, did you ask Joshua Torres to take a lie detector test?"

Clearly, a smug Chandler thought he was about to spring a trap on Tom. Tom thought that the defense lawyer was trying to give the jury the impression that Josh had passed the test, without allowing Tom to tell the whole truth.

"Yes, I did," Tom replied.

"And did he take a lie detector test?"

"Yes, he did—and he failed," Tom said, with relish, in a loud voice.

Chandler had walked, smiling, into a trap set for Josh nineteen months earlier by Tom and Louie. Josh's lawyer was stunned. If the detective had volunteered the information without being asked, it might have been grounds to stop the trial—but Chandler had asked the question, and insisted on an answer. It was a rare and dramatic moment. The jury had seen the defense's secret weapon explode in Josh's face. The look of incredulous shock that hung over Josh's features was unmistakable.

"Strike out the last part: 'took the lie detector test,' " Demakos ordered the court reporter.

"Judge!" Chandler screamed, slamming his papers down on the defense table, and throwing his hands in the air. "I ask for a mistrial!"

"Your honor . . ." Gene began.

"Holy shit," Tom thought on the witness stand, "I hope I didn't screw up here."

"No," Demakos ruled. "Please," he said, stopping Gene in mid-sentence. "Motion for mistrial denied."

"Thank God," Tom thought.

"I have no further questions," said Chandler, giving up, and sitting down next to his confused client.

"Do you have any?" the judge asked Gene.

"Just one," said Gene, struggling to keep a smile off his face. "This test was taken months before his arrest, wasn't it?"

"Yes," said Tom.

"You never told him the results of the test, did you?"

"No, I didn't."

"Thank you—no further."

The following day, Luis Negron testified that his nephew Joey gave a tape to the family after saying that he had done something so bad that he could never get into Heaven. The following week, Josh's friend George told the court that Josh had borrowed a pair of pants and a jacket on the night Kim was killed. Antonette Montalvo told jurors about how Joey was gunned down by a "shadow," and failed to point Josh out as the killer.

Rich Tirelli took the stand and gave crucial testimony about Josh admitting that he had bought the gas can—only after Rich had faked Josh out by claiming that he had been caught on videotape at the gas station. Chandler's cross-examination did not shake Rich. In fact, as the defense grilling drew to a close, it seemed obvious that the jury did not share the defense's moral outrage that an NYPD detective had told fibs to a man he suspected had burned a girl alive.

"Now, Detective," said Chandler, "is it fair to say the statement that you made to him—saying that you had fingerprints—was a lie?"

"Yes," Rich replied.

"And would it be fair to say the statement that you made to him concerning the video of him at the gas station, was a lie?"

"Yes," beamed Rich, who could not help smiling.

As he did, most members of the jury also smiled. It was not a good omen for Josh's chances of acquittal. Chandler sat down.

The next day, November 14th, the prosecution rested its case, and Chandler mounted a brief—but lively—defense case of just two witnesses. First, the defense put Redrum's girlfriend *Leila Barnes on the stand to say that she and Redrum had been with Josh the night Joey was gunned down. Josh's girlfriend April, who supposedly was also with Josh the night Joey was shot, never came into court or took the oath. Redrum, said Barnes, worked as an office cleaner but was off work on the day of Joey's murder. On cross-examination by Gene Reibstein, Barnes admitted that she had spoken to her childhood friend Joshua Torres since his arrest—including the very night before she came to court to testify on his behalf. But she denied ever discussing Josh's arrest with her common-law husband, Redrum.

"Not one time?" Gene pressed.

"No," Barnes answered.

"Miss Barnes?" he prodded in a skeptical tone.

"No."

"That's your testimony? Your close friend is arrested, you find out about it a couple of hours later, and you know it couldn't be true—and you never talked about it with the father of your children? Yes or no?"

"No."

"Not once?"

"Not about that particular night . . ."

"In fact, you told our detectives not only did you fall

asleep at around one a.m., but you slept most of the night holding the baby on the couch, right?''

"That's not exactly what I said."

"The first time that's what you said, and then you changed it, right?"

"No, I said the same thing both times. What I said was I was asleep on the couch, but that they were playing video games. I had my son, it's not like I was in a dead sleep—I wasn't knocked out . . ."

"The father of your children is Peter Rodriguez. His nickname is Redrum since he's been about sixteen?" Gene asked.

"Objection!" shouted Chandler yet again.

"No, I'll allow it," the judge said.

"Yes."

"It is. And is Redrum the nickname?" Gene asked.

"Yes."

"That's 'murder' spelled backwards, isn't it?"

"Objection!" Chandler said again.

"Yes."

"She answered the question," Demakos pointed out.

"Now, you love Peter Rodriguez, don't you?" Gene asked in a suddenly gentle voice.

"Yes, I do."

"If he's in trouble, you would try and help him, wouldn't you?"

"Yes, I would."

"So Peter Rodriguez is driving that car for Josh Torres at one o'clock in the morning—while you were asleep?"

"Objection!" Chandler shouted. "I ask for a mistrial."

"Overruled," Demakos said. "Your application for the mistrial is overruled."

"You don't know where Peter Rodriguez, April, and Josh Torres were at one o'clock, June twenty-third—because you were asleep, isn't that right?"

"Objection," Chandler said.

"I'll allow it," said the judge.

"Yes or no?" demanded Gene.

"Yes, I do know where they were."

"While you were asleep?" Gene said sarcastically, as a parting shot. "Thank you."

Redrum took the stand next. After he swore to tell the truth, he told the court that Josh was with him on the afternoon and evening of June 22nd, 1995. First, said Redrum, he and his girlfriend Leila and their two children had played handball in the sunshine at a local park with Josh and another woman. After handball, they all went to pick up April, and played video games at her apartment in Canarsie. Redrum told the jury that he and Josh only left the apartment once for twenty minutes—to pick up snacks. After munching the food, the girls and children fell asleep, he said, but he and Josh played video games until five or six in the morning, when Josh drove Redrum, his girlfriend, and their son and daughter home. Listening to the testimony, Gene took Redrum at his word. He felt that if Redrum claimed that he and Josh were together all night, Gene believed him—but Gene did not believe they were playing video games while someone shot a nine-millimeter slug through Joey's head. When he rose to cross-examine Redrum, Gene began with a question that seemed to be from left field.

"Mister Rodriguez, how old is your daughter?" asked Gene.

"My daughter just turned one," Redrum answered, somewhat perplexed.

"What's the birthday?"

"November 17th, nineteen ninety . . . Oh, man . . ." sputtered Redrum.

"Well, if this is November, ninety-six, so, if she just turned one, she was born November nineteen ninety-five—right?"

"I be with my daughters too much," Redrum offered.

"The question is, were you with your daughter?" Demakos directed.

"No."

"Your daughter didn't exist, but you just swore to that?"

Gene asked, in a tone of disbelief reserved for those who might have committed perjury.

"Strike that last remark by the DA," Demakos ordered.

"The girls were asleep, right?"

"Yes."

"He's your friend, isn't he?"

"Yes."

"He is in trouble. You will try to help him, wouldn't you? Yes or no?"

"No, depending on the trouble . . ."

"How many times did you talk to your wife about the fact that Josh couldn't have done this because you and her were together at the time—tell me how many times you talked about it?"

"I don't remember, a few," Redrum replied, contradicting Barnes's testimony—which was still fresh in the minds of the jury.

"When was the first time you spoke about it?" Demakos asked the witness.

"When, I guess, he found out he was being accused of the crime, I guess," Redrum said.

"You talked about it then?" Gene asked, looking at the jury.

"Yes."

"You talk after that?"

"Yes."

"Talk about it more than that?"

"Yes."

"Talked about it a bunch?"

"Not a bunch, no."

"Your wife wouldn't have forgotten these conversations, would she?" It was a polite, lawyer-like way of calling Barnes a liar.

"Objection, Your Honor," said Chandler.

"Sustained."

Gene then established that Redrum was unemployed when

Joey was slain—not off for the day, as Barnes had just testified.

"So you were not employed on June twenty-second?" Gene asked.

"Right," Redrum confirmed.

"Your wife forgot about that," Gene added in a sarcastic tone.

"Objection!" Chandler said.

"Sustained," said Demakos, who again questioned Redrum. "How long were you employed prior to June twenty-second?"

"I don't remember stuff like that," Redrum huffed.

Gene then quizzed Redrum on his drug arrest, for which he was still on probation.

"Did Josh tell you before he drove you on June twenty-second that he was going to shoot anybody?"

"No," said Redrum.

It was an interesting moment. There seemed to be only three possibilities. Either Redrum was telling the truth, or he was lying to protect a friend—or he was the wheelman on the hit, and had the colossal gall to come into court to try and get Josh off.

"It was a surprise to you when he did it?" Gene asked, in mock sympathy.

"Objection, Your Honor."

"Sustained."

"Did you speak to Josh last night?"

"No."

"Your wife talk to Josh?"

"No." Redrum was not in the courtroom, so he could not have known that Barnes had just told the court that she had spoken to Josh the night before.

"You didn't get on the phone with him?"

"I wasn't there."

"Have you spoken to him since he was arrested on the case?"

"Yes."

"How many times?"

"A few times. I don't know—I didn't count, a few times," said Redrum, getting a bit testy.

"Did you tell him, 'Hold your head up—stick to the story'?"

"Objection!"

"Sustained."

"No further questions for you, Mister Rodriguez," Gene said, dismissing Redrum with a contemptuous wave of his hand.

"I'll object for this, and I'll ask for a mistrial again," Chandler said.

His motion was again denied.

"Any other witnesses, Mister Chandler?" Demakos inquired.

"No, Your Honor, the defense rests."

Chandler's only witnesses had been for Joey's homicide, and they had been savaged on the stand. Their stories were at odds with each other, and the Assistant District Attorney had all but accused Redrum of complicity in Joey's murder, and implied that both Redrum and his girlfriend had lied under oath. Within minutes, Chandler stood and addressed the jury in his summation for the defense:

"This is a horrendous case," said Chandler.

"What occurred here was horrendous, and it makes your job all the more difficult. You see Mister Antonakos is here," he said, gesturing to Tommy sitting in the audience. "You see his grief, and it's hard to put that aside, and look at the testimony to make a determination. Your conviction of the wrong person will not satisfy anyone—not Mister Antonakos, not God, not anybody."

Chandler claimed the entire defense rested on what Josh had allegedly told Rich Tirelli, and the testimony of Jay. He called Gene "a master story-teller," who had woven a case of innuendo against his innocent client. Josh had refused to go into the church to pray with Tommy, he said, not because he feared to enter the House of God, but simply because Josh was not religious. In fact, said Chandler, if Josh had been the criminal mastermind behind Kim's kidnapping, "it would seem to me that another conclusion could be reached—that he would have gone in, and faked it." The defense lawyer criticized Gene for putting a lot of witnesses on the stand, and noted that the prosecution never played Joey's tape in court. There were no independent eyewitnesses to Kim's abduction, her murder, or to Joey's execution who came forward to identify Josh, his lawyer told the jury. Also, Jay was a liar—not to be believed, said Chandler.

"He would sell his soul not to be charged with a murder, or as an accomplice in a murder," the lawyer said. In fact, Jay was the only one who said Kim's abduction was a kidnapping. He told the jurors that if Rich Tirelli lied to Josh about being videotaped in a gas station, "The question is—is he lying to you?"

Chandler took his seat and Gene then delivered his summation.

"Your Honor, Mister Chandler, ladies and gentlemen of the jury. Joshua Torres killed Kimberly Antonakos," said Gene. "Josh Torres killed Kimberly Antonakos on March fourth, nineteen ninety-five—and you know that now." He again described how Kim was marooned "for three days, taped around the mouth, around the eyes with the contact lenses, which were hurting before he ever had her grabbed— no food, no water, no human voice, in a freezing basement . . .

"Joey Negron, who told his God-fearing uncle—you heard on the stand—he had done something so terrible that even the Lord couldn't forgive him. That's his friend, who he is in telephone contact with," Gene said, gesturing toward the defendant.

Josh, he said, felt Kim's pulse and knew that she was still alive—but told his co-conspirators that she was dead. The fire Josh set was to kill Kim, Gene said. Otherwise, why would Josh order the refrigerator shoved against the basement door to block a rescue effort?

"By March fourth," said Gene, pointing at Josh, and staring him down, "he knows the whole scheme has gone out
of line. Because you're way over your head . . .

"He has got to make her dead," Gene told the jurors.

Later, he said, Josh killed Joey for the same reason—to
avoid arrest.

"On June twenty-third, at one o'clock a.m., when one of
his alibi witnesses is asleep, and the other was certainly with
him—because somebody drove that car, while he ran back
to it," Gene said, Jay "didn't fudge, he didn't hedge, he
didn't duck any question . . . You know in your gut he told
the truth, from what you saw."

Gene said that Nick and Joey were "morons" impressed
with Josh.

"They're stupid to do this kidnapping. They've got everything all backwards—those morons can't even do it right."

"Objection!"

"Overruled."

Gene walked through the sequence of evidence for the
jurors. Gene said Josh had made a mistake by not walking
across the street to see if Kim's car was there on the morning
after she disappeared, and then telling Tommy Antonakos
that he had looked.

"Because he didn't look, because he knew she was kidnapped, in his control, and he is too stupid to realize it—he
is a stupid guy, after all—smarter than some of those others,
but still stupid." Gene told the jury that it was "interesting"
Josh went under a bridge with the big rats "but he wouldn't
go with him into a church." Everyone, said Gene, "draws
the line someplace, and even Josh Torres isn't going into the
Lord's house on the holiday, while he is doing the work of
the Devil . . .

"He is obviously guilty of the murder of Joey Negron.
He had the motive, the opportunity, the reason, the car . . .
You don't stick a gun to somebody's head without meaning
to kill them . . . You know he deliberately set her on fire—
guilty of arson—therefore, he is guilty of the two counts of

felony murder of Kimberly Antonakos . . ." Gene told them.

"Well, ladies and gentlemen, he'll get justice. Whatever your verdict is, will be just," said Gene, who asked them to find Josh "guilty as charged, guilty as proven. Thank you, ladies and gentlemen."

The trial was over, and the judge charged the jury, instructing them on the law and how to determine reasonable doubt. When Demakos finished, he gave the case to the jury at 11:30 a.m., and they retired to consider their verdict. They could look at any piece of evidence that had been introduced at trial. They were free to examine the three pictures of Kim's burned body and hands, her singed clothing, or any of the documents in the case, including what Josh had allegedly told Rich Tirelli. Josh was taken in handcuffs back to a holding cell in the courthouse basement. The press returned to the Press Room on the ground floor, and the prosecution team returned to their offices to wait it out. Gene, Julian, Rob, Louie, Tom, Rich, and the others were anxious, as were Tommy Antonakos and his family. Even after a powerful prosecution and a weak defense, no one could really predict what a jury would do once that Jury Room door closed behind them. After all, there were no independent eyewitnesses to the murders, no fingerprints, no DNA evidence, no gun, no bullet pointing to Josh as the killer. The strongest witness against him was involved in the kidnapping, and had a criminal record. Would the jury believe Jay, or would they dismiss it all as circumstantial evidence, and the effort of a co-conspirator to get off? Most often, juries would methodically weigh the evidence, as the judge ordered, and emerge with a verdict based upon the heft of the facts. But a jury was composed of a dozen human beings, and there was always the chance that one or more of the jurors could turn out to be a wild card with a secret agenda, or a holdout who might force a jury deadlock and a new trial. After the infamous O. J. Simpson acquittal for two murders in California, no prosecutor, detective, or victim's family in the country could ever really banish doubt at such a moment. The image of Lady Justice wielding the Scales of Justice was an apt one. Everyone felt the sway of the moment beneath them, almost as if they were teetering up and down on a giant scale, which could only be stopped by a verdict.

Behind the wooden door of the Jury Room, the jurors were fighting. One lone man made it clear to his fellow jurors at the outset of their secret deliberations that he did not intend to convict Josh of anything. There was no evidence, he said, to prove Josh was guilty of either murder—and he would not budge. The man did not say that he believed Josh was innocent—but said there was not enough evidence to convict. At least one juror felt that the law was not a game, and, as jurors, they had to use their hearts, as well as their heads. After some polite discussion, several other jurors became angry at the man's intransigence.

"There's a man's life at stake!" the man argued.

"This man gave up his rights when he killed someone," said another male juror, a young man who was angry because he suspected the holdout was simply balking at the onerous duty of finding Josh guilty of intentional murder, and sending a killer away. It was a difficult thing to do—but each juror had promised to do it if the evidence warranted it. It was now time to step up to the plate.

Later in the day, the jury sent a note to the judge, and everyone rushed back into the courtroom. Justice Demakos told the lawyers that jurors had requested read-backs of the testimony of Rich Tirelli and Jay Negron, and he directed the court reporter to locate his transcripts, those thick stacks of narrow paper that issued from the stenographer's strange little typewriter in the well of the court. Once the testimony was located, the jury was called back, and the court reporter began reading the testimonies of the prosecution's star witness and the detective who'd tricked Josh into admitting he was involved. The court reporter intoned the witnesses' words in a loud, unemotional voice, as the jury listened intently. As they did, the lawyers on both sides scrutinized the jurors' faces, and tried to read their minds. Was the request beneficial to the prosecution or the defense? It was usually impossible to tell whether a jury wanted to hear a particular witness's testimony in order to prove a point—or to disprove it. But one observer noticed that only one male juror in the front row was looking at the court reporter as he read—the other eleven jurors were all staring at that juror. They did not seem to be happy with him. Were they trying to convince a holdout? After the read-backs, the jury retired again. Dinner came and went, and still there was no verdict. The crowds in the courthouse left, and the building closed, but Demakos let the jury continue with their deliberations into the night. Soon, however, he would have to stop them for the evening, and direct that they resume in the morning.

Back in the Jury Room, eleven jurors were still arguing, trying to convince their holdout to convict. Even after the read-backs, and the discussions that followed, the man stubbornly held on—then he held out for a lesser charge in the indictment, murder by depraved indifference. Depraved indifference was closer to manslaughter than murder—it meant that he must have known that pouring gasoline on a human being, and setting it ablaze with a match, was likely to cause serious injury or death, but he did it anyway. Some of the jurors were furious that the holdout could actually believe that burning someone alive was not murder. They were convinced that Josh had intentionally killed Kim. Under pressure, the holdout caved in—after the other jurors agreed to find Josh not guilty of one of the crimes.

At 10:30 that night, after ten hours of deliberation, the jury announced that it had reached a verdict, and Demakos' courtroom quickly filled up with Kim's family and friends, DA Richard A. Brown, and the press. Josh was brought into court by the court officers, who took off his handcuffs and seated him at the defense table. Tommy Antonakos sat with his family, and Louie and Tom and Rich, in the audience. Tommy and the others had already been warned that the jury would probably not convict Josh for the murder of Joey Negron, due to lack of evidence. Tommy was thinking how appropriate it was that the verdict was coming ninety minutes before midnight. The next day, November 15th, would have been Kim's twenty-second birthday. Louie Pia was an experienced homicide detective and the veteran of many trials, but he had goose bumps as the jury filed in. A hush fell over the courtroom. The judge asked the jury if they had reached a verdict, and the foreman said they had. Demakos asked the defendant to stand, and Josh got to his feet.

"How do you find the defendant on count one of the indictment, murder in the second degree?" the clerk asked the forewoman.

Count one was the murder of Joey Negron. The forewoman read the verdict aloud:

"Not guilty."

Many people in the courtroom gasped, not realizing that it was for the Negron homicide—shocked at any not-guilty finding. Many faces wore expressions of stunned confusion. Tommy Antonakos' knees began to shake with involuntary fear. Louie cursed to himself. Even though he expected it, the verdict galled him. He felt that Josh had just gotten away with murder. Was it possible that he could also get away with Kim's murder? The clerk then asked the forewoman for the verdict on the felony murder charge.

"Guilty."

Applause erupted at the verdict. Josh faced a twenty-five-year-to-life sentence for the crime, but his face remained blank. A broad smile spread across Tommy Antonakos' face. He sighed, as if a heavy burden had been lifted from him, looked up, and spoke to Kim, as if she were in the courtroom, sharing the victory.

"We did it, baby," he said, pumping his fist in the air.

Cautious smiles began to appear on some of the troubled faces in the audience. Next, the clerk asked for the verdict on the depraved indifference murder charge.

"Guilty." More applause, even louder, came from the spectators.

Tommy and his family hugged, and many began crying—

releasing their pent-up emotions. As depicted on the court-house mosaic, a single human heart had outweighed the life-less lawbook, and tipped the scales to the side of Justice. The clerk called for the first-degree kidnapping verdict:

"Guilty."

He then asked for the kidnapping with the death of the victim charge:

"Guilty."

Josh faced another twenty-five-years-to-life in jail on the kidnapping charge, and now faced a minimum of half a century in prison. More and more satisfied smiles appeared in the audience, as the clerk asked for an arson verdict.

"Guilty."

"We're done with part one," said Louie.

Demakos set a date of December 10th for sentencing, and it was over. Tommy watched as the cold-blooded killer of his only child was handcuffed and led away to jail. Josh wore a cool expression that Tommy interpreted as a sly one. He glared at the convicted killer, trying to project his thoughts through his eyes.

"If you're thinking of ever getting out of jail, forget it," Tommy thought. "I will be right there. If I die, then my brother will be there."

It was part of his continuing promise to Kim to see justice done. Of course, Josh could not read Tommy's thoughts, but the look on Tommy's face spoke volumes. Now, every year on Kim's birthday, Tommy would know that it had been another year that Josh had spent behind bars. The jurors were thanked for their service, and released. One juror told a reporter that the jury did not believe everything that Jay told them, but they agreed Josh "was guilty of murder."

"There were very few things to believe or not believe," one male juror said. "This case was not crystal-clear. What-ever was available, we used."

A stern DA Brown said the case "cries out for the max-imum penalty permitted by law. At sentencing, we will ask the court to see to it that the defendant never again walks the streets of this city.''

Outside the courtroom, a jubilant Tommy spoke to reporters, who asked how he felt about the verdicts.

''It doesn't do anything for my daughter, in terms of bringing her back—but at least she could rest in peace,'' he told the cameras and microphones as he left the courthouse.

Tommy called his ex-wife Marlene in Florida, who had not been up to the ordeal of attending the trial every day, as Tommy had done. She was happy to hear of the conviction and screamed over the phone:

''The rat bastard got what he deserved!''

Tommy drove back to Staten Island and went directly to Kim's grave.

''We did it, baby!'' he repeated to the pink granite of the vertical mausoleum slab that bore a smiling picture of Kim.

The next day, after a night's sleep, the young juror who had gotten so angry at the holdout juror drove out to Staten Island. He went to the Moravian Cemetery, asked for directions, and went directly to Kim's grave. He felt that he had done his duty, as a juror and as a human being, and had come to quietly pay his respects. After a while, he left— leaving behind a note to Kim on the stone:

''You're in a better place.''

That day, Tommy told a reporter he was resigned to going through it all a second time—when Nick Libretti went on trial.

''I have no life,'' a sad-eyed Tommy said. ''Kimberly was my princess. If she hadn't moved out, if she hadn't had that extra room—there are so many ifs.'' He explained to *New York Post* reporter Mark Stamey that Kim's spirit had been with him every day since her murder.

''Today's her birthday,'' said Tommy, looking at a photo of Kim, with tears in his eyes. ''She would have been twenty-two today. This conviction is a bittersweet birthday present to give a daughter, but it's all I have. At least now she can rest in peace. I knew she was there in the courtroom waiting for the guilty verdict.''

"She used to confide in me a lot," said Kim's heartbroken grandmother Betty, 78, tears running down her cheeks. "I'm going to miss her very much. I love her."

Stamey asked if Tommy was sad that Josh had never faced the death penalty.

"As for him, death is maybe justified in some cases, but for him it's too good," said Tommy. "Let him rot for fifty years."

On December 10th, Justice Demako's third-floor courtroom was filled again for the sentencing of Josh Torres. There was one additional spectator—Kim's mother Marlene, who was in the courtroom for the first time. She had been told by Tommy that Kim had been chased by her kidnappers, and had crashed her car and died while fleeing them. Tommy had hoped to spare her the same agony he was still enduring. Marlene took a seat up front with the family, because she, like Tommy, intended to see that justice was done.

Gene Reibstein rose first to speak.

"Joshua Torres kidnapped and killed Kimberly Antonakos," Gene told the court. "This monstrous crime was conceived and carried out by that man—who decided that Kimberly Antonakos represented nothing more than an item of commerce, a commodity, to be taken from her home, and offered for sale to her father, and her family."

He noted that Josh had begun his criminal career by offering eight-year-old boys in his neighborhood twenty dollars and bringing them into Manhattan to be sexual tools of middle-aged pedophiles, who were paying several hundred dollars for this privilege. "That's how he started his criminal convictions, selling human beings," said Gene. "It should be no surprise that he now moved up to this step. Joshua Torres is evil, Your Honor. Anyone who knows anything about the facts of the case knows that." Gene said, staring at Josh—who glared right back.

"In addition to being evil, he is also incompetent, and a

fool. He was unable to carry this scheme out in the manner he originally conceived it, and, therefore, the Antonakos family, which is present here today in their grief, never got the opportunity to ransom their daughter Kimberly—who had never done anything but show kindness to this monster sitting here.

"Because he is a coward and his fear of capture became so great, he ended this crime in fire. Once again, being incompetent, this fire did not keep him from being caught . . . The People now ask that he be sentenced to every single day that the law allows for this crime that he has committed, for each of the crimes for which he was charged, indicted, and convicted," said Gene distinctly, his voice vibrant with purposeful anger as he stared at Josh. "And it is the People's hope that not one day on the Earth should ever see Joshua Torres outside the prison walls again—until he's inside a coffin, being buried. Thank you, Your Honor."

As he intoned the words, Gene wanted Josh to feel as if he were already confined, that he might as well be in his coffin already. The judge asked Chandler if he wished to say anything on behalf of the defendant.

"Your Honor," Chandler responded, "Mister Torres wishes to make a statement on his own behalf."

Kim's family gasped. Since Josh had not taken the stand, no one had expected him to speak.

"All right, Mister Torres, I'll hear you," Demakos said.

Josh then stood up and addressed the court. Characteristically, his eye already on his appeal, Josh stuck with his Big Lie, as he donned wire-rimmed eyeglasses and read a prepared statement from a piece of yellow paper:

"I give my condolences to Kimberly Antonakos' family for losing such a precious jewel in such a hideous way," Josh said, imitating the lawyerly tones he had heard in court.

Gene was shocked at what Josh had said. Gene felt it was outrageous and revolting, that Josh, who had hurt the Antonakos family enough, would now inflict more pain on them with a lying pretense of injured innocence.

"It is now apparent Tommy thinks I was responsible for the murder of Kimberly," Josh said, in a wounded voice. "This case has proven that the district attorneys Reibstein and Wise used unsupported evidence and manipulated witnesses to seek a conviction for public notoriety—and were never interested in the truth. Throughout this trial, we heard many people testify, and commit perjury—except for Tommy Antonakos, and Elizabeth Pace. The stenographer was incapable of maintaining accurate minutes," he grumbled, causing a few snickers throughout the court.

"This injustice, along with tainted information provided by the media, made it impossible for me to receive a fair trial."

"Anything else?" Demakos asked.

"No, Your Honor," Chandler replied.

"Well," Demakos said to Josh. "Number one, regarding your claim of innocence, the proof of guilt was overwhelming here—you were guilty, and so the jury found you guilty."

Demakos said that "this crime here, that this defendant Joshua Torres committed, was especially heinous and brutal and also cries out for the death penalty . . . What revolted me the most, is the manner in which she was killed—pouring gasoline over her head, and around her, and igniting her by the striking of the match."

"What?" cried Marlene in her seat—learning for the first time how her daughter had died. The mother burst into tears. She was not the only family member who was crying.

"I must admit that this, that hearing this testimony almost brought me to tears, and the most horrifying of all was that she was alive at the time," said Demakos. "What can be more inhumane and depraved than the act of burning someone alive? You deserve the maximum penalty I can impose under the law."

Marlene could be heard sobbing hysterically as the judge sentenced Josh to four twenty-five-years-to-life terms on four counts—two for murder and two for kidnapping. Josh also got 8⅓-years-to-25-years for arson. Both murder and kidnapping terms were to run concurrently—which meant that Josh was going to spend 58⅓-years-to-life in an upstate pen. The earliest that Kim's killer would be eligible for parole would be sometime after his eighty-first birthday.

"Instead of him getting the death penalty, this is better," a tearful Tommy Antonakos told reporters outside the court. "Let him suffer for the rest of his life. I hope every day of it is a nightmare—the same kind of nightmare that he gave my daughter."

Josh "didn't even deserve to have anything to say," said Kim's Aunt Francine. "It was disgusting. They should torture him—every one of his fingers should come off . . . he's an animal."

Tommy said he was going to hold a Christmas vigil at Kim's gravesite, and would decorate it with a two-foot-tall Christmas tree, and a Santa Claus figurine with a music box that played a yuletide tune. He said he would decorate the tree with cartoon characters like Sylvester and Tweety—just as they had done when Kim was a kid:

"That way, when I'm not there, she will at least have 'Jingle Bells,' " Tommy said. "I'll just bundle myself up and hope, and hope it doesn't get too cold. If it is, I'll sit in the car, and hang out all day—that's where she is now, so that's where I'll be.

"I've always been with her at Christmas."

CHAPTER THIRTY

TRIBULATIONS

Jay was sentenced to his short prison term before Nick came to trial. After his court appearance, Jay was placed into a holding pen at Rikers Island. He sat down and waited to be called by a guard to leave for the trip to his upstate prison, where he would serve his term. Jay glanced around at the milling group of inmates standing close by, and his eyes stopped on one.

Nick Libretti.

Nick, his eyes darting around nervously, looked down at Jay and then looked away. Jay had heard that Nick had broken his promise to Jay not to speak ill of each other. Jay had been told that Nick had made a statement against him. Nick did not recognize Jay because Jay had shaved his head, and had pumped up with muscles. He had become a warrior. Jay had resolved to live every day as his last—because it might be. Jay startled Nick by tapping him on the shoulder.

''What's the deal, killer?'' Jay said.

Nick wheeled around, ready for another attack. When he saw Jay, he just stared, dumbfounded, with zombie eyes, for what seemed like an hour to Jay. It was like Nick was looking at a ghost. Perhaps he feared Jay would set him on fire and make the Madrina's prophecy come true.

''Damn, you got big,'' Nick said, at last.

Jay stood up, and Nick braced himself, fearing an attack.

"Why'd you play yourself?" Jay demanded. "Why'd you flip on me?"

Jay, who'd ratted on Josh, was asking why Nick had ratted on him. Before they went their separate ways, they spoke about how "everything fell apart," but Nick did not answer the question. Jay felt that Nick was haunted, not by what he had done to Kim, but by the abandonment of his spiritual guardian. He seemed tormented, terrified that he would die in prison—in flames.

Tommy had to go through the whole thing again, almost a year later, in October, 1997—for Nick Libretti's trial. Rob Ferino opened for the People, and Andrew Worgan returned as Nick's defense lawyer. Perhaps the most dramatic moment of the trial came when Louie Pia at last took the stand. As he was testifying about how Nick had confessed to his part in burning Kim, Louie was interrupted by shouting from the audience.

"I can't believe it!" Nick's mother Helen Libretti screamed. "Not my son!"

She continued ranting at Louie, apparently accusing him of lying about her little boy.

"Hold on, Officer," Demakos told Louie, who continued after Mrs. Libretti piped down.

When the prosecution announced they were about to show Nick's video confession to the horrible crime, Mrs. Libretti bolted from the courtroom. She did not return until after the tape had been played. Neither her shouting, nor the lawyer she had hired, prevented her son from being convicted on all counts. It was another victory for the prosecution, and the end of a long road for Tommy and Kim's relatives and friends.

"Nicholas Libretti is one of those soulless individuals, Your Honor," Gene told Demakos at Libretti's sentencing on November 13, 1997—two days before what would have been Kim's twenty-third birthday. "He has had previous contact with the criminal justice system, and he has been given break after break—and at this time he should be sentenced to serve every single day of imprisonment that the law permits for this crime," Gene said.

"The rest of society should be ensured that Nicholas Libretti will never walk another day as a free man among free people. He doesn't deserve it, and the rest of society doesn't deserve to have him within its midst. He should never be free again, Your Honor, never, ever again."

Nick, sporting a shaved head, and wearing a wrinkled sweatshirt and a pair of blue jeans, also spoke to the court. It was the short version of Josh's remarks at his sentencing.

"Your Honor, I just wish to say that, you know, that the crime was a terrible crime and I'm sorry it happened—but I'm innocent," the twenty-one-year-old told the court.

"Anything else?" Demakos asked.

"That's it," Nick said.

Demakos said that "burning her alive was most depraved and inhumane, and he deserves the maximum penalty—as I did with Joshua Torres and, certainly, I don't know whether he had compassion for the act that he did." The judge's sentence was a carbon copy of Josh's penalty—Nick also got 58⅓-years-to-life up the river.

"Go to Hell, and live in Hell," Tommy Antonakos said.

Libretti "was convicted of depraved murder and he is depraved," Gene Reibstein told reporters.

"Justice was done," Louie Pia said. "I just hope this brings some sense of closure to the Antonakos family."

"Kimberly, you know it's all over with now," Tommy told his daughter's gravestone after the sentencing. "You had to live with the Devil for three days, and then God took you away from the Devil, and me, too."

Tommy went every day to Kim's grave in the peaceful glade of the Moravian Cemetery. He spoke to her and gave her the news of various goings on—such as the fact that her friend Tara had had a bad car accident, but was recovering.

Two years earlier, as the first anniversary of Kim's murder had approached, Tommy felt that he could not face the day at home. Before the awful date arrived, Tommy went to Kennedy Airport with his passport, and literally got on the first plane out of the country—one bound for South America. But when he arrived in Bogota, Colombia, he realized that there was nowhere on Earth where he could hide from the awful reality of Kim's death. In tears, he called Tom Shevlin, and then Louie Pia on Long Island. Tommy spoke to Louie for more than an hour, long distance—which cost about $400. He had to speak to someone who understood. It was also painful for Louie, Tom, Rich, Gene, Julian, Rob, and others who had become very close to Tommy—and who wished they could do more to ease his enduring agony. They had put away his daughter's killers, but no one could bring Kim back.

Joey had received the death penalty for his part in Kim's death. Josh and Nick were serving their virtual life sentences, and so was Tommy. He was serving a life sentence without Kim. The only difference was, Tommy could never be paroled. Tommy had dreaded the preparations, hearings, trials, delays, and sentencings that had dragged out over two years. But now that it was all over, Tommy had less to look forward to, less to do. The driving force that kept him going was to keep his promise to Kim, and he had done that—her killers had been caught and punished. Tommy let go of his computer firm but maintained other real-estate and business interests from his home office—which was a shrine to Kim's memory. Smiling pictures of Kim, from childhood to college, filled the room. Portraits in small frames adorned the desktop. Others were displayed on an adjacent table. Over a couch were two large, framed photos of Kim taken when she was in grammar school.

One day, Tommy, who was plagued by severe headaches, was accosted at the grave by Mike Castillo. Mike said he wanted to collect the $10,000 reward that Tommy had posted. At first, Tommy was unsure who the young man was. Gene Reibstein and Louie Pia had warned Mike to stay away from the grieving father, but he ignored them. He wanted the money.

"I turned Joshua in," Mike explained. "My mother is sick."

Tommy reached in his pocket, and gave the man whatever cash he had—three hundred dollars—and Mike went away, unsatisfied. After Mike's mother died, Tommy donated $500 for the funeral of the woman, whom he had never met—but Mike did not get the reward money. The cash was still sitting in an escrow bank account. Although it had looked like Blondie would get the cash, her arrest ended her chance to be the one to convict the killers in court. Mike did not testify either. No one expected Tommy to give a reward to Jay, who had put Josh away, but was an accomplice in Kim's kidnap and murder. His reward was a light sentence.

Later, Tommy brought the news to Kim that Tara was getting married. It was heartbreaking to Tommy, who was, of course, very happy for his daughter's best friend. But, as the wedding date approached, his anxiety level began to rise. For years before her death, Tommy had been looking forward to giving Kim away as a beautiful bride. He was invited to Tara's wedding, but he did not know if he could stand to see Kim's girlfriend walk down the aisle. Tommy tried to avoid the pain by sending a gift, and his best wishes. Then he boarded a plane to Miami, where he went on a cruise ship alone for a week to find some respite from his grief among happy strangers. It actually worked—for a week. At the end of the cruise, Tommy went shopping in a souvenir shop, where they featured little sand castles that could never be washed away with the tide. Tommy had always bought Kim a present when he went on vacation, and this time would be no exception. A small, white figurine caught his eye—a little angel with a vial behind her wings that contained perfume. Tommy brought it home and gave it to Kim, gently placing it at the foot of her grave. He prayed that she was happy where she was.

Tommy knew there was no place on Earth where he could

really escape. He only felt comfortable with Kim, at her grave. But there were always places in his memory where he could take a brief vacation in the past. He remembered the last happy religious occasion, and how proud and happy he was at Kim's glittering First Communion party at the Tavern on the Green in Central Park. Many people had compared the elaborate feast to a wedding. Perhaps, Tommy thought, there was a reason. Maybe it was because her communion with God, and their celebration of it, were as close as Kim would ever get to a wedding. Sadly, the only time Kim was carried over a threshold "like a bride" was when Joey lifted her into the empty house that became her death trap.

Tommy would always remember sweet little Kim filing down the church aisle in a line of other little girls in short, white flouncy dresses, always see her head bowed solemnly at the church altar during the service. Tommy could still see Kim arriving at the party in her carriage, her dark eyes sparkling with happiness and wonder. In her diaphanous, snow-white dress, Kim shone in the middle of the joyous celebration like a laughing angel—whose visit, no one knew, would be all too brief.

EPILOGUE

Josh Torres is currently serving his fifty-eight-years-to-life sentence at the Auburn Correctional Facility in upstate New York. I wrote letters to him requesting an interview for this book, but he twice declined to give one. Instead, he requested that I grant him a secret, off-the-record visit. I wrote back informing him that I had not granted such a request for any other person interviewed for the book. Months later, close to my deadline, he finally responded. Again he repeated his demand for a secret interview, and said that it was "because I want to know what you know"—before telling me "the truth and only the truth." He did not explain how learning what I knew about the murders could possibly influence the "truth" he might tell me. I informed him that I wished to interview him—not the other way around. He did not write back, except to inquire when the book would be published. Josh has an appeal pending, and, no doubt, hopes to overturn his conviction. If he loses in court, Josh will have more than half a century to ponder the fact that his actions—and his own big mouth—will keep him behind bars until the year 2053.

Nick Libretti also expressed a willingness to be interviewed for this book—but also stalled. I spoke to his lawyer, Andrew Rendiero, who assured me that he and Nick would speak to me and introduce me to several people who would back up Nick's claims—but Nick's mother Helen rejected the idea. As the book was almost complete, I spoke to the lawyer and to Helen Libretti. This time I was told that neither Helen nor Nick would speak to me—only the lawyer. I am still waiting to hear from him. Nick was initially incarcerated at the Downstate Correctional Facility in upstate Fishkill, but was later transferred to the Walsh Regional Medical Unit at the Mohawk Correctional Facility in Rome, New York. Authorities would not say why Libretti needed medical care, citing medical confidentiality. Nick also has an appeal pending, and will do the same time as Josh if he fails to prove that he was an innocent man, wrongly convicted. His mother is still fighting to help her son, but would not comment on the record.

Brooklyn Criminal Court Judge Bernadette Bayne, who had set Nick's $1000 bail in the armed robbery case, has retired from the bench, as has Supreme Court Justice Nicholas Coffinas, who continued the bail.

Rep. Edolphus Townes, the congressman who wrote a letter to Supreme Court Justice Michael Gary in Nick's previous criminal case, declined to be interviewed for this book. "He doesn't have anything to add," said Townes' spokeswoman Karen Johnson. "This whole thing was very tragic. I think he feels dreadful for the poor family."

Justice Michael Gary revealed that Nick Libretti was given light treatment for his first arrest at the request of the prosecution—because he had no prior record and agreed to testify against his friends. Because Nick cooperated with authorities, the record was sealed and Gary took an undeserved hit in the press for setting Nick free to kill. Gary said he did not know the congressman:

"I am appointed, and not elected," Gary said. "I have stepped foot inside a political clubhouse only once in my life—to attend a retirement party. I vehemently deny that the congressman's letter had anything to do with my treatment of Mr. Libretti's case."

The third bad guy, Joey Negron, almost certainly made the anonymous call to Louie Pia, mentioning his own name, but he is not alive to confirm that. Perhaps the strongest proof that Joey was the caller was the fact that, after the bad guys were locked up, no one else came forward to claim that they were the caller deserving the $10,000 reward—only the authorities and the caller knew about the call.

The fourth conspirator, Jay Negron, was interviewed for this book, and was very helpful. Jay maintains his claim on the witness stand that he did not think Kim was going to be kidnapped, despite the fact that Josh spoke of his plan in advance. He also said that no one set out to kill Kim, which is likely. Jay is out of jail after serving a two-year term, as per his plea-bargain deal. He said he currently works at two jobs. His day job involves construction and refinishing of cabinets. At night, Jay is a male stripper. Both day and night, Jay says he lives only for the moment, and is ready to die—looking over his shoulder for the expected retribution for his violation of the code of the street. He claimed that a convict who "got tight with Josh in jail" was released, and was seen prowling the neighborhood with his picture—with murder on his mind. Jay was very secretive, and never revealed to me his home address or the locations of his places of work.

"I guess, for me, this nightmare will live on 'til my last breath," said Jay. "When my number comes, I'll be waiting for it. I live life for today, and never look forward to the next day, 'cause I know sooner or later, I'll meet my fate—but I'll always be ready to go out in gunsmoke," Jay said. "I live in a gangster's paradise."

When asked if his warrior live-for-today philosophy made it difficult to plan for the future and make friends, Jay responded:

"I have no friends."

Jay blames the whole affair on Josh's determination to get something for nothing.

"It was greed—his lust for things he didn't deserve," said Jay. "I guess it has to do with growing up on the dark side."

Jay, who also calls himself "Q, the real one," a shortened version of his B-Q nickname, believes he "was supposed to be somebody in life, and not a loser. Those days haunt me and control my dreams."

He said that Kim was his "soul mate, and I lost her 'cause of what people call friendship and loyalty. It's something that has me waking up in a sea of loneliness every night, and feeling so cold to the touch, that I begin to believe I myself have joined her."

Jay has admitted that he knew his friends kidnapped Kim and he did nothing, even after her death. He confessed to me that he had agreed to kill Blondie and Mike Castillo at the behest of Josh and Nick—although he claimed he never intended to carry out the contracts. He also revealed to me Josh's plan to murder Nick, Nick's betrayal of Joey, and Joey's plan to kill him and Josh.

Julian Wise, in a view not shared by the other prosecutors, suspects that Jay was involved from the beginning of the kidnapping, and has "probably gotten away with murder. He should not be on the street right now. I believe Jay will make some family shed tears at some point in the future." Gene Reibstein and Rob Ferino disagree. In fact, Jay could have walked out the door with his lawyer, rather than place his life in danger by testifying against Josh. He decided to come clean and that is the only reason Josh and Nick are serving long jail terms.

"Give the Devil his due—he got Joshua," said Rob Ferino.

Of course, if Jay had not tried to lure Blondie—who probably fled on her dope run to avoid assassination—things might have ended differently. Blondie might have testified, and put Josh away. If so, she might have collected the reward money and lived happily ever after, instead of going to jail. But Blondie went south, and Jay took her place in the catbird seat. Jay, who claims to have renounced the black magic of Santeria, said he felt betrayed by Josh and the others, who he said, were "evil" and "felt the wrath of the Almighty . . . for this is the beginning of the Hell they have created for themselves. As for me, I live with the horrible choices I've made in my life, and I, as well, pay for my mistakes very dearly.''

Jay told me he was doing well, but only time will tell if he turns his life around, or returns to the dark side. He said that his big mistake was following his upbringing, which taught ''a stupid street code that will continue to cause a lot of pain for whoever follows it.''

The record shows that Josh, Nick, and Jay followed the ''code of the street''—but only until they were caught. Once under arrest, each one quickly ratted out one or more of the others in an effort to get a deal. No honor among thieves. Nick identified Josh as the prime mover, as Jay did later, and Josh named Jay as the ringleader. They all pegged Joey as the main kidnapper. They all pointed to someone else. Jay and Josh both claimed Joey's role of reluctant, remorseful accomplice who refused to enter the home where Kim was set on fire. Josh's claims were overwhelmed by facts, but Jay's were validated by the prosecution.

Jay told me that neither he nor Josh made ransom calls to Tommy Antonakos. Jay said that Joey and Nick made the ill-fated calls and then asked Josh to give it a try. Jay said Josh agreed to do it, but never made the call. Nick, in his written confession, claimed that Josh was the one who bungled the ransom calls. If Nick simply wanted to shift blame, why didn't he just blame the dead Joey? Again, each man pointed to someone else with self-serving claims that exempted himself from the dirty deeds. Certainly, they were all motivated to try and lessen their individual guilt, and blame it on someone else. This book tells the prosecution's version of the story as validated by Nick's and Jay's written confession. The prosecution claims that Josh made the calls. It is, however, possible that at least two or three of the conspirators made the ransom calls. Only Josh, Jay, and Nick know the truth.

The backgrounds of Josh, Jay, and Joey were similar—childhoods scarred by violence and poverty. Nick certainly was involved in a violent incident—the death by gunshot of his cousin—but could not claim poverty as an excuse.

It is certainly interesting that in a desperate time of crisis, danger, and confusion, both the criminals and the victim's family turned to female spiritual advisors for help. The paid consultants—one using alleged extrasensory perception, the other alleged pagan magic—gave advice that was unique, but ultimately useless. Claire Day, the psychic, told Kim's family, correctly, that she was not in Brooklyn, and was tied up in a cold basement and not wearing her shoes. But she also claimed that Kim was tied to a bed, which was incorrect. She hit a bull's eye with the letter 'J,' something that terrified three out of four bad guys, whose names all began with that letter. Her statement that the house was not abandoned also seemed to fit the Woodhaven home. She hit a partial bull's eye when she said the crooks had fled to California. Only Nick had gone to the West Coast. Her most glaring error was in her prediction of the outcome: Kim, unfortunately, never found her own way out of her predicament. Of course, Day also failed to identify the pictures of Josh and Jay, never said it was a kidnapping, or ever mentioned a gray house, a barking dog, or Woodhaven. But, even so, her box score was 75%—distinctly better than chance. Of course, true believers might argue that, since the killers had already been to La Madrina, who gave them beads to protect them from other magic, Claire Day may have been blocked by the Santeria sorceress. Those true believers might also claim that Joey was murdered because he was not wearing his protective beads around his neck when the gunman came up behind him. Non-believers would only be impressed by a psychic who is incredibly wealthy—from picking winning Lotto numbers. What is undisputed is that the Madrina's exorcism did not work—one of her customers was killed and the other three were arrested and convicted. Also, Nick Libretti is alive in his prison cell. The Madrina's prediction that Nick might be burned alive in his cell has not come true, at least not yet. In fairness to the priestess, it should be noted that her clients ignored her advice to stay away from each other. That left open the unlikely possibility for the faithful that Josh, Nick, Joey, and Jay would have gotten off scot-free—if they had only done what the witch doctor ordered.

Two years after Kim's murder, in March, 1997, former criminal and rap artist Charles Wallace—better known as "Biggie Smalls" and the "Notorious B-I-G," who recorded the "I'm Ready to Die" album that Kim played on the night she was kidnapped—was himself shot to death in a drive-by shooting in Los Angeles.

"Blondie" is still serving her fifteen-year sentence for drug smuggling and perjury in a federal penitentiary. Originally jailed in Florida, she later contracted cancer and was transferred to the Carswell Federal Medical Center prison in Fort Worth, Texas—where she underwent several surgeries and chemotherapy. In phone calls and letters, she told me that her treatment had been successful, and that she was in remission. Late in 1998, she was transferred to a federal lockup in Connecticut, in order to be closer to her family and children. I was able to confirm many things she told me—but not the part of her story that the jury did not believe. Jay confirmed that he tried to lure her to meetings as part of a plot to kill her and Mike Castillo. But I was unable to find any evidence that mysterious figures held her children hostage and forced her to become a drug courier. Nevertheless, Blondie is sticking to her story. She, also, has an appeal pending, and hopes to hug her kids outside jail walls sooner, rather than later. "I am no criminal," she said. She was flabbergasted when I told her that Jay was free.

"He's out?" Blondie asked, incredulously. "I can't believe it!"

"Redrum," the man Blondie feared so much, is also a free man. He was never charged with threatening her, or with any crime in connection with the murders of Kim Antonakos or Joey Negron.

"Psycho," too, is on the street. Detective Phil Tricolla, who was promoted to the Brooklyn South Homicide Squad, ran into Psycho during the summer of 1998. Psycho was polite and was not under suspicion for any crime.

Detectives in Manhattan arrested several suspects in the machine-gun murder of Kim's former boyfriend Shawn Hayes. The alleged killers in the drug revenge slaying have not yet come to trial.

Jeanette Montalvo deeply regrets not doing anything about her barking dog, the noises she heard, or the lights she saw in the neighboring house where Kim died.

"If I had known, I would have called the police," she told me. "I would have gone over there and released her myself. May God rest that girl's soul. Joshua—I never met that bastard—he should rot in Hell. Nick is a cold-hearted devil. I hope those two rot in Hell."

Her daughter Antonette misses Joey.

"He was a good person," she told me, tears streaming down her face. "He just got caught up in something."

Every June, on Joey's birthday, her son Bobby releases his birthday balloons into the Queens sky "to Poppa Joey in Heaven."

Joey's uncle, Luis Negron, told me that he knew his nephew would never hurt a woman and was "taking steps to correct" the situation when he was slain.

"I guess that's where he drew the line with these people," Luis said. "If he hadn't had a change of heart, there would have been no reason to kill him. I guess he wanted the truth to come out, one way or another."

Luis said he watched Josh Torres' face as he testified against him in court. But the devout Christian said that it was not too late for Joey, and it was not too late for Josh.

"As evil as he is, if he asks God's forgiveness, he will be forgiven," Luis said.

April Dedely still works as a legal secretary, and is raising Josh's son Timmy.

Kim's friend Tara Pappaccio married her fiancé Steven.

Liz Pace has also married, and is raising a young infant.

Ruth McCook, absentee owner of the house where Kim died, passed away. Her sons sold the house to a family who are apparently unaware of the nightmarish history of the house.

Former prosecutor Julian Wise is a lawyer for a large Manhattan law firm specializing in real-estate law. Julian now has time to play golf and watch the LA Raiders. But every time he smells something burning, it brings him back to the horror in the Woodhaven basement.

"I immediately think of Kim and get nauseous—I picture it," Julian said.

Julian believes that he will have that reaction as long as he lives. He does not regret his decision to leave the DA's office, although he is proud of having put away criminals like Josh and Nick.

"The world is a better place," he said.

Rob Ferino married his girlfriend Helen. They had a son named Anthony and moved to Brooklyn. Rob also left the DA's office but not because he hated the job—he needed more money to support his growing family. He works as a lawyer for an insurance company. When asked his thoughts about Josh Torres, Rob paused before saying:

"There is a special fucking place in Hell for him."

Gene Reibstein still works long hours supervising homicide prosecutions, and trying cases in the Queens DA's office as the Coordinator of Trials for the Major Case Division. His office clock is still hopefully stuck at one minute to five. Gene still inspires hope among middle-aged pedestrians with his antics on roller blades and his skateboard. He is still married to his college sweetheart, Cathy, and they live on Long Island with their two sons, Zack, 19, and Luke, 14.

His boss is still DA Richard A. Brown, and both men are glad to greet Tommy Antonakos, who calls and sometimes drops into the office for chats.

The amiable, and "nosey," Detective Johnny Wilde, who first heard Blondie's tale, retired from the job on New Year's Eve, December 31, 1998, after twenty-five years on the job.

Detective Rich Tirelli is still on the Queens Homicide Squad. He is also a delegate for the Detectives Endowment

Association, whose motto, rightly, is "The Best Detectives in the World." In 1996, he and Louie Pia were two of several detectives who obtained confessions and statements from Heriberto "Eddie" Seda—the Zodiac Killer.

Tom Shevlin retired after his accident, but he started a family tradition—his eldest son, Tom Shevlin, Jr., entered the Police Academy in August, 1998. He still lives on Long Island with his wife and children.

Louie Pia is still doing The Job, locking up killers, but he is no longer a Marlboro man. In June, 1998, he gave up smoking, finally yielding to his daughter Erin's pleas. The only loose end that troubles Louie is the reward money. He felt that the $10,000 reward should have been divided between Blondie's four children and Mike Castillo, but the money remains in the bank.

For several years, Tommy Antonakos was paralyzed with grief. He lost interest in his business and spent most of his time at home or at Kim's grave. He reproached himself for letting Kim move out of the house, for having an answering machine message with a pause, and a long list of "what-ifs"—a normal emotional reaction to such a tragedy. Like Phil Tricolla, he was beating himself up for not being psychic. Tommy said that when he remembered Josh "helping" him look for Kim, but refusing to go into the church, "it haunts me." In 1998, Tommy made an effort to get out of the house more, and spend less time at Kim's grave—often going only every other day. In November, 1998, as the painful day of Kim's birthday approached, Tommy opened an office, and began a new business. He began to live again.

Perhaps the worst thing that can be said about Kimberly Antonakos is that she was too generous, too open, too trusting with people. Most twenty year-olds are not overly critical of their friends and associates, and Kim was no exception. Unfortunately, many of the people around Kim were not like her, and saw her as an income opportunity—not as the giving human being she was. Kim was kidnapped because Josh Torres wanted an expensive car that he was too lazy to earn. He was able to do it because Kim had invited him into her home, and Josh was able to recruit some mutts, who were as greedy and evil as he was, to help him. Kim was tormented because of their stupidity and cowardice. She died because none of the confederacy of dunces could tell the difference between hypothermia and death, and were willing to set a human being on fire to avoid punishment for their crime. Perhaps Josh did not know that he was burning Kim alive, but the kiss he gave her before dying—accompanied by flippant, cruel words—marked him as an evil man.

Kim's murder and Josh's duplicity touched a deep nerve inside those who read about it in newspapers, or saw it on television—not to mention those who investigated and prosecuted the crime, and those who wrote the stories. It left no one unmoved. The cruel act of burning a beautiful young woman alive evoked primal disgust and outrage. It also inspired fear. The case forced us all to remember that evil was not just a quaint word used in the Bible or comic books. Evil was alive and well today—hiding, unsuspected, behind a smiling face, perhaps a face we have passed on a crowded street on a warm, sunny day.

The only remedy we have for everyday evil is justice, and that was accomplished in this case. But it could never be enough for Tommy Antonakos and his family. Only one thing would make them happy and whole again—but that is not a reunion that will take place in this world.